Praise for *Vulnerability and Resilience: Body and Liberating Theologies*

"A sobering but hopeful read! The essays in this wide-ranging volume tackle an immensely important and yet peculiarly controversial topic: bodies in which we live. These thoughtful and provocative analyses will enable us to see various precious bodies that are being denigrated or violated bodies in our world today. They will further embolden us to embody our theological thinking and emend our theological practice."

—Tat-siong Benny Liew,
College of the Holy Cross (USA)

"This volume of collected essays is a 'daring' project that disturbs and unsettles the biblical text and traditional theological understandings. Almost all of the essays deal with subject matter—'body' and 'liberation'—that is seldom interrogated in a sustained way in theological seminaries and churches around the globe. Of note is the diverse range of authors that bring together the experiences of marginalized groups across continents, ensuring that notions of vulnerability and resilience are interrogated as they intersect with transnational locations."

—Beverley Haddad,
University of KwaZulu-Natal (South Africa)

"Through a transnational lens, *Vulnerability and Resilience* brilliantly interweaves the stories from those whose bodies have been categorized as vulnerable and, thus, not fully human. However, these stories create a courageous space to challenge the traditional understandings of vulnerability, oppression, and liberation by unfolding the theological meanings of the embodiment of resilience. This book plainly shows how vulnerable and despised bodies, in fact, produce the critically transnational and deeply theological knowledge of resilience, resistance, and liberation. I highly recommend this book to anyone who wants to meditate on the deeper meaning of the vulnerable body of Jesus in various transnational contexts. Readers will appreciate the critical voices filled with love, hope, resilience, and resistance from the vulnerable who have never lost the power of agency."

—**Kuen-Joo Christine Pae**,
Denison University (USA)

"If the first part is a confronting, visceral, poetic, embodied, and liberating vulnerability (with some humor thrown in for good measure), the second part is a challenging, theoretically, pastorally, and theologically embedded program for transformation. Together the two parts of this book provide a glorious, erotic powerhouse for the metamorphosis of contemporary Christian theology and praxis."

—**Anita Monro**,
Grace College, University of Queensland (Australia)

"Highly commendable. A moving, challenging, and liberating collection of essays that explore the subversive nature of resilience. In this book, the meaning of vulnerability as powerlessness is challenged to demonstrate that the vulnerable have agency with the power to speak. Resilience comes with the courage to talk back to the powers that bind."

—**Seforosa Carroll**,
World Council of Churches (Switzerland)

Vulnerability and Resilience

Theology in the Age of Empire

Series Editor: Jione Havea

In these five volumes, an international collective of theologians interrogate Christianity's involvement with empires past and present, trouble its normative teachings and practices whenever they sustain and profit from empire, and rekindle the insights and energies within the Christian movement that militate against empire's rapacity.

Titles in This Series

Religion and Power, edited by Jione Havea
Scripture and Resistance, edited by Jione Havea
People and Land: *Decolonizing Theologies*, edited by Jione Havea
Vulnerability and Resilience: *Body and Liberating Theologies*, edited by Jione Havea

Forthcoming

Mission and Context, edited by Jione Havea

Vulnerability and Resilience

Body and Liberating Theologies

Edited by
Jione Havea

Foreword by Collin Cowan

LEXINGTON BOOKS/FORTRESS ACADEMIC
Lanham • Boulder • New York • London

Published by Lexington Books/Fortress Academic
Lexington Books is an imprint of The Rowman & Littlefield Publishing Group, Inc.
4501 Forbes Boulevard, Suite 200, Lanham, Maryland 20706
www.rowman.com

6 Tinworth Street, London SE11 5AL, United Kingdom

British Library Cataloguing in Publication Information Available

The hardback edition of this book was previously catalogued by the Library of Congress as follows:

Library of Congress Cataloging-in-Publication Data

ISBN: 978-1-9787-0363-6 (cloth : alk. paper)
ISBN: 978-1-9787-0365-0 (pbk. : alk. paper)
ISBN: 978-1-9787-0364-3 (electronic)

∞™ The paper used in this publication meets the minimum requirements of American National Standard for Information Sciences—Permanence of Paper for Printed Library Materials, ANSI/NISO Z39.48-1992.

This book was made possible through the kind contribution of the Council for World Mission.

Contents

Figure

Foreword

Collin Cowan

Incarnational theology, which embodies the vision of the Word becoming flesh (John 1:1–18), is at the heart of Christianity. This articulation of the divine speaks of God's mission as embodiment of love, and in Jesus, the amazing grace in vulnerability and resilience murmurs in the sweet sounds of transformation and freedom.

Jesus was embroiled in the bodies of the people, the land, and the politics of his time. He was moved by the hurting of human bodies, he responded to the turbulence of the land and the seas, and he confronted the power politics of Rome and of the Temple. He transgressed the rules that objectify the vulnerable bodies of women, of sick people, and of minorities. In his encounters, his daily ministry, and, ultimately, his death, he experienced the vulnerability of human liminality. And yet, with resilient and audacious hope he demonstrated that rising to life is the divine endowment that liberates and empowers.

The Gospels often point to the visceral responses of Jesus, how he was moved to his guts (with compassion, Matt 9:35–38, NIV) by situations. In confronting the purity laws and holiness codes of the Temple, Jesus pointed the way to dismantle the myriad ways that religious systems confine, define, deny, and occupy the bodies, souls, and minds of others. Every time Jesus healed a leper, ate with an outcast, embraced a scandalous woman, or made room for a stranger, he announced a new world of freedom that is rooted in faith, hope, and love.

This volume of essays outlines in powerful ways this mission and ministry of Jesus, God incarnate, whose body and blood we hallow and whose spirit we seek. Yet, in another way, the essays also confront us with the myriad ways that churches rebuilt what Jesus sought to tear down. Mission agencies like Council for World Mission (CWM) have a shameful history of using religious power to occupy and denigrate the bodies and spirits of human beings. Racism, patriarchy, homophobia, and ableism find their voices in the past and present of missionary Christianity. Conversion has been seen in terms of particular norms of an era or culture despising and disrespecting the people—normal, respectable church people—in whom Jesus continues to embody himself. The authors of these essays make themselves vulnerable to these domineering forces in religion.

As CWM seeks to amplify the voices in this collection, we pray for grace and resilience to remain committed to placing their causes and claims at the heart of mission.

Collin Cowan
General Secretary, CWM

Chapter 1

Tell Us

Jione Havea

Harvest is on the lips of the community. Grains have been gathered, and spread over a mat-like cloth to air out and dry up. The whiff of fresh seeds dances in the open air where the wind distributes it as far as the unseen corners of the imagination, and draws in the craving of hungry creatures who are within sniffing distance. The sniffles of harvest draw many needy creatures in, to the pile of grains on the ground. Among them, a blackbird dives in. Eyes closed, bill extended, the blackbird lunges in. It could sniff the feed on the ground, seeds of the land, but it cannot reach in to peck at the pile of grains. Its legs are caught in a string. *Trapped.* It awkwardly turns its head down, but it cannot reach down to join in. It wants to be in, but it is strung up. And kept out.

Yesudas's *Trapped* (the artwork on the cover of this book) gives a traumatic view of the blackbird, which embodies the harassment suffered by other creatures (many of whom are black bodies) who are strung up so that they cannot reach what could give them satisfaction. The harvest is withheld (by a string that only human hands would weave) from the seed-eating creatures of the land. Vulnerability. For those trapped creatures to reach and to nourish, they need release. For the seeds of the land to sprout life for those trapped creatures, they need release. Yesudas's *Trapped* thus highlights a critical call. Release. Emancipation.

The contributors to this collection write out of the realities and hopes of subjects who are trapped in situations of vulnerability. We (the contributors) write in order that vulnerability does not have the final word. We write in order to tell the stories of real subjects (plus some of our own stories) who are trapped because of their queer bodies, because of the color on their skin, because of their dirtied profession, because of the roots of their ancestors, because of the biases in the Bible, because of the imperial cultures in the society, because of the doctrines and practices of the Christian church, and because of so many other no-good reasons. We write out of solidarity with subjects who are vulnerable to two or more of these traps, telling personal and communal stories, and as a collective we propose ways through which those who are trapped in situations of vulnerability might endure. Resilience. And find release. Liberation.

The overall tone of the essays in this collection, individually and as a collective, flows from trapped body (of individuals, of collectives, of positions and teachings) to liberation (of bodies, minds, cultures, and theologies). Similarly, in terms of the theological and theoretical engagements that we (as authors) undertake, the overall flow of the book is from body theology to liberation theology. These flows do not mean that the two, body and liberation, are separate as if liberation is "post" body. As theological movements, the limits between the two—body and liberation theologies—are porous so that they interpenetrate. Put simply, body needs liberation and liberation needs body. This is one way of saying that this book, like a hungry bird in my musings earlier, dives in at the intersection of body and liberation theologies.

TO TELL OR NOT TO TELL

Creatures need bodies to live, and stories to keep us alive. With all due respect, Shakespeare missed a necessary prior question. While *to be or not to be* is important, a more critical question in the interests of vulnerable subjects is to first ask whether *to tell or not to tell*. This is a critical first question for the authors of this collection, who become more vulnerable and agitated in telling their stories and the stories of trapped subjects whom they advocate. Advocacy is empowering, as well as risky. And risk taking, the burden of activists in all colors, is also agitating. In this spiral of connections, vulnerability can be empowering for the weak and their advocates.

To tell through writing (with the rules of correct grammar and proper expressions, required by the language used) could be seen as a trap, because the story thereby becomes caught in a *string* (recalling Yesudas's *Trapped*) of words. But writing can also emancipate, and provide the meeting point (intersection) for vulnerability and resilience. Our words, our stories, when written, make us vulnerable—anyone and everyone has access to our words and stories and they can ridicule, condemn, or reject us on the basis of what we have written; and the very same words and stories, when written, make us resilient—our words and stories are not lost, for anyone and everyone who have access to what we have written are informed. But our words and stories could be ignored, or even distorted, and these are the challenges for the stories (re)told in the following pages (and in other pages where vulnerable subjects and advocates opt *to tell*).

It is not necessary, in my humble opinion, to repeat here the theories of and examples for the telling of stories—autobiographical, ethnographical, or otherwise, with Western, Eastern, and/or indigenous native leanings—in theological exercises. It is also not necessary to explain how stories are at the heart of scriptures and theology, or to illustrate how stories are like the wind in the sails of life. Stories are everywhere. Everything is storied. But not all stories are told. And not all telling find emancipation. Hence this collection of essays.

My task here is not to nail another list of theses onto the storehouse of stories but to outline what the authors tell in the following pages, which are divided into two overlapping sections.

DARE TO (RE)STORY

The authors in the first section tell stories of vulnerability and resilience at the intersections of body and theology. They tell their stories around matters of sexuality and gender, context and color, masculinity and coloniality, and the oppressive ways of (hetero)normative and binary thinking.

Adriaan van Klinken follows a suggestion by Marcella Althaus-Reid that queer theologies are necessarily first-person theologies—autobiographical, embodied, self-disclosing—and therefore have the potential to debunk T-theology (totalitarian theology, or the heteronormative, racist, disembodied theology of empire). Following this suggestion, van Klinken engages in embodied autobiographic storytelling—talking about his experiences with black bodies, sexuality, and HIV in South Africa, as well as his HIV status. Employing the notion of (the church as) the body of Christ, van Klinken explores the obscenity of the HIV+ body of Christ and discusses how it opens up a space of vulnerability and publicity where we are constituted politically toward embodied solidarity, disrupting the logic of empire. Hence the body of Christ is a site of self-disclosed sexual and otherwise embodied storytelling, and through such storytelling our vulnerable erotic bodies are embraced and revalorized.

Karl Hand proposes that Jesus's masculinity is an indigenous masculinity in a colonized land. Hand reads Jesus's indigenous masculinity drawing on Raewyn Connell's work on hegemonic masculinity and Hand's own white Australian (hegemonic) masculinity. Hand situates narratives of Jesus at table in Luke within the context of his subordinated masculinity in a cultural world where the conqueror's masculinity is understood to have feminized the conquered men. This reading creates space for theological critique of the contemporary Australian gender discourse which regards Adam Goodes's indigenous war dance as a public obscenity, and in which Aboriginal fathering is subject to mockery in political cartoons.

Masiiwa Ragies Gunda reflects on how Christianity struggles with the human body. Gunda engages with three attitudes toward the human body: rejection of the body as an obstacle to communion with God, mastery of the body's sexual needs, and affirmation of the body. Through these various attitudes, Christian faith has played into the hands of empire, whose goal is to exploit the human body for profit and for the selfish interests of the elites. The support for empire through the rejection of the human body can be direct or indirect. Gunda posits that Christian faith is meaningless outside the human body. Through a reading of Gen 1–2, Gunda contends that Christian faith must affirm the body as willed by God. In affirming the body, we acknowledge the importance of the body to Christian faith and we challenge the ways of empire which make bodies vulnerable.

Nienke Pruiksma retells two stories of boys born without the physical intervention of a man. One a well-known biblical narrative, the story of Mary becoming mother for Jesus; the other a lesser-known narrative of the Gavião people of Rondônia, Brazil. Pruiksma proposes a deconstructive kaleidoscopic approach to hegemonic religious interpretations, colonial binary epistemologies, and female bodies and sexuality. She weaves an indigenous tale about the introduction of corn into the Gavião community with the Lucan narrative of the annunciation, and with notes referring to theologies looking at sexuality, bodies, and the indigenous proposal of *bem viver* (translation from the Kíchwa *sumac kawsay,* the Aymara *suma qamaña,* or the Guarani *nhandereko*), into a radical (de)constructive proposal for transformative societies, relations, and views of life. The chapter investigates how theologies that reflect on human sexuality and bodies may learn from indigenous approaches such as *bem viver* to include a wider imagination on life, justice, bodies, and interdependence beyond humanity.

Brian F. Kolia appeals to the Samoan practice of *fāgogo* (storytelling event) as a way of reading biblical texts in which one does not lose the magic of storytelling, and as a reminder that stories are *telling* truths as opposed to telling *the* truth. Stories communicate values and morals. With regard to reading biblical stories, Kolia invites readers to assume the role of the listeners and *faalogo* (hear) the story as though one of our elders (*matua*) was recounting it. *Fāgogo* is the hermeneutical framework for Kolia's rereading of the story of Eve and the serpent in Gen 3:1–19 as a love story, inspired by the Samoan tale of Sina and the *tuna* (an eel). In the spirit of *fāgogo,* how could there have been something "forbidden" in the garden?

Monica J. Melanchthon reflects on the functioning of gender and violence within empires—empires of sex, caste, class, religion, language, ethnicity—all of which are explosive within the Asian context. Melanchthon focuses on the manner in which texts of various kinds—written, oral, visual—oppress and/ or liberate women. How might we read those texts for the sake of women, for their empowerment, resilience, and flourishing?

Melanchthon's question applies to all the stories in this section: how might we hear the magic in those stories (like in a *fāgogo* event) so that the subjects in the stories are not trapped, and in order that those stories do not trap other vulnerable bodies?

DARE TO (RE)IMAGINE

The second section shifts the focus to the intersections of body, liberation, and the practices of theology (in general). The authors call for liberation at multiplying platforms: liberation of the body, liberation of the mind, liberation of the Christian movement, liberation of public workers, liberation of black and blackened bodies, liberation of the liberation movements, and liberation of the usual business of doing and teaching theology in church and academic settings.

Wanda Deifelt addresses how, during its development, Christianity often failed to actualize Jesus's teachings of resisting oppression and advocating for the liberation of oppressed and trapped subjects. Christianity gradually ceased to be a movement of liberation and affirmation born within Judaism to become the stronghold of imperial ideologies. Human bodies suffered under these concepts. The church's adoption of a Greek way of thinking and a Roman mode of administration perpetuated a dualistic and hierarchical approach that gave priority to the salvation of souls instead of the well-being of bodies and of the creation, down below. By affirming an embodied theology, Deifelt reclaims the teachings and ministry of Jesus, who preached life in abundance, and posits its implication for Christian discipleship today.

Dwight N. Hopkins revisits the ways in which empire has the heaviest impact on the black working class. In this connection, Hopkins calls upon black liberation theology (BLT) to pay attention to and deal specifically with the working class. Hopkins's definition of working class comes from Martin Luther King Jr.'s public ministry. King Jr. gave his life for the working class and linked the working class with empire, a link that was evident in the stories of working-class slaves in Egypt as well as in Luke 3–4 and Matt 28. The early black power movement and BLT focused on workers and empire, and Amilcar Cabral provides analytical clarity on unhealthy relations between workers and empire in his writings from the Guinea Bissau, Cape Verde, and the struggle against Portuguese colonial empire. Cabral gives clarity for understanding what King Jr. preached and died for, as well as the drive for liberation in the early BLT and in the Bible. In their footsteps, Hopkins affirmed that Another. World. Is. Possible.

Luis N. Rivera-Pagán develops the links between the Iberian conquest and Christianization of Latin America and the Caribbean with the emergence of modernity, global empire, and capitalism. Latin America and the Caribbean became the cradle of Western imperial domination and missionary enterprises. It was an imperial process vindicated, but also contested, by theological arguments and scriptural hermeneutics, as attested by the writings of Francisco de Vitoria, Bartolomé de Las Casas, Juan Ginés de Sepúlveda, José de Acosta, and others. Those forerunners invite engaging with the voices of oppressed peoples and articulating decolonizing perspectives. This is the context for the emergence of contemporary decolonizing theologies, in conjunction with the exodus paradigm and the hope for God's kingdom that characterize Christian scriptures. These theologies dare to discern critically the signs of times and radically engage the imperatives of human liberation.

With the background of Deifelt's review of the dissing progress of Christianity and the review of two liberation theologies by Hopkins (black American) and Rivera-Pagán (Latin Caribbean), the remaining chapters of this section turn to the intersection of the practices of theology and the shaping of future theologies and theologians.

Cláudio Carvalhaes presents a decolonizing perspective around three questions: Is there anything outside of nature? Is there anything outside thinking? and Is there anything outside of losing? The first two questions challenge the binarial structures of modern theological thinking that stress culture over nature and abstract thinking over bodily epistemologies. Using the knowledge of indigenous communities, the work of Eduardo Viveiros de Casttro, Déborah Danowski, and Boaventura de Sousa Santos, Carvalhaes calls for theological thinking that considers the earth, indigenous sources, multinaturalisms, and the "epistemologies of south" as fundamental sources for thinking to counter and offer alternatives to the binary, abstract, hierarchical, and power-dominated multicultural frames of mainline (which is the old, expired, line) theological thought. Carvalhaes considers the coloniality of power structures that keep the suffering of vulnerable marginalized communities and looks at the daily religious and liturgical symbols of resistance from marginalized communities to foster new forms of living and thinking. Resistance is at the frontline of resilience.

The floodgates are open, damage is done, and for Stephen Burns, there is no return to naivety about the extent of harm caused to young and vulnerable persons, the massive diminution of the churches' reputation, or well-founded suspicion of its representatives. In Australia—where Burns is located—recent Royal Commission investigations into ecclesial-institutional abuse have recently opened up far too many tragedies. While some sensitive work has been done about the special care needed around liturgy with and for abused persons, still, not enough work has been done on how authoritarian church cultures conspire to create conditions for abuse, and less attention again has been directed to how such authoritarian cultures can be reinforced in liturgy. Burns opens up for scrutiny a range of un-/underexamined liturgical dynamics—hierarchical ceremonial scenes, ritually constructed power-distance, inherited ascriptions of the divine and human beings, unison prayer, and so on. Gathering and amplifying insights of feminist theologians especially, Burns challenges aspects of liturgical traditions and calls for reform and relinquishment.

Sarojini Nadar and Sarasvathie Reddy seek to queer the academy. They engaged with the scholarly position that queering should be regarded as a responsibility that goes beyond the inclusion of LGBTI perspectives in the curriculum, toward transformation of the ways in which knowledge is produced. "Queerying" is regarded as a commitment to destabilize academic empires which control what kind of knowledge is produced, how such knowledge is produced, for whom, and by whom. Queering therefore includes giving consideration to embodying pedagogy, to decolonizing the curriculum, and to recognizing the resources both teacher and student bring to these processes. It also includes, Nadar and Reddy argue, a recognition of the ways in which the act of queering itself can become an act in embedding the very empires we wish to destabilize. Nadar and Reddy explored these themes through a case study of their embodied experiences as teachers within a transdisciplinary master's program that seek to produce knowledge at the intersections of gender, religion, and sexual and reproductive health rights.

Jenny Te Paa Daniel winds up this collection with an invitation to imagine seminaries anew, as openly subversive sites of theologically daring spiritual and intellectual endeavor. This requires coming out of the shadows of generally older white male clerics from whom virtually all institutionalized academic theology derived. Their voices enjoined to the voices of the classical philosophers and theological writers of the earliest Christian times comprise de facto the legacy of intellectual authority, of intellectual genius, of intellectual credibility, which even into the twenty-first century is upheld as being that against which the theological academy proudly and uncritically benchmarks itself. Te Paa Daniel identifies the key points of intervention needing attention if twenty-first-century seminaries are to be transformed into intellectually courageous spiritual communities. She envisages public theologians who dare to critique and disrupt the stranglehold of institutionalized theology and to dream of a seminary tradition freed of the inherent North Atlantic colonially inspired constraints of racism, sexism, classism, and homophobia.

TELL ON

Many stories, bodies, minds, cultures, theologies, and institutions of faith and of learning are trapped. And vulnerable. The authors in these pages tell and reflect on the stories of some of these vulnerable subjects with the hope that in telling and engaging with their stories and realities, these "trapped birds" might endure. Also, that these "black birds" might be unstrung. So that they might fly, and sing freely. And find more than resilience. Release. Emancipation.

BLACKBIRDS

I add the story of another trapped bird, this time in Pasifika, the *kumul*— the indigenous name (known to nonnatives as the *cenderawasih* or bird-of-paradise) for the national bird of Papua New Guinea (PNG). While the female *kumul* is smaller in size with greyish brown shades and a golden head, the male *kumul* is full of colors which stream down long feathers that he showcases during courting and mating rituals. The *kumul* is the national bird of PNG because of the strong and beautiful male *kumul*, but the often-overlooked story is that his beauty comes out because of the scent and presence of the greyish brown female *kumul*.

The *kumul* was chosen to be PNG's national bird in part because the island of Papua, the largest island in Pasifika (larger than Aotearoa, or New Zealand), is in the shape of a male *kumul* (head to the west and tail to the east). While the native people of Papua are *one people, one soul, one destiny*, as the activist musician Airileke Ingram put it,[1] the island is divided between two nations: Indonesia (which occupies West Papua, at the head and upper body of the *kumul*) and PNG (tailing off to the east of the island).[2] Appealing to Yesudas's *Trapped* as presented at the opening of this essay, Indonesia is the string that stops West Papua from eating freely.

West Papua has several stories of occupation.[3] The Netherlands occupied West Papua together with Indonesia until 1949 when it gave independence to Indonesia but kept West Papua as a Dutch colony. Through the 1950s the Dutch government prepared West Papua for nationhood and after a congress at which the native people declared independence, the Morning Star flag of West Papua was raised on December 1, 1961, to the fervors of a national anthem. Soon afterward the Indonesian military invaded and occupied West Papua, and after several discriminating and unjust negotiations the "New York Agreement" (on August 15, 1962) of the United Nation handed control over West Papua to Indonesia. This is only one of West Papua's many stories of occupation, but it is the bloodiest one because over 500,000 native bodies have perished due to Indonesia's ongoing genocide (see many stories of slaughter told by the Free West Papua campaign at freewestpapua.org). These native bodies are slaughtered "black birds," but they are survived by many black bodies that are vulnerable to Indonesia's "bloody string."

Where's the key? is a collaborative work created by a group of Pasifika activists named the Youngsolwarans (young saltwater [solwara] people) during a seminar at Madang, PNG (August 2014, at which Airileke Ingram was among the participants). This work depicts the *kumul* as being torn apart, thus separating West Papua from PNG (represented by the two flags painted onto the island) but held together by two hands: a brownish black hand from the side of PNG and a greyish ashy hand from the side of West Papua. Papua is divided, but the hands of *one people, one soul, one destiny* reach across to hold the island together as *one land* as well.

Where's the key? calls for collaboration on three tasks: first, to stitch and mend (represented by the needle and roll of string[4]) the island of Papua so that the native peoples across Indonesia's border (sanctioned by the United States

Figure 1.1 Youngsolwarans, *Where's the Key?* (oil on canvas, 2014). Used with permission.

and UN) may come together as one; second, to remove the blindfold (represented by the cloth placed over the "face" of PNG, at the top of the island) so that neighbors and foreign nations may see the plight and vulnerability of West Papua; and third, to remove the chain and lock held by a strong arm (which represented Indonesia) around the neck of the *kumul*. The title of the work—*Where's the key?*—challenges viewers to look for the key that will unlock the chain and let this blackbird (Papua) fly again. The urgency of this challenge is felt by the vulnerable "blackbirds" in Papua, and by natives on other island groups in Pasifika that are still under occupation by foreign powers, including

- Micronesia, Hawai'i, and Tutuila, under occupation by the United States;
- Kanaky and Ma'ohi Nui, under occupation by France; and
- Rapa Nui, under occupation by Chile.

I use "blackbird" intentionally because it is a term that brings to mind the slave trade in Pasifika. As the transatlantic slave trade (abolished by the Slave Trade Act of 1807) was slowly ending in the 1860s, the slave traders (called "blackbirders") turned to Pasifika. In the case of my home island, Peruvian blackbirders reached Tonga between 1862 and 1864 and took natives from 'Ata (the southernmost island in the Tonga group) and Niua Fo'ou (to the north, closer to Samoa than to the capital island of Tongatapu) but did not succeed in their attempt at 'Uiha (in the Ha'apai group). There were other slave traders who took native Pasifika bodies to other parts of the world, including to our neighbor Australia, and those blackbirds were also *trapped* and in need of allies to *find the key* and unlock the chains of occupation and enslavement.

From the blackbirds of the 1860s to the native bodies from occupied (is)lands in Pasifika of the 2020s, and to the trapped bodies and minds on other (occupied) lands of the current time, many stories of vulnerability and resilience await telling and engagement. The essays collected in this work are invitations for engagement with the stories told in these pages, and for the telling of more stories of vulnerability and resilience.

TELL US

Stories often get stolen. Like when i add my own twists to make my neighbor's story my own. Or when my other neighbor tells her story and i respond with "tell me about it," and then i roll my eyes as if i already know what she wants to tell me. Instead of listening in and paying proper respect to my neighbors and their stories, i shut them up and take over their stories with my own. Whether one calls these behaviors as appropriation or contextualization does not pardon my sins as a thief of stories. Tell me about it!

On the other hand, stories can also be creative, restorative, and formative. Stories are not just products to be shared, traded or stolen, lost and forgotten but events that *tell me into being* as well as *tell me into something else* (i.e., into an alternative being). I am created, restored, and transformed in hearing the stories of my neighbors, and i sincerely hope that the stories that we (the contributors) tell in the following pages have a similar *affect*. In other words, may these stories *tell us* (contributors and readers) into being. As well as *tell us* into other kinds of being. Not the kinds that trap. But the kinds that release the trapped.

NOTES

1. See *Sorong Samarai* (2016) performed by Airileke Ingram and the Rize of the Morning Star (https://www.youtube.com/watch?v=faJfu-FJVt0 accessed December 1, 2018).

2. Geographically, a few kilometers north of the international waters of Australia, Papua is at the meeting point of Asia and Pasifika. The head of the *kumul* is in the region of Asia, and its tail extends into the waters of Pasifika.

3. See Jason MacLeod, *Merdeka and the Morning Star: Civil Resistance in West Papua*. Peace and Conflict Series (St. Lucia: University of Queensland Press, 2015).

4. String has a restoring function in this artwork, compared to its ensnaring function in Yesudas's *Trapped*.

Part I

DARE TO (RE)STORY

Chapter 2

Stories Telling Bodies

A Self-disclosing Queer Theology of Sexuality and Vulnerability

Adriaan van Klinken

In empire, self-disclosure and self-disclosive acts by gay and lesbian people are penalized by repression, expulsion, and sometimes death.

—M. Shawn Copeland[1]

Denise M. Ackerman has written that "our stories are our lives. Telling stories is intrinsic to claiming our identity and, in the process, funding impulses for hope. For those living with HIV, there is a need to claim and to name their identities in order to move away from the victim status often thrust upon them."[2]

Autobiographic, embodied, and sexual storytelling is of great political and theological significance. Through such acts of self-disclosure our messy bodies and lives become a source of knowledge disrupting the hegemonic narratives that govern and discipline human existence. In Christian and other religious contexts, those hegemonic narratives are rooted in what Argentinian queer theologian Marcella Althaus-Reid has called T-theology (totalitarian theology). T-theology, for Althaus-Reid, refers to "theology as ideology, that is, a totalitarian construction of what is considered as 'The One and Only Theology' which does not admit discussion or challenges from different perspectives, especially in the area of sexual identity and its close relationship with political and racial issues."[3] T-theology, so to say, is the theology of empire: colonial, patriarchal, heteronormative, racist, disembodied. Althaus-Reid suggests that this theology can be radically unshaped by queer theologies, which she describes as being necessarily first-person theologies, "diasporic, self-disclosing, autobiographical and responsible for its own words," and embodied theologies since "sexuality and loving relationships are not only important theological issues but experiences."[4] Following this suggestion, storytelling, specifically the telling of autobiographic sexual stories, is a key theological method, as it enables a dialectical reflection on queer lives—"the strangers at the gate of Christianity, that is the people whose life and experiences do not fit with T-theology"—in relation to the queer God—"God as the sexual stranger at the gates of theology."[5]

I-THEOLOGY

Taking up this challenge of doing I-theology, in this essay I allow my body to speak, or perhaps better: I read and narrate my own body in conversation with other theological texts. Thus, in line with the DARE vision of radical theology involving engagement and requiring theologians "to come out of the closet," I engage in self-disclosure as an act of resisting empire and its T-theology of decency.[6] As Althaus-Reid puts it:

> At the bottom line of Queer theologies, there are biographies of sexual migrants, testimonies of real lives in rebellions made of love, pleasure and suffering. On this point, paraphrasing Kosofsky Sedgwick, we may say that Queer theologies are those characterised by an "I" because the Queer discourse only becomes such when done in the first person.[7]

This essay gives, indeed, insight into the biography of a sexual migrant, with a real life and a real body at its core—a body that travels (in this case, to South Africa), makes love, enjoys pleasure across boundaries of place and race; yet also a body that is vulnerable. As womanist theologian Shawn Copeland reminds us, "the vulnerability and marginality of gay and lesbian people makes a claim . . . on the body of Christ."[8] Indeed my act of disclosure explicitly performs such a claim, since as I argue the body of Christ opens up a space of vulnerability that enables solidarity and publicity. Along the way I also reclaim my own "polluted body"—to use the words of Malaysian queer theologian Joseph Goh—as a "prophetic body," "crafting alternative self-perceptions of sexuality, serostatus, and faith."[9] Indeed, this essay is my attempt to make some autobiographic and theological sense of my recent diagnosis with HIV.

South Africa I

This story starts more than ten years ago. In 2006, as a master's student in theology in The Netherlands, and in my early twenties, I studied for three months in South Africa. At the University of KwaZulu-Natal I joined the program on HIV, AIDS, and Theology, and I did research for my MA thesis about the work of African women theologians on issues of religion, gender, and HIV and AIDS. I encountered the realities of the HIV epidemic with my own eyes through exposure trips to community-based organizations, both in KwaZulu-Natal and in Swaziland (two regions heavily affected by the pandemic, which around that time was at its peak). It made an everlasting impact, as then and there I discovered not just intellectually but in a very embodied way what it means to do contextual theology. Since then, the religious responses to, and theological reflections on, the realities of HIV and AIDS in Africa have been one of my academic interests. It was the topic of the first academic paper I wrote as a PhD student a few years later, which got published in the South African theology journal *Missionalia*: a study of the ways in which African theologians seek to overcome the silence and stigma surrounding the HIV epidemic by creatively employing the classic theological metaphor of the church as the body of Christ, leading them to make the radical statement that the body of Christ is HIV positive and has AIDS.[10]

Through my time in South Africa, I not only learned about the value and significance of contextual theology; through my study of African women theologians I also encountered a particular genre of contextual theology, based in narrative methods and autobiographic storytelling. The theologies of each of the three theologians I studied for my MA dissertation—Isabel Phiri, Beverley Haddad, and Fulata Moyo—have narrative and autobiographic elements which are in line with the work of African women theologians more generally who, in the words of Mercy Oduyoye, "accept story as a source of theology and so tell their stories as well as study the experiences of other women . . . in Africa whose stories remain unwritten."[11] Telling women's stories is key to reclaiming history as her-stories, and to developing her-theologies.[12] I found Moyo most fascinating in this regard. She does not just engage in autobiographic storytelling but in sexual storytelling—as she writes about her embodied experiences of gender, marriage, widowhood, and sexuality and reflects upon these from biblical and theological perspectives.[13] According to Moyo:

> Telling our stories helps us bring about a fourfold yield: 1) engaging in dialogue with others helps us relate personal hurt and search for healing with academic reflection; 2) it will provide other perspectives that enrich our own; 3) singing our own songs and reflecting on them in dialogue with existing songs by others will help us shift from positions of helplessness as victims to being agents who make a contribution to theologies of life and wholeness; and 4) the act of narration is in itself therapeutic.[14]

Moyo was a PhD candidate at UKZN while I was a visiting student, and our conversations about her work, in particular about her (equally autobiographic, I assume) notion of sexual orgasm as a foretaste of eschatological hope, formed the beginning of a friendship that continues today. If the current essay comes anything close to being authentic, embodied, and self-disclosing, this is thanks to what I have learned from her and other theologians who dare to write from the experiences of their own erotic bodies and intimate lives.

In relation to the fourfold yield identified by Moyo in the preceding quotation, the narration presented in this essay is, indeed, therapeutic as it helps me to make sense of, and come to grasp with, my own recent embodied experiences, and to find healing. It also allows me to become an agent, taking control over how I want people to learn about my story, and shaping the story into my own "song" (to use Moyo's words). I hope and trust that my story will be further enriched by others, in the same way as it has already been enriched by the stories and perspectives of friends, writers, and thinkers who have inspired me. Paraphrasing the preceding quoted words of Nadar I suggest that in addition to telling women's stories, it is also of vital importance to tell queer stories, in order to reclaim history as queer-story and develop queer theologies.

My 2006 visit to South Africa was academically stimulating and personally enriching. However, it was also emotionally disturbing—not only because of the exposure to AIDS but also because of the exposure to the complex realities of race in postapartheid South Africa. Until then, my knowledge of South Africa was shaped by what I had heard about apartheid, liberation, truth, and reconciliation in the media, and by a late 1990s visit of a racially mixed South African school choir while I was at secondary school myself (a visit during which two beautiful black girls stayed at our house—with my sisters teasing me that I was in love with one of them—who taught me South Africa's national anthem with its closing stanza referring to "the call to stand together, and united we shall stand"). The togetherness and unity the anthem refers to seemed far away at the Lutheran Theological Institute (LTI) in Pietermaritzburg where I was staying and where I struggled to find my place and make friendships, as there was an obvious tension between the white and black South African students living there. Added to the problem of race, I felt insecure with regard to my sexuality: the homophobic statements made by some of the students, both in the UKZN program and at the LTI, made me careful not to disclose my gay identity or my relationship status. (I had a picture of my boyfriend on my desk but told people that he was my brother.) I did befriend one of the black LTI laborers to whom I gave swimming lessons in the pool, and who turned out to be gay himself; but when the friendship became closer and a sexual tension emerged, I distanced myself from him while referring to my boyfriend waiting for me at home. Sticking to the moral principle of "faithfulness" as I understood it at that time meant that I missed an opportunity for intimate racial and sexual boundary crossing and for bodily expressing, enjoying, and strengthening our nascent friendship.

South Africa II

Since 2006, I have returned to South Africa frequently. Most recently in 2016, for a three-month visiting fellowship at the Stellenbosch Institute for Advanced Study (STIAS), in Stellenbosch, close to Cape Town. My first visit to Stellenbosch, in 2015, was a very strange experience. Flying from Amsterdam for eleven hours to finally arrive in an overwhelmingly Afrikaans-speaking town with typical Cape Dutch architecture, and staying in a hotel located at Dorpsstraat (Afrikaans/Dutch for "town street"), one might think that I couldn't feel more at home. Yet for me it was alienating, as it was such a completely different face of South Africa than the one I had seen and come to appreciate during previous visits to KwaZulu-Natal. This town was clean, ordered, and pretty, and the locally produced wine was great; but it also felt like a conservative place where apartheid was somehow still in the air. Attending a conference on queer theology at the University of Stellenbosch, one evening we went out with a group of delegates, including old and new friends. We formed a queer bunch of people—of mixed gender, mixed race, mixed nationalities, and in all LGBT varieties. Obviously, we were too queer for Stellenbosch, and I was shocked by the expressions of racism and homophobia we encountered that night.

A year later I was back in Stellenbosch for a three-month visit, to work at STIAS on a research project on Christianity and queer politics in Africa. The slogan of STIAS is, "A Creative Space for the Mind," and indeed I had an academically productive and intellectually stimulating time, not at least thanks to the exchanges with other visiting fellows from all over the world. At the same time, the institute felt like a bubble in a town that is already an enclave in an otherwise enormously complex and dynamic (if not boiling) society. Moreover, the slogan's reference to the mind reinforces the idea of academia being a rather disembodied activity. I admit that the way STIAS caters to the bodies of its fellows through daily lunches at the institute is rightly renowned. Yet of course the body, at least my body, has also desires and needs other than food-related. Thank God, my boyfriend of ten years ago (who in the meantime has become my marital partner) and I have grown in our relationship and have come to realize that the faithfulness, commitment, and love we share are too rich and meaningful to be limited to a narrow idea of sexual exclusivity. Thus different from the previous time, during this three-month period in South Africa I could and did explore opportunities for intimate sexual boundary crossing, including the crossing of racial boundaries (which in a place like Stellenbosch might be even more transgressive).

Not long after my return back home (which is now in the UK), I went for a regular sexual health check. When a week later I received a phone call and was asked to come to the clinic for the results, I knew that something was wrong, which could mean only one thing. I had been tested positive. On the basis of the blood test results, the excellent staff at the Leeds Centre for Sexual Health reconstructed the transmission history and gave a close estimate of the infection date. In all likelihood I had contracted the virus in South Africa, during my fellowship at STIAS. Half way through that period I had been quite seriously ill for about a week. It started over the weekend, and that Sunday I wrote on Facebook (as one does when feeling bored and miserable): "To everyone who envies me for my travelling abroad, I want you to know that this weekend I've just been feeling a little (home)sick, cold and lonely," with the hashtags #WhyKeepUpAppearances? #MissingMyHubby #TomorrowWillBeBetter. However, instead of feeling better the next day I felt even more unwell. It took three more days before I went to see a doctor, according to whose diagnosis I had tonsillitis. One friend—or shall I be honest and say, lover?—came to see me several times, and his attention and care helped me to feel better. Only the next weekend I felt my energies coming back. Retrospectively, my sickness must have been the phase of seroconversion: the period, usually one to three weeks after the initial infection, when the body starts developing HIV antibodies, accompanied by heavy cold and flu-like symptoms.

THE POLITICS OF BEING POSITIVE

So here I am, and this is where the preceding narrated stories about my trips to South Africa come together. I contracted HIV in South Africa, ten years after I visited the country for the first time as a visiting student working on HIV and AIDS. I contracted HIV eight years after my first peer-reviewed publication appeared in a South African theology journal, about the body of Christ with AIDS. I contracted HIV on the African continent while working on a research project dealing with queer activism and politics in Africa, specifically Kenya. In this project HIV was not planned to be a major theme, yet it became one of the subthemes as it appeared to be relevant in each of the case studies I'm writing about.

Since hearing the news about my status, I have been wondering about a range of questions. Does it make a difference for my research and writing that I'm now HIV positive? Does it make a difference that the virus transmitted to me most likely came from a black South African male body? Does it make a difference that I contracted the virus on the continent that has been central in my writing about gender, sexuality, and, indeed, HIV and AIDS? I keep thinking about these questions and don't have any final answers yet. I do, however, think that it is remarkable and indeed meaningful how my transmission history connects to my long-standing interest in, and engagement with, issues of sexuality and HIV and AIDS in Africa.

One reason why this is meaningful relates to the classic insider-outsider problem that not only haunts the study of religion but also the study of Africa. As a white European academic working in the field of African Studies I'm painfully aware of the long-standing history of the othering of Africa in Africanist scholarship. Writing about the problem of Western representations of Africa (as the Other par excellence), Cameroonian postcolonial philosopher Achille Mbembe has argued:

> The theoretical and practical recognition of the body and flesh of "the stranger" as flesh and body just like mine, the idea of a common human nature, a humanity shared with others, long posed, and still poses, a problem for Western consciousness.[15]

More than before, my HIV status has made me realize the extent to which my flesh and body, my identity, are indeed enmeshed with the black African bodies I have come to know through my work in various parts of Africa. This is part of the reason why I want to share this part of the story of my life: because it has become so intricately connected to the life stories and bodily histories of those on the African continent who are living with the virus or who have died as a result of its disruption of their immune system. I wish to share this part of the story of my body because it is now so closely tied to the many HIV infected and affected bodies inhabiting this continent—some of which I've come to know intimately, have had pleasure with and made love to. Zimbabwean theologian Edward Antonio has rightly critiqued the recolonization of African sexuality in Western public health discourses about HIV that echo "a long history of stereotypical Western portrayals of Africans as sexually immoral, exotic, aberrant, and totally other."[16] When I state in this essay that I likely received the virus from a black African body, this is not to blame that body for my infection but to acknowledge that if Africans are "immoral and aberrant sexual beings"—as colonial discourse has it—then I am one, too, which is another way of overcoming the othering of Africa and of African sexuality. (To be honest, I'd prefer overcoming that othering by pointing at the beauty of black bodies but that entails the risk of being accused of another colonial gaze, of objectification and eroticization.)

More generally, what I did realize, more or less immediately (very much to the surprise of the nurse who disclosed the test result to me), is that my HIV status is political. The classic feminist slogan of the personal being political certainly applies to a bodily infection with a virus that, more than three decades after its discovery, is still associated with moral taboo and is surrounded by silence—simply because it is sexually transmitted. I have read enough about the power of stigma to know that the only way of overcoming it is by breaking the taboo and silence—by being open and honest and sharing one's story, that is, if one has the necessary personal courage and social support. Thanks to the latter I think to have gained the former.

VULNERABILITY AND SOLIDARITY
IN THE BODY OF CHRIST

My decision to disclose is motivated by the deep insight beautifully, almost poetically, captured by American feminist philosopher Judith Butler: "Each of us is constituted politically in part by virtue of the social vulnerability of our bodies—as a site of desire and physical vulnerability, as a site of a publicity at once assertive and exposed."[17] I discovered the physical vulnerability of my body as even my commitment to safe sex could apparently not prevent transmission of the virus. I experienced the social vulnerability of my body as immediately when I received the test results there was this unavoidable question: to disclose, or not to disclose? Butler's insight underlines the importance of assertively claiming our bodies as a site of publicity, turning vulnerability into strength. It also underlines the need to let our bodies speak truth about desire and love, even if this truth transgresses (as it often does) heteronormative standards of monogamy and so-called decent sexual behaviors. At this point it may be good to evoke the words of Althaus-Reid that "the body of the libertine, that nomadic body par excellence, has never been considered in a theological dialogue. Without doing that, God may also be condemned to never come out of the confessionary closet."[18]

Butler's words suggest that bodily vulnerability and the precariousness of life are essential to what human beings have in common and therefore are the basis of community and solidarity. This reminds me of St. Paul's notion that in the body of Christ,[19] when one member suffers all members suffer together (1 Cor 12:26). This notion has been taken up by several African theologians to argue that if one member is HIV positive all members are positive, and that indeed the body of Christ itself is HIV positive. For instance, biblical scholar and HIV activist Musa Dube from Botswana writes:

> 1 Corinthians 12, which defines the church as a body with many parts, is cited as a key part of the foundation of compassion. If one member suffers, we all suffer with him/her. If one member of the church is infected, the church cannot separate itself. If one member is suffering from AIDS, the church cannot separate from his/her suffering. . . . The church, in other words, should not shy away from saying, "We have AIDS."[20]

Further elaborating on this, South African theologian Tinyiko Maluleke evoked the words of the prophetic *Kairos Document* critiquing apartheid to argue that the HIV epidemic constitutes a new *kairos*—in the sense of both "crisis" and "moment of truth"—for the church in Southern Africa and indeed for the world as a whole.[21] In some of my academic writings I have engaged this idea of the body of Christ being HIV positive, reflecting upon its ethical, political, and theological consequences as a metaphor of solidarity within contemporary global Christianity and in a globalizing, postcolonial, fragmented world.[22] Within the body of Christ, one could argue, I-theology becomes we-theology—not to transcend the particularities of I-theologies but to acknowledge the interconnectedness of experiences narrated in these theologies.

Employing postcolonial theorist Homi Bhabha's notion of interstice, I have suggested elsewhere that the body of Christ can be considered an interstitial or intervening space, giving birth to "interstitial intimacy," that is, an "intimacy that questions binary divisions through which . . . spheres of social experience are often spatially opposed"—to begin with, the division between those who are, and who are not HIV positive.[23] Ironic or not, several years after writing about this, another embodied (literally, this time) form of intimacy has now inscribed me and my body into the history of HIV in Africa. The division between me and the members of Christ's body who are HIV positive has been overcome. I now literally share their HIV status. However, other spatial divisions remain, such as between those who have access to antiretroviral treatment and those who have not, and between those who can be open about their status without fear of serious repercussions and those who cannot. So even though I am now HIV positive myself, the interstitial intimacy within the body of Christ continues to make me critically aware of the very different social and bodily experiences within that body, which relates to location, class, race, economic privilege, and the varying scales of sexual oppression and freedom.

THE OBSCENITY OF THE BODY OF CHRIST WITH HIV

The image of the body of Christ with HIV is a disruptive one. It is radically disruptive because it reminds us that Christ's body is not just metaphorical. It is a real body, constituted by the total of the bodily experiences of its members. As Althaus-Reid points out, references to the body in Christian theology—such as the body of Christ and the body of the church—tend to be abstracted and disembodied: "these theological bodies have usually been bodies without flesh, without bones or brains, bodies without nervous systems of blood—and, we may add, bodies without menstruation or sweat or without malnutrition and bodies without sexual relationships."[24] The image of the body of Christ with HIV reminds us that Christ's body consists of blood—blood that can bring life but also blood that can be infected with a virus that potentially is deadly. It further reminds us that Christ's body is sexual—meaning that it can make love, enjoy pleasure, and reach orgasms; it can penetrate and be penetrated (oral, vaginal, and anal); but also meaning that it is vulnerable to sexually transmitted diseases. Added to this physical vulnerability comes social vulnerability as Christ's body will be exposed to the stigma and exclusion associated with HIV. As a sexual body, the body of Christ with HIV is also omnisexual, polyamorous and promiscuous as it comprises a variety of heterosexual and nonheterosexual bodies, as well as heterosexual and nonheterosexual loving patterns of relationships many of which "exist outside that theology of relationships from the centre which has become normative."[25] What Althaus-Reid writes about the Trinity-as-an-orgy can also be applied to Christ's body: it is "composed in relation to multiple embraces and sexual indefinitions beyond oneness, and beyond dual models of loving relationships."[26]

Many African theologians writing about issues of HIV and AIDS have frequently done so in a discourse that tends to victimize people living with HIV and "suffering from" AIDS. Thus, they have drawn attention to the link between the risk of HIV transmission, poverty, and unequal socioeconomic structures. African women theologians, in particular, have drawn attention to the fact that women in Africa often get infected with the virus as a result of their relative powerless position in sexual decision making and in gender relations more broadly.[27] As a white European same-sex loving person holding many privileges, including power and freedom of sexual decision making, I am careful not to deny or downplay these realities. Yet there is a risk that such discourses reinforce monolithic representations of African women as powerless, and of African sexuality as lacking of mutual pleasure, love, and intimacy.[28]

It is well possible that the narrative of victimization and suffering in relation to HIV and AIDS is easier to accept in mainstream theological discourse, as it relates to more general (nonsexual and disembodied) notions of compassion in the body of Christ. However, in Africa and elsewhere HIV is not always and only passed on as a result of unjust social structures and unequal power relations between partners. Both in hetero- and homosexual contexts, HIV transmission is part of the risk to which we expose our bodies when being intimate with others, when making love to others, when enjoying pleasure with others. Even methods of safe sex do not offer 100 percent protection. This physical vulnerability, which is inherent to sexual intimacy and indeed to human embodied existence in general, is acknowledged by and incorporated in the body of Christ with HIV. That is how the image of the HIV positive body of Christ becomes much more than a metaphor of compassion and solidarity in situations of disease and bodily suffering. It radically affirms sexuality and embraces intimacy and erotic love, while simultaneously acknowledging the vulnerability that this entails.

Referring to the theological obscenities caused by the images of the black Christ in black theology, and of the female Christ or *Christa* in feminist theology, Althaus-Reid points out that "any uncovering of Christ needs to follow that pattern of obscenity as disruptive and illuminating at the same time, because Christ and his symbolic construction continue in our history, according to our own moment of historical consciousness."[29] The image of the HIV positive Christ is yet another obscenity. In addition to uncovering the racism under the guise of a white Caucasian Christ and the androcentrism under the guise of the male Christ, this image disrupts and uncovers the asexual and disembodied nature of Christ in T-theology; it illuminates Christ's fundamental capability to engage in embodied intimacy, with Christ's body constituting a site of desire, physical vulnerability, and social vulnerability. It is a radically queer image, reminding us that the body of the queer Christ, in the words of Shawn Copeland, "embraces all our bodies passionately, revalorizes them as embodied mystery, and reorients sexual desire towards God's desire for us in and through our sexuality."[30]

UNDETECTABILITY AND THE ONGOING NEED FOR DISCLOSURE

The suggestion that the body of Christ with HIV is sexually affirmative might sound blasphemous to those who have in mind the images of the HIV epidemic in the 1980s to the early 2000s. In this period in Africa, but of course also elsewhere, HIV caused large-scale disease, illness, suffering, and death, not seldom among people in their twenties and thirties. In the United States and other parts of the West, this reality began to change in the mid-1990s with the development of anti-retroviral treatment (ART); the enormous trauma and tragedy of AIDS is now part of these regions' history. In Africa the introduction of ART was slowed down, by the industrial patents that kept the prices of these medicines too high. However, over the past ten years, the availability of, and accessibility to, ART in Africa has increased significantly. As a result, the face of the HIV epidemic on the continent and its impact on the lives of those who are infected have changed dramatically. Every year, a smaller number of people are *dying from* AIDS in Africa, while many people are *living with* HIV. From a medical perspective the virus may constitute less of a *kairos* these days, yet the stigma surrounding it still makes the epidemic, in Maluleke's earlier quoted words, a "moment of truth," in Africa and elsewhere.

The new phase in which the epidemic has become manageable raises new ethical and theological questions. Where initially theologians stated that the body of Christ has AIDS, this later changed into the body of Christ being HIV positive; and in the current situation we may ask whether the body of Christ has become undetectable. Undetectability means that the viral load has become very low—so low that the virus almost disappears from the body, to the extent that an HIV test may even give a negative result. My body responded very well to ART and within a few months after starting the treatment I was undetectable. Clearly, even if there is not yet a cure for HIV, thanks to ART the body of Christ has become a site of healing, a site where a positive test result is no longer a death sentence but the beginning of a period of renewed hopeful and grateful living. Perhaps more critically, the image of the body of Christ being undetectable creates a particularly queer space of fluidity and ambiguity in which any rigid boundaries between HIV positive and negative are dissolved and become more or less meaningless. Undetectability further means that the risk of transmission of the virus has reduced to almost zero, and one may wonder what the implications of this are for the ethics of disclosure.

With HIV becoming manageable in most parts of the world, one may argue that there is no longer a need for disclosure. However, even if HIV is no longer a death sentence, the stigma around it remains strong, simply because it is sexually transmitted—and sexuality is still disciplined by the heteronormative regime of empire. Personally, the image of the body of Christ with HIV encouraged me to disclose my status. In my understanding, the earlier quoted words from Judith Butler become particularly meaningful in relation to Christ's body which is perhaps more than any other body "a site of desire and physical vulnerability, [and] a site of a publicity at once assertive and exposed." If we are serious about imagining ourselves as part of that body, we are constituted politically not only by virtue of the vulnerability of the body of Christ but also by virtue of its publicity. In the body of Christ, Paul reminds us, our embodied experiences—both of suffering and of joy—are not private but shared. The queer and HIV positive body of Christ, then, is a site for self-disclosure and embodied storytelling, including sexual storytelling. It is a site where we are all naked, not able to hide the secrets of our bodies but more importantly without a need to hide the secrets of our bodies. It is through sharing our nakedness that we come to acknowledge our common embodied human existence and are united with Christ. After all, "the only body capable of taking us all in as we are with all our different body marks is the body of Christ."[31] Hence, if there is one site that constitutes us politically in such a way that it enables public disclosure of our HIV status, or any other body mark that in the heteronormative, patriarchal, and racist logic of empire leads to exclusion, marginalization, and stigmatization, it is the site of Christ's body.

CONCLUSION

As much as I have just stated that principally, within the body of Christ we are all naked and have no secrets, I am very much aware that the aforementioned attempt toward autobiographic and self-disclosive theology through storytelling is selective. I have disclosed some crucial parts of the story of my body and life but have hidden other aspects. The voyeuristic or otherwise curious reader may want to know many more details about my intimate, emotional and relational life, about the impact of living with HIV and my experiences of disclosure. However, a key principle of autobiographic narrative theology and storytelling is to respect the agency of the storyteller and their power of dis/closure. The preceding account reflects how I, at this moment, want to share my story, as an attempt to make some theological sense of my body, of my life. I hope that this will encourage others to share their stories, too. It is through sharing the vulnerability of our bodies that true solidarity becomes possible and that a queer world is made in which indeed there is no longer reason to disclose selectively. Then and there our bodies shall know fully and are fully known.

NOTES

1. M. Shawn Copeland, *Enfleshing Freedom: Body, Race and Being* (Minneapolis: Fortress Press, 2010), 74.

2. Denise M. Ackermann, "From Mere Existence to Tenacious Endurance: Stigma, HIV/AIDS and a Feminist Theology of Praxis," in *African Women, Religion, and Health: Essays in Honor of Mercy Amba Ewudziwa Oduyoye*, ed. Isabel A. Phiri and Sarojini Nadar (Maryknoll, New York: Orbis Books 2006), 231.

3. Marcella Althaus-Reid, *The Queer God* (London and New York: Routledge, 2003), 172 n.4.

4. Ibid., 8.

5. Ibid., 60.

6. CWM (Council for World Mission), *Discernment and Radical Engagement (DARE), Concept Note* (Singapore: Council of World Mission, 2017), 1.

7. Althaus-Reid, *The Queer God*, 8.

8. Copeland, *Enfleshing Freedom*, 74.

9. Joseph N. Goh, "From Polluted to Prophetic Bodies: Theo-Pastoral Lessons from the Lived Experiences of Gay, HIV-Positive Christian Men in Singapore," *Practical Theology* 10.2 (2017): 133–146.

10. Adriaan van Klinken, "'The Body of Christ Has AIDS.' A Study on the Notion of the Body of Christ in African Theologies Responding to HIV and AIDS," *Missionalia* 36.2/3 (2008): 319–336.

11. Mercy Amba Oduyoye, *Introducing African Women's Theology* (Cleveland: The Pilgrim Press, 2001), 10.

12. Sarojini Nadar, "Her-Stories and Her-Theologies: Charting Feminist Theologies in Africa," *Studia Historiae Ecclesiasticae* 35 (2009): 135–150.

13. Fulata L. Moyo, "Navigating Experiences of Healing: A Narrative Theology of Eschatological Hope as Healing," in *African Women, Religion and Health: Essays in Honor of Mercy Amba Ewudziwa Oduyoye*, ed. Isabel A. Phiri and Sarojini Nadar (Maryknoll, New York: Orbis Books, 2006), 243–257; Fulata L. Moyo, "'Singing and Dancing Women's Liberation': My Story of Faith." In *Her-Stories: Hidden Histories of Women of Faith in Africa*, ed. Isabel A. Phiri, Devaraksham Betty Govinden, and Sarojini Nadar (Pietermaritzburg: Cluster, 2002), 389–408.

14. Moyo, "Navigating Experiences of Healing," 244.

15. Achille Mbembe, *On the Postcolony* (Berkeley: University of California Press, 2001), 2.

16. Edward P. Antonio, "'Eros', AIDS, and African Bodies: A Theological Commentary on Deadly Desires," in *The Embrace of Eros: Bodies, Desires and Sexuality in Christianity*, ed. Margaret D. Kamitsuka (Minneapolis: Fortress Press, 2010), 187.

17. Judith Butler, *Precarious Life: The Power of Mourning and Violence* (New York: Verso Books, 2004), 20.

18. Althaus-Reid, *The Queer God*, 52.

19. As a theologically imagined community centering around what has been called "solidarity of Others," see Anselm Kyongsuk Min, *The Solidarity of Others in a Divided World: A Postmodern Theology after Postmodernism* (New York: T&T Clark, 2004).

20. Musa W. Dube, *A Theology of Compassion in the HIV and AIDS Era. Module 7 of the HIV and AIDS Curriculum for TEE Programmes and Institutions in Africa* (Geneva: WCC Publications, 2007), 76.

21. Tinyiko S. Maluleke, "The Challenge of HIV/AIDS for Theological Education in Africa. Towards an HIV/AIDS Sensitive Curriculum," *Missionalia* 29.2 (2001): 125–143.

22. Adriaan van Klinken, "When the Body of Christ Has AIDS: A Theological Metaphor for Global Solidarity in Light of HIV and AIDS," *International Journal of Public Theology* 4.4 (2010): 446–465.

23. Homi K. Bhabha, *The Location of Culture* (London and New York: Routledge, 2010), 19; see also Adriaan van Klinken, "Western Christianity as Part of Postcolonial World Christianity: The 'Body of Christ with AIDS' as an Interstitial Space," in *Contesting Religious Identities: Transformations, Disseminations and Mediations*, ed. Bob Becking, Anne-Marie Korte, and Lucien van Liere (Leiden: Brillvan Klinken, 2017), 39–58.

24. Althaus-Reid, *The Queer God*, 114.

25. Ibid.

26. Ibid., 57.

27. Isabel A. Phiri, Beverley Haddad, and Madipoane Masenya, eds. *African Women, HIV/AIDS and Faith Communities* (Pietermaritzburg: Cluster Publications, 2003); Teresia M. Hinga, "AIDS, Religion and Women in Africa: Theo-Ethical Challenges and Imperatives," in *Women, Religion and HIV/AIDS in Africa: Responding to Ethical and Theological Challenges*, ed. Teresia M. Hinga, Anne N. Kubai,

Philomena Mwaura, and Hazel Ayanga (Pietermaritzburg: Cluster Publications, 2008), 76–104.

28. A similar criticism has been made by Musa Dube in her assessment of African women theological writings about HIV and AIDS, when she writes that these writings have "a tendency to present the African woman monolithically: she is always the helpless victim of a range of cultural atrocities and marked by a lack. . . . [T]he African women lacks the power to say no to sex; she lacks property rights; she does not have power to say where and when sex takes place" (Musa W. Dube, "HIV and AIDS Research and Writing in the Circle of African Concerned African Women Theologians 2002–2006," in *Compassionate Circles: African Women Theologians Facing HIV*, ed. Ezra Chitando and Nontando Hadebe [Geneva: WCC Publications, 2009], 183).

29. Marcella Althaus-Reid, *Indecent Theology: Theological Perversions in Sex, Gender and Politics* (London and New York: Routledge, 2000), 111.

30. Copeland, *Enfleshing Freedom*, 80.

31. Ibid., 83.

Chapter 3

Jesus's Colonized Masculinity in Luke

Karl Hand

In Virgil's *Aeneid*, Aeneas recalls his father's advice to him as a prophecy: "When, my son, after you have been driven to unknown shores, hunger compels you to eat your tables once you have consumed your meal, then in your weariness remember to hope for a home and there to locate your first dwelling with your own hand and to build up ramparts."[1] This prophecy has been fulfilled for many white settlers in Australia, who have built their homes with walls to keep out indigenous and other migrant peoples. Traces of such exclusivist and supremacist attitudes are also evident in Australian biblical scholarship.

That the overwhelming majority of Australian biblical scholars are (like most theologians in the history of Christianity) ethnically privileged males makes it very easy to "go stealth" and assume that such a perspective is simply "objectivity." Perhaps, in the case of white Australians, with an occasional allusion to colonial sentimentality, or a hint of culture cringe.

WHITE AUSTRALIAN MALE CRISIS

It is an act of privilege to conflate one's personal perspective with "objectivity." The way that white Australian males claim to speak from a universal viewpoint has been exposed by Chris Budden.[2] It is Budden's project which inspires me, a white Aussie male, to press forward in defining my point of view and making it visible. But there is something unavoidably problematic about this project. The defining of whiteness and of masculinity is as much a privilege of white men as leaving it undefined. Whether I do it or leave it undone, I do so on my terms, my timeline, and to suit my agendas. Marilyn Frye once observed a similar situation which arises when white feminists listen to black women: "It seemed like doing nothing would be racist and whatever we did would be racist because *we* did it . . . no decision I make here can fail to be an exercise of race privilege. (And yet this cannot be an excuse for not making a decision.)"[3]

The way forward is articulated by Toula Nicolacopoulos and George Vassilacopoulos in their call for a white Australian manifesto, a truthful account by white Australians of our own story, which names the space we inhabit and our relationship to it.[4] This is needed because, when indigenous Australians ask us, "I come from here. Where do you come from?" we lack any coherent answer. This situation, which Nicolacopoulos and Vassilacopoulos characterize as both onto-pathology and Nietzschean resentment, is a deeply inauthentic place from which to speak. I suggest that this situation is at the root of the white Australian man's inability to create a philosophy and history of his own.[5] It is this failure that I am seeking to redress by articulating my own subjectivity here.

Framing the articulation of white Australian male subjectivity as an authentic account of who white men really are in Australia addresses the problem I raised earlier regarding white male privilege. The demand for an authentic account comes not from the agendas of colonizing men but by the demands of indigenous survival and resistance themselves, in particular, by the Tent Embassy. As Gary Foley writes, "The underlying premise of the Tent Embassy was that the indigenous people regarded themselves as 'aliens in their own land,' and therefore—like other sovereign nations—they would have an embassy to represent their interests in the Federal capital."[6] The embassy is a tangible demand that white Australia gives an honest account of who we are in this land. Former prime minister John Howard's famous quip, "a nation does not make a treaty with itself" is a refusal to answer this question.

The question was often raised whether my approach is simply replacing an old essentialist masculine ideal with a new one, one in which "authenticity" is the new hegemony. I admit that I cannot answer this question with a clear "no." Perhaps hegemony will be unavoidable for the foreseeable future, and the best we can do is seek to make it more honest, allowing indigenous voices and interests to frame the questions we answer, and thus subvert the role hegemonic masculinity plays in justifying colonialism.

In either case, I write this essay as a white Australian male and as a pastor, seeking to be honest about who I am in this land. The specific location from which I seek to follow Jesus and lead others to do so is white masculinity. I assume that position in a historical situation often described as a "crisis of masculinity," in which it is increasingly impossible to even state clearly what masculinity (let alone white masculinity) *is*. Michael Kimmel suggests that any sense of social usefulness for men has collapsed with the emergence of Western modernity, resulting in a sense of aggrieved entitlement.[7] If this is true, finding sources of meaning and identity for men will be a difficult task.

As a student of the Jesus tradition, one point of departure for me is to ask the question of how my masculinity relates to his masculinity. Historically, his is brown and colonized while mine is white and coloniz*ing*. But that is not how it is usually appropriated in our world. Rather, Jesus is presented as an exemplar of ideal or hegemonic masculinity. Curiously, he is presented in this way not only in uncritically macho Christian circles but also by feminist and pro-feminist gender-critical studies of Jesus's gender. The fact that his masculinity is in some way troubled is largely unnoticed.

Is Jesus a masculine exemplar for me to follow, as he is so often portrayed in popular Christian sources? Alternatively, is his masculinity a problem for me, since he held a privileged gender identity in his own social world, and therefore, following him at all should be seen as form of ideological devaluing of femininity?

HEGEMONIC MASCULINITY

My starting point for a solution is Raewyn Connell's work, especially this insight:

> Hegemony works in part through the production of exemplars of masculinity (e.g., professional sports stars), symbols that have authority despite the fact that most men and boys do not fully live up to them.[8]

When hegemonic masculinity was first identified in the 1980s by Connell, it was defined as the "currently most honoured way of being a man," which required all other men to define themselves in relation to it, and provided the ideological ground for the global dominance of men over women.[9] A quarter-century later, Connell reformulated the concept.[10] The original idea had suggested a single and global pattern of hegemonic masculinity. The reformulation took into account the variety of local and regional gender structures, and the agency of women and subordinated men in creating and even in using hegemonic masculinity for their own ends.

Of particular interest to this essay is that the new definition shifted from viewing hegemonic masculinity as a globally unified means of oppressing women only, to emphasizing the variety of "protest masculinities" which may be used as strategic responses to marginalization on the basis of race, ability, class, or sexuality. These alternative masculinities open up the prospect of reading Jesus's masculinity differently. Is he portrayed by the Gospel writers as exemplifying hegemonic masculinity, or is his masculinity somehow troubled in these texts?

MASCULINITY AT TABLE

In order to situate my colonial masculine subjectivity and Jesus's historical position in the gender hierarchy, I will explore a specific biblical theme. It strikes me that nowhere in scripture is Jesus quite so masculine as when he is sitting at table eating a meal. This theme is explored most prominently within the Gospel of Luke.

While a number of critical commentaries treat Lukan meals as nothing more significant than the setting in which Jesus's teaching is presented,[11] L. Timothy Johnson identifies the table-setting as a feature of Lukan Christology. He notes that this setting places Jesus's teaching in the Hellenistic literary form of a *symposium*, which highlights his identity as a prophet and a philosopher.[12] According to Darrell Bock the table-setting is a context in which Jesus's wisdom is shared with others.[13] The table-setting also has social and political import. John Dominic Crossan's portrayal of the historical Jesus highlights how Jesus used open commensality as a strategy to subvert social exclusion. This is significant in an honor-shame society, in which meals were expected to be shared with people of similar honor, and in which seating arrangements indicated relative honor among the guests.[14]

This table practice of Jesus is a key theme in Luke's theological presentation of faith community.[15] The community which Luke prefigures and founded in Acts breaks down all kinds of social barriers by engaging in culturally subversive table-fellowship. This is outlined in programmatic form in Jesus's speech in the Nazareth synagogue, and given concrete expression through scenes where Jesus is seen with unexpected table companions. It is then expanded as Jesus is shown in fellowship with women, with the whole spectrum of social classes, with social outcasts, and with both Jews and Gentiles.

Examples from the Gospel of Luke include the welcoming of a sinful woman at a Pharisee's table (7:36–50), the critique of excessive purity rituals at table (11:37–54), two sets of parables about the value of welcoming outcasts to the table (14:1–24 and 15:1–32), and a speech at table with Zacchaeus about the importance of making restitution to the poor (19:1–10).[16] In these stories, boundaries of gender, class, and ethnicity are subverted by Jesus's actions at table.

This theme is certainly no minor concern to Luke. Once it is noticed, it is suddenly everywhere in the Gospel. In addition to the instances cited earlier, Jesus is at table with Simon (4:39) and Levi (5:29) after their callings, and visits Mary and Martha at table (10:38–42), institutes the Lord's Supper at a table (22:7–38), and reveals himself after the resurrection at tables in Emmaus (24:30) and Jerusalem (24:41–43).

If this use of meals is indeed an expression of hegemonic masculine privilege, then an apparent problem becomes evident for the liberating readings of Crossan and Squires. If Jesus is assuming the male privilege of teaching at table in order to explain and teach social inclusion, then his actions don't match his words. Could it be that Luke portrays Jesus mansplaining the inclusion of women?

CONTEMPORARY MASCULINE CHRISTS

According to Mary Douglas, "If food is treated as a code, messages it encodes will be found in the pattern of social relations being expressed. The message is about different degrees of hierarchy, inclusion and exclusion, boundaries and transactions across the boundaries."[17] Three different ways of reading Jesus at table have followed this principle, while assuming that he is indeed speaking from a place of hegemonic masculinity in texts like these Lukan *symposia*.

The Exemplary Male Jesus of the Men's Movement

"When we are studying the life of Christ, we're studying all the ways to be a man," he said.[18]

Jesus's hegemonic masculinity is celebrated by the Christian men's movement. Susan Faludi investigated the 1990s phenomenon of The Promise Keepers, which she describes as a "Christian Quest for Manhood." The message of Promise Keepers was that men could save their marriages and overcome their moral and financial failures by taking back their rightful place as servant leaders of their families.

Faludi notes how this spiritual quest is connected to a particular image of Jesus. Contrasted with the medieval image of Jesus as mother, the Victorian picture of Jesus as the loving husband, and the 1920s boom-time picture of Jesus as the successful businessman, Promise Keepers found in Jesus an affectionate older brother who modeled a loving relationship with a heavenly Father. The restoration of parental masculine affection could restore their damaged manhood.[19]

The portrayal of Christ as masculine exemplar is found in popular literature on masculinity and faith. I focus here on popular literature since this is *not* a prominent theme in theologically sophisticated defenses of traditional gender roles, such as the work of John Piper and Wayne Grudem.[20] One example of popular literature is John Eldredge's *New York Times* best-selling book *Wild at Heart*. It claims that there is a masculine heart and a feminine heart, and that God has placed three desires in the masculine heart: a battle to fight, an adventure to live, and a beauty to win. The feminine heart was given three matching desires: to be fought for, to share an adventure, and to unveil her beauty. In the second chapter of his book, Eldredge portrays Christ as the exemplar of the three masculine desires. In Eldredge's picture, Jesus engages in a battle against the forces of evil to save his people. He takes the risky adventure of creating a world with freewill, and living in dynamic relationship with unpredictable people. He seeks to win the beauty of his bride, the church.[21]

Feminist Critique of Jesus's Masculinity

We would expect that Eldredge's vision of a restored traditional masculinity would be susceptible to a feminist critique. But, at least with regards to Luke's Gospel, feminist critical studies have often agreed with Eldredge in portraying Jesus as a masculine exemplar. Feminist readings of Luke's Jesus show a considerable disparity between positive and negative assessments of Luke's approach to patriarchy. While it is widely admitted that he is affirming and kind toward women, such readings nevertheless portray Jesus's relationship to women in terms which conform to Greco-Roman patriarchal norms. Because of this, Amy-Jill Levine claims, "The Gospel of Luke threatens any attempt made by women . . . to find a voice in either society or church."[22]

Katherine Corley, in her study of women's place at meals in the Synoptic Tradition, has shown how Luke portrays women conforming to Greco-Roman table manners by excluding themselves entirely from participation in public meals, and from taking the role of serving (διακονέω) at table.[23] Corley analyzes Luke's redaction in Luke 4:39, where Luke politely removes any bystanders from the scene (as in Mark 1:29) in order to make Peter's mother-in-law's service a private affair.

Mark 1:29–31 (NRSV, my italics)	Luke 4:38–39 (NRSV, my italics)
29 As soon as they left the synagogue, they entered the house of Simon *and Andrew, with James and John.*	38 After leaving the synagogue he entered Simon's house.
30 Now Simon's mother-in-law was in bed with a fever, and they told him about her at once.	Now Simon's mother-in-law was suffering from a high fever, and they asked him about her.
31 He came and took her by the hand and lifted her up. Then the fever left her, *and she began to serve* (διηκόνει) *them.*	39 Then he stood over her and rebuked the fever, and it left her. *Immediately she got up and began to serve* (διηκόνει) *them.*

The use of διακονέω (serve) holds significant implications for the place of women in the Lukan community, since, "when men 'serve'. . . the community it symbolises a leadership role . . . had Peter's mother-in-law 'served' several men . . . it might have had scandalous overtones."[24] By surrounding Jesus with such appropriately behaved women in table scenes, Luke highlights his exemplary Greco-Roman masculinity and protects his leadership role.

Critical Perspectives from Masculinity Studies

This assessment of the Lukan Jesus's masculinity as hegemonic is supported by the critical study of masculinity. I emphasize *critical* study to differentiate this topic within the discipline of gender studies from the broader "uncritical celebration of traditional masculinities"[25] as, for example, by the men's movement I discussed earlier.

An early critical treatment of Christ's masculinity is found in David Clines's study "Ecce Vir," which lists a series of components of "biblical masculinity" (such as strength, violence, and womanlessness), and shows how Christ exemplifies each of them. Drawing on Clines's work, Susan Haddox proposed that biblical masculinities are not monolithic but plural and diverse. While certain properties such as honor, potency, and wisdom are key components of masculinity,[26] biblical texts often show favor to subordinated masculinities such as younger sons, and speak disapprovingly of more traditional masculinities, such as Genesis' condemnation of the dominating and retributive violence of Cain's descendants in Gen 4.[27] In the Deuteronomistic History, masculine domination and strong military leadership by figures such as Samson, Saul, and David, when carried out without regard for the instructions of Yahweh, are often portrayed as leading to a loss of masculine attributes such as self-control or even sanity.[28]

A methodological shift was clearly observable in the 2004 collection of studies entitled *New Testament Masculinities*, where Clines's canonical category of "biblical" masculinity was replaced with a methodological trend toward reading texts within their own cultural constructions of gender, such as Imperial Roman masculinity.[29] There is one exception in this volume to the interpretation of Jesus's masculinity as hegemonic. That is, Chris Frilingos's interpretation of the Lamb's wounds and exposure to the gaze of other men as feminization.[30] In this reading, however, the Lamb's masculinity is quickly regained by his vengeance on all those who pierced him.

SUBORDINATE MASCULINITY

While it is dangerous to apply biblical masculinity unthinkingly to our own context, because it developed in a culture with different gender assumptions, the favored masculinities in the biblical text offer a wide variety of gender performances, more than is often allowed for "real men" today.[31]

What if the masculinity of Jesus was not hegemonic at all but actually functioned as a subordinate or even protest masculinity? I will now argue that Jesus's masculinity was far from ideal in his social world. In fact, as a conquered subject and an itinerant, whatever masculinity he had must be considered subordinate due to a number of factors.

Bruce Malina describes first-century Mediterranean masculinity as operating within a "moral division of labor," which is gendered. This culture's ideal of masculinity is best understood as the aggressive pursuit of honor. Since honor was understood as a limited commodity, there was constant competition for it.[32] The role of males was to seek to acquire and defend honor for one's own kinship group, whereas the role of females was connected to shame and required sensitivity to the perception of the kinship group's honor by outsiders. To challenge someone's honor is to make a claim to enter their social space, and this is understood in strongly sexual terms. The claim to honor is, according to Malina, symbolled by the testicles, while the protection of one's social space is symbolized by the hymen.[33]

That a male who belongs to a conquered people would be viewed as feminized by the penetration of his space is attested in ANE sources (including Israelite ones) and Greco-Romans sources. This can therefore be understood as a cultural assumption firmly established in Jesus's social world, and recognized by the conquering Romans and the conquered Palestinian Jews.

ANE Contexts

ANE men acquired honor through penetration, and lost it by being penetrated. According to the Middle Assyrian Laws, "if a man has sex with his comrade and they prove the charges against him, they shall have sex with him and they shall turn him into a eunuch."[34] However, in Assyrian dream oracles, for a man to penetrate his social equal from behind is an omen that the penetrating partner will become a leader.[35]

This contest for honor can be carried out through the invasion of physical space as well as the penetration of bodies. John White has documented the extensive use of architectural metaphors for female genitalia and virginity in love poetry throughout the ANE world, in biblical texts discussing female sexuality (Gen 29:31, 30:22; Song 4:12, 8:2, 9, and especially 5:2–8) and in Second Temple and Rabbinic literature.[36] In this metaphorical world, entering a private space is a form of penetration in which the space entered is feminized, and the one entering is making a claim to masculine power.

This sexual imagery is similarly evident when invading armies claim masculine honor upon invading the territory of another king. In such contexts, the defeated king becomes feminized by the penetration of his space. According to Cynthia Chapman, "for an Assyrian king, the battleground was the performance venue for achieving masculinity."[37] In battle, Assyrian kings portrayed themselves as "without rival amongst the princes" and therefore part of the achievement of ideal masculinity was to portray the enemy as having forfeited or failed masculinity, or being feminized. This is notable in royal accounts of battles which portray foreign kings fleeing or surrendering,[38] and curses placed on conquered vassals, which describe them as women and prostitutes.[39] Assyrian palace reliefs take up the same metaphors, portraying enemy soldiers physically impaled on Assyrian weapons, sexually exposed, and their city walls penetrated by phallic-looking Assyrian battering rams—they have become women in defeat.[40]

What is fascinating in Chapman's study is the way that Israel, as a conquered people, adopts these metaphors for themselves. In Old Testament texts, Israelites appropriate the same basic set of metaphors for defeat by Assyria, gendering their conquerors masculine, and themselves as feminine. Early texts such as Hosea and Amos portray Israel as a woman who, by being conquered, has committed adultery against Yahweh. Later, Isaiah and Zephaniah and Nahum expand on the metaphorical complex and describe the city of Jerusalem as a woman who abandoned Yahweh as Father/Husband, and went after Assyria as a poorly chosen lover, who treated her unkindly. Biblical texts also feature feminization curses on Israel itself, such as Nahum 3:4–5, 13, in which Israel is threatened with sexual humiliation. Deutero-Isaiah describes the way that Yahweh's slighted masculinity is reclaimed by the restoration of Jerusalem as a bride.

It is therefore part of Jesus's tradition as an Israelite that as a *conquered* man, he is a feminized man. Such a categorization is also a feature of his lived situation, the Roman occupation of Palestine.

Greco-Roman Contexts

Drawing on Foucault's *History of Sexuality*, David Halperin has argued that the Western concept of sexuality as a mutually pleasurable expression of a private and internal psychological and physical drive is foreign to the ancient world. Analyzing such texts as Plato's *Symposium* and Caelius Aurelianus's account of homoerotic behavior in *De Morbis Chronicis*, Halperin argues that in classical cultures, masculinity is similarly identified with phallic penetration, and that it is therefore unmanly to be penetrated.[41]

In classical Athenian attitudes and behaviors, for example, a sexual act is not seen as an interaction between two people but rather an action performed by one person on another. The sexual act is phallic penetration, and the one who performs it claims his domination of the penetrated sexual object, and asserts his manly status by so doing.[42]

Halperin's argument has been demonstrated with numerous ancient textual examples by Martti Nissinen.[43] Particularly relevant here is the Eurymedon vase, which celebrates the victory of the Athenians over the Persians, by depicting a Greek soldier approaching a Persian, holding his erect phallus, and intending to rape the conquered enemy.[44] The categories of thought assumed here make remarkable sense of the wider Mediterranean attitudes to conquest in Assyrian and Israelite texts described earlier. They also predict rather effectively the relationship between Jesus's conquered masculinity and the ideal masculinity of the invading Romans.

The sense of phallic domination by the Romans may even be reflected in the nervousness shown by Jews so diverse as Herod (as portrayed by Josephus)[45] and the Rabbis[46] about leaving Jewish boys alone with Roman guardians. Daniel Boyarin also noticed a passage from the Mekhilta of Rabbi Ishmael (Amaleq 1) in which a conquered Israelite king is depicted being subjected to rape by a foreign conqueror.[47]

The Protest Masculinity of Jesus

There is no written record of the structure of Galilean family life from a Galilean perspective, other than what we know from archaeology and Josephus's often tangential comments. As in all agrarian societies, one's social standing was completely determined by one's relationship to the oldest male relative.[48] There is some evidence that the division of labor in Galilean households was less rigidly determined by gender than even in Judean Jewish homes.[49]

Galilean masculinity is therefore distinct from its Roman counterpart. The Jewish *mishpahah*, for instance, was an extended family or clan, in contrast to the nuclear Roman *familias*. The patriarchs of Jewish households (except rarely, when they were Roman citizens) were less powerful than a Roman *paterfamilias*.[50] Jewish patriarchs did not have power of life and death over their sons, or sexual access to subordinate members of their households other than their own wives.[51]

Jesus's masculinity may have been culturally different to the hegemonic masculinity of the Romans; Jesus's was a subordinated masculinity. The Roman penetration of Israelite space through military occupation feminized Jewish men, and spoiled their masculine honor. In that case, the assumption that Jesus's table ministry in Luke represents masculine power seems to be misplaced. If Jesus asserted male privilege at table, or if he is portrayed as doing so by Luke, he does so in order to reject the hegemonic masculinity of Roman dominance. He cannot be understood as enacting it himself.

Jesus's masculinity in Luke should be viewed as a form of "protest masculinity," which Connell and Messerschmidt define as

> a pattern of masculinity constructed in local working class settings, sometimes among culturally marginalised men, which embodies the claim to power typical

of hegemonic masculinities in Western countries, but which lacks the economic resources and institutional authority that underpins the regional and global patterns.[52]

To avoid anachronism, we here read "working class" as "peasant" and "Western" as "Greco-Roman," but the point holds. Jesus's masculine behavior is not supporting global patriarchy. Rather, it is challenging it in a democratizing way.

None of this is to suggest that ethnically subordinate (or protest) masculinities are unproblematic. Michelle Wallace's critique of "black macho" argues that the black (i.e., African American) man in the 1960s "accepted a definition of manhood that is destructive to himself."[53] That is, emasculated by slavery and segregation, black men sought to claim their masculine status in Western society by emulating and aspiring to the oppression of women they saw in the white man.

But "black macho" is not comparable to Jesus's masculinity in the Gospels. Wallace's complaint is that the black man's own definition of masculinity had been displaced by the white perspective on manhood. But Jesus's ministry clearly doesn't comply with Greco-Roman patriarchy. Instead, it calls on disciples to leave their patriarchal village life and follow him (Luke 9:57–62).

JESUS'S COLONIZED MASCULINITY AND THE WHITE AUSTRALIAN MALE SUBJECT

With the relationship between Jesus's masculinity and mine clarified in this way, I can begin to articulate my vantage point as a reader of the Bible, and especially as one who would seek to appropriate the Jesus tradition and apply it to his own context. Jesus's protest masculinity helps me to locate my own subjectivity as a reader. My white Australian masculinity is not comparable to that of Jesus. Rather, Jesus's masculinity is a *protest* against the very masculinity that I embody. And as such, Jesus's masculinity is no example for me to follow but rather it is an affront to my masculinity.

In many ways, white Australian men are like Aeneas and his companions in the opening quotation from the Aeneid. We seek to validate our masculinity and fulfill the aspirations of our forefathers through colonizing land, and then by eating on it. We find ourselves eating the land itself, and in this way, consuming the original connection of indigenous people. Jesus, a man indigenous to Palestine, stayed at the head of the table throughout his ministry, and retained his masculine dignity as an act of resistance against such erasure of his culture and identity. White Australian men should experience this as a protest against them, rather than an example for them.

Indigenous masculinities challenge colonizing masculinities because of the uncomfortable truth they expose. White Australian exemplars of masculinity all seem to reflect a need to assert a natural connection to the land. Swagmen, convicts and bushrangers, sporting legends, and so on are portrayed outdoors, in the countryside, enjoying the natural features of surf and sun, completely in control of the rigorous natural environment.[54]

The average white Australian man, perhaps living in suburbia, working a trade, and raising a family, relates to this process of erasing and then replacing indigenous masculinity with a naturalized white masculinity in mundane ways. He need not live in the outback or brew tea in a billy, because these cultural icons have evolved into that mainstay of Australian suburban entertaining: barbequed sausages with tomato sauce, coleslaw, and beer in the backyard.

Particularly interesting in our case is David Dale's claim that Australian men's love of meat is a reassertion of the ancient male role as a tribal hunter,[55] claiming for white men a form of masculinity associated with indigenous men. An action so innocent as burning sausages while the ladies are tossing salads in the kitchen contains a culturally encoded erasure of indigenous masculinity, and its replacement with an indigenized white Australian masculinity.

It is because white Australian masculinity is founded on this falsehood that it finds indigenous masculinity so unbearable. A scandal in the Australian Football League illustrates this problem aptly. In 2013, a thirteen-year-old girl heckled Adam Goodes, a Sydney Swans player of Andyamathanha and Narungga descent, calling him an "ape," and she was asked to leave. In 2015, Goodes celebrated a goal by performing a war dance with a symbolic spear-throw gesture, resulting in further outrage. In Goodes's own words,

> I haven't had an opportunity to show that passion, and that pride about being a warrior and representing my people and where I come from. . . . There was nothing untoward to the Carlton supporters. It was actually something for them to stand up and go, "yep we see you, and we acknowledge you—bring it on."[56]

Here, Goodes is asserting his indigenous masculinity as protest in the same way that Jesus asserts his masculinity in Lukan symposia. Not surprisingly, the white Australian outrage was hostile enough to echo the Pharisaic backlash against Jesus. Take, for example, the words of a popular radio commentator, Alan Jones:

> They're booing Adam Goodes because they don't like him, they don't like his behaviour, they don't like the spear-throwing and the running in and doing a war dance and so on and provoking people. They simply don't like the fellow and Adam Goodes can fix all this by changing his behaviour.[57]

Jones's comments reveal a strange double standard. Displays of masculinity are surely normal on a football field if nowhere else! And yet, in that very context, indigenous masculinity provokes public upset and outrage. Protest masculinity is upsetting to hegemonic masculine readers.

I hope that the interpretive possibilities arising from this essay will be possible to translate into exegetical writing and teaching within the theological academy but also to the preaching and devotional reading of biblical texts. Jesus's masculinity will remain a feature of the Gospel tradition. But it should not be used to deify our own traditional gender roles. Instead, it must critique and destabilize them.

NOTES

1. *Aeneid* 7.171–76a; quoted from *The Aeneid of Virgil*, trans. and with an introduction by Kevin Guinagh (New York: Holt, Rinehart, and Winston, 1953), 170–171.

2. Chris Budden, *Following Jesus in Invaded Space: Doing Theology on Aboriginal Land* (Eugene, Oregon: Pickwick, 2009).

3. Marilyn Frye, "On Being White: Thinking toward a Feminist Understanding of Race and Race Supremacy," in *The Politics of Reality: Essays in Feminist Theory*, ed. Marilyn Frye (Berkeley: Crossing Press, 1983), 112–113.

4. Toula Nicolacopoulos and George Vassilacopoulos, *Indigenous Sovereignty and the Being of the Occupier: Manifesto for a White Australian Philosophy of Origins* (Melbourne: re.press, 2014), 11.

5. Nicolacopoulos and Vassilacopoulos, *Indigenous Sovereignty*, 13–14.

6. Ibid., 29–30.

7. Michael Kimmel, *Angry White Men: American Masculinity at the End of an Era* (New York: Nation Books, 2013), 20. Kimmel's claim is used very effectively by Susan Faludi to describe many examples of Western masculinity in decline. See Susan Faludi, *Stiffed: Betrayal of the Modern Man* (London: Random House, 2011), 3–47.

8. Raewyn W. Connell and James W. Messerschmidt, "Hegemonic Masculinity Rethinking the Concept," *Gender & Society* 19.6 (2005): 846.

9. Raewyn W. Connell, *Gender and Power: Society, the Person and Sexual Politics* (Sydney, Allen & Unwin, 1987), 183.

10. Connell and Messerschmidt "Hegemonic Masculinity," 832, 846–853.

11. See, e.g., Joseph A. Fitzmyer, *The Gospel According to Luke X–XVV* (Garden City: Doubleday, 1985), 1039–1041.

12. Luke Timothy Johnson, *The Gospel of Luke* (Collegeville, MN: Liturgical Press, 1991), 225–226.

13. Darrel L. Bock, *Luke: 1:1–9:50* (Grand Rapids, MI: Baker Books, 1994), 1253.

14. John Dominic Crossan, *The Historical Jesus: The Life of a Mediterranean Jewish Peasant* (San Francisco: HarperCollins, 1991), 261–264.

15. John T. Squires, *At Table with Luke* (Sydney: UTC Publications, 2000), 23–24.

16. Ibid., 51–52.

17. Mary Douglas, "Deciphering a Meal," in *Myth, Symbol and Culture*, ed. Clifford Geertz (New York: W. W. Norton and Co, 1971), 61.

18. Faludi, *Stiffed*, 238.

19. Ibid., 264–267.

20. In such literature, a far more common biblical rationale is found in the created order, Adam's failure to lead Eve to resist Satan's temptation, Jesus's decision to appoint male apostles, and even Jesus's kind treatment of women. However, these references are generally grounds from which doctrines about the nature of gender roles are inferred rather than examples of a masculine role. The portrayal of the relationship between Christ and the church is arguably the central theological argument put forward in this literature. However, they do not generally pay any attention to the masculinity of Jesus *as a historical figure*. See John Piper and Wayne Grudem, "An Overview of Central Concerns: Questions and Answers," in *Recovering Biblical Manhood and Womanhood: A Response to Evangelical Feminism*, ed. John Piper and Wayne Grudem (Wheaton, IL: CrosswayPiper and Grudem, 2006), 60.

21. John Eldredge, *Wild at Heart: Discovering the Secret of a Man's Soul* (Nashville: Thomas Nelson, 2001), 20–38.

22. Amy-Jill Levine, "Introduction," in *A Feminist Companion to Luke*, ed. Amy-Jill Levine (London: Sheffield Academic, 2002), 1.

23. Kathleen E. Corley, *Private Women, Public Meals: Social Conflict in the Synoptic Tradition* (Peabody, MA: Hendrickson, 1993), 109.

24. Ibid., 121.

25. Stephen D. Moore, "'O Man Who Art Thou?' Masculinity Studies and New Testament Studies," in *New Testament Masculinities*, ed. Janice Capel Anderson and Stephen D. Moore (Atlanta: Society of Biblical Literature, 2003), 4.

26. Susan E. Haddox, "Is There a Biblical Masculinity? Masculinities in the Hebrew Bible," *Word & World* 36.1 (Winter 2016): 6–7.

27. Ibid., 7.

28. Ibid., 10–11.

29. Moore, "'O Man Who Art Thou?'" 20.

30. Christopher A. Frilingos, "Sexing the Lamb," in *New Testament Masculinities*, ed. Janice Capel Anderson and Stephen D. Moore (Atlanta: Society of Biblical Literature, 2003), 306–309.

31. Haddox, "Is There a Biblical Masculinity?" 14.

32. Bruce J. Malina, *The New Testament World: Insights from Cultural Anthropology* (Atlanta: SCM Press, 1981), 30–33.

33. Ibid., 42–48.

34. Marti Nissinen, *Homoeroticism in the Biblical World: A Historical Perspective* (Minneapolis, MN: Augsburg Fortress, 1998), 25.

35. Ibid., 27.

36. John Bradley White, *A Study of the Language of Love in the Song of Songs and Ancient Egyptian Poetry* (Missoula, Mont: Scholars Press, 1978), 93, 96, 152.

37. Cynthia R. Chapman, *The Gendered Language of Warfare in the Israelite-Assyrian Encounter* (University Park, PA: Eisenbrauns, 2004), 20.

38. Ibid., 33–39.

39. Ibid., 41–58.

40. Ibid., 161–163.

41. David M. Halperin, *One Hundred Years of Homosexuality: And Other Essays on Greek Love* (London, New York: Routledge, 1990), 21–24.

42. Ibid., 29–38.

43. Nissinen, *Homoeroticism in the Biblical World*, 57–88.

44. Ibid., fig. 3.

45. Ibid., 94.

46. Ibid., 99.

47. Daniel Boyarin, "Are There Any Jews in 'The History of Sexuality?'" *Journal of the History of Sexuality* 5 (1995): 339–340.

48. Richard A. Horsley, *Galilee: History, Politics, People* (Valley Forge: Trinity Press International, 1995), 196–201.

49. Ibid., 200–201.

50. Martin Goodman, *Rome and Jerusalem: The Clash of Ancient Civilizations* (London: Penguin, 2008), 222–223.

51. Ibid., 229.

52. Connell and Messerschmidt "Hegemonic Masculinity," 848.

53. Michele Wallace, *Black Macho and the Myth of the Superwoman* (London: Verso, 1999), 79.

54. This vision of masculinity is hardly unique to Australia. Faludi has chronicled a parallel process in that other great settler-colonial country, the United States. According to Faludi, this was a response to the crisis of masculinity, and loss of any social usefulness for men as breadwinners and role models (Faludi, *Stiffed*, 40–42). In the United States, the masculine exemplar that emerged was Davy Crockett, the wastrel on the frontier, asserting control over his natural environment (Faludi, *Stiffed*, 11). In Australia, Ned Kelly has played this role: the outlaw on horseback.

55. Simon Carey Holt, *Eating Heaven: Spirituality at the Table* (Melbourne: Acorn, 2013), 36–37. A Baptist pastor and sociologist, Holt has traced this culinary construction of Australian masculinity back to a variety of origins, such as the English belief in the virility of roast beef dinners, to the late nineteenth-century conviction that our access to meat three times a day was a historically unprecedented consequence of our radically egalitarian society.

56. Michael Safi, "AFL Great Adam Goodes Is Being Booed across Australia. How Did It Come to This?" *The Guardian* (July 29, 2015). http://www.theguardian.com/sport/blog/2015/jul/29/afl-great-adam-goodes-is-being-booed-across-australia-how-did-it-come-to-this?CMP=soc_567.

57. Greg Denham, "Adam Goodes Booing Controversy: 'Can't blame him if he quits,'" *The Australian* (July 29, 2015).

Chapter 4

"I Am My Body"

Toward a Body-affirming Faith

Masiiwa Ragies Gunda

There are many issues that confuse Christians who live on earth but believe that our destiny is in heaven. Among such issues is the attitude toward the human body. The history of Christianity is littered by groups that struggle with the question of the human body and some go to the extreme of rejecting the body while others appear to affirm the body in an extreme way. While there are differences on how we view and value the human body, there is no conflict in the view that the human body is central to the way we reflect about God and the universe.

> The human body is the primary lens through which we view, encounter and engage the world around us. It is no surprise then to find a wide range of theological reflection upon the human body, from those that affirm the human body as something very good, through to other more negative views where the body is something to be marginalized or escaped from.[1]

The complexities surrounding the human body have been exposed in the discussions on sex, gender, and sexual practices. The traditional fault lines between body-affirming faith and body-rejecting faith have been exposed in the way different groups respond to the realities of sexual practices and relationships. This essay engages with the theology of the body, the scriptures, and the designs of empire in a bid to find a position on faith and the body. This study begins with an overview of traditional Christian faith and the human body, and then shifts to a consideration of the rejection of the body and the designs of empire. A scriptural basis for a body-affirming theology focusing on Gen 1:26–28 and Luke 10:27 will be proposed, leading to a proclamation that we are our bodies. Any attempt to reject the body opposes what it means to be created in the "image of God."

TRADITIONAL CHRISTIAN FAITH AND
THE REJECTION OF THE BODY

The question of the human body constituted a major focal point in early
Christianity. The quest to attain salvation revolved around the mastering of
the human body, especially its desires. "The body in early Christianity was
not only a temporary earthly container for the eternal soul; it was also seen as
a threat to living a good and sin-free earthly life. The source of this threat was
its sensuality, a quality seen as simultaneously inescapable and destructive."[2]
Central to the problems created by the body for the believers was sexual
desire. In fact, traditional teaching from prominent early Christians regarded
sexual desire as the end of all senses of the human body. Everything leads to
sexual desire.

A theology of the body emerged, therefore, as "an inquiry into the identity
and existence of divine beings, divine activity in history and nature, the purpose and destiny of human life as these are revealed by a being called 'God'
to others called 'persons.'"[3] A theology of the body sought to establish what
was the acceptable attitude toward the body by those who wanted to please
God. Among early Christians, three different positions regarding the human
body emerged: (1) that the human body was an obstacle to true spirituality
hence sexual desires had to be conquered by foregoing sexual intercourse;
(2) that the human body and its sexual desires are the epitome of the freedom
gained through Christ hence sexual intercourse had no problem and could
even be done by everyone with anyone; and (3) that the human body has
desires that must be tamed hence sexual intercourse can be done only within
the institution of marriage and only for procreation purposes. This third view
is particularly interesting in our quest to expose designs of empire and will be
pursued further in subsequent sections. While the actual ideas of the different groups among early Christians may differ here and there with these three
broad lines of thought, I think these three sum up the main lines of thought.
However one looks at these three thought patterns, it is clear that the human
body was not to be trusted entirely.

Various groups emerged in the early centuries with teachings on the human
body and sexuality. Among these early Christian groups were followers of
Marcion, who taught against sexual intercourse because they believed that
sexual intercourse was the "knowledge" they had gained in the Garden of
Eden, seen as the cause of human sinfulness.[4] Closely connected to this
group, "Gnostic teaching associated the body with active evil that threatened the acquisition of true knowledge. Procreating children was therefore
procreating further evil."[5] Picking on some biblical texts, especially Gen 3
and materials from Paul, these groups exalted individuals who could conquer
their sexual desires and forego sexual intercourse in their lives. Following the

teachings of these groups arose some Christians pursuing castration as a way of renouncing their sexuality. In fact, "when religions arose, this disassociation became even more pronounced as the 'you are not your body' belief. Countless people in East and West throughout the ages have tried to find God, salvation, or enlightenment through the denial of the body."[6] Indeed,

> the renunciation of the body and its sensuality was to lead eventually to the establishment of monasteries as retreats from the temptations of the world and its carnal pleasures. Early Christian sexual morality demanded the "death of the senses" through the practice of bodily asceticism in extreme forms. Yet there was little confidence that such self-denial was effective in killing off the desires of the flesh, especially when in closer contact with women.[7]

During the first four centuries of Christianity, the body became associated with evil; with ignorance and bestiality; and with lack of control. More specifically, sexual desire was identified as both the proof and exemplar of these claims.[8] The Manicheans taught that "since the body is the work of the devil, the propagation of the body is evil; and marriage, considered as the institutional means of procreation, is also evil."[9] In general terms, some forms of early Christianity taught that

> [S]ex was the original sin and that the carnal and spiritual were forever irreconcilable. One could not live in the world of the spirit and of the body at the same time. In order to live and grow spiritually in this world, and thus enter the next, the body must be renounced. This view depended upon the interpretation of Genesis 1–3 that sex was the original sin. For Ambrose and Jerome, and the earlier Church Fathers who advocated virginity (Chrysostom and Tertullian, for example) there was no sex in paradise. Before the fall, Adam and Eve were as sexless as were the angels.[10]

There were other Christian groups who stood on the other extreme in the discourses regarding the human body and sexuality. Opposed to Marcion and his group was "the libertine group, the Carpocratians who apparently participated in licentious sexual acts because they believed they were imitating the primordial powers who had intercourse with one another in order to create the universe."[11] A libertine approach to sex was considered dangerous to the general moral fiber of society, especially a society organized patriarchally where the control of women and children became a prized asset for men. As Christianity became an institution it also wanted a sustainable way of managing relations and creating a conducive environment for organized increase in numbers through procreation. Interestingly, in that regard, Christianity and empire appeared to move closer to each other against Libertine and Ascetic groups. While there were Christians who advocated a libertine approach to the body and its desires, these were already few in number when compared to those who advocated the renunciation of the body and its desires. These two extreme positions, however, were not accepted by the major institutions (religion and empire) hence the rise of the third and alternative view, which over the centuries became the "official teaching of Christianity," with varying nuances depending on the teacher and context.

It is within this third group that key figures such as Augustine and Clement may be placed. This third group appears to have been influenced by the Stoic teachings of the time, which were quite prominent in the Roman Empire. "Stoics taught that sexual pleasure, more than any other sensation, caused man to lose his reason, a view that is also evident in Classical antiquity. Yet they also believed that the intellect and will could counteract the temptations of bodily desire and that marriage provided an ideal context for this to be demonstrated."[12] One of the leading Stoics, Musonius, thought pleasure was a bad reason for sexual intercourse, which is meant for procreation.[13] Moderation was the name of the game; everything that human beings did had to be done moderately and must never be driven by desire but by reason. When arguing against the Manichean teaching on the evil of marriage and sexual intercourse, "Augustine offers the counter-thesis that it is precisely the goodness of procreation which makes marriage good."[14] Similarly, we can understand Clement's teaching in this light when he says Christians should

> [D]o nothing from desire. Our will is to be directed only towards that which is necessary. For we are children not of desire but of will. A man who marries for the sake of begetting children must practice self-control so that it is not desire he feels for his wife, whom he ought to love, and that he may beget children with a chaste and controlled will.[15]

As Seneca famously put it,

> A wise man ought to love his wife with judgment, not affection. Let him control his impulses and not be born headlong into copulation. Nothing is fouler than to love one's wife like an adulteress.[16]

While the two dominant views in early Christianity are different—one completely rejects bodily desires surrounding sexual intercourse and the other accepting the necessity of sexual intercourse for procreation—one can conclude that generally, early Christianity (many Christians may silently still share such fears about the potential to sin through sexual intercourse) had a negative perception of the human body and sexual intercourse.

Theologies that reject or renounce the body are based on a reading of the Bible, especially Gen 3. Gail Hawkes accordingly argues that through a reading of Gen 1–3 most early Christians associated original sin with sexual intercourse between Adam and Eve.[17] The assumption is that the fruit they shared was responsible for arousing sexual desire and they therefore ended up having sexual intercourse not because of the will to procreate but because of the desire they had aroused in themselves. Along this line, early Christians read Matt 5:29–30 as a basis for renouncing the body, as they sought to achieve eternal life and salvation.

REJECTION OF THE BODY: PLAYING INTO THE DESIGNS OF EMPIRE

Empire is an institution that is all encompassing and that seeks to control the totality of human life to serve its own interests. Empire is the aggregate of political, military, economic, and religio-social powers that harnessed to rule and exploit for profit, a reality that is seen and felt all around us. The human body has been very central to the designs of empire because without it, empire cannot survive. From ancient to contemporary empires, the desire to control the human body has not wavered, but the actual control has taken various forms. It is within this context that we can appreciate the rise of slavery in the ancient empires and why it continued for so long in human history. This desire is also behind the apparent downgrading of the woman's body into some form of machine designed to make babies to strengthen empire and its designs. The convergence of empire and organized religion can, therefore, be seen clearly. In fact, in most ancient empires, religion was developed by and in order to serve the interests of empire. In this regard, we can confidently assert that Christianity, as a continuation of Israelite theology and faith, was found to challenge empire and its forms of religions and not to aid empire in its designs. In Christianity, we have a religion that started as a movement to stand up to empire and its machinations. This is particularly clear in Luke 4:18–20, Jesus's manifesto on the ministry and movement that started off in Galilea.

A critical reading of the Babylonian creation myth, the *Enuma Elish*, illustrates the convergence of religion and empire and shows in no uncertain terms that religion was subservient to the designs of empire. In the myth, human beings were created to serve the gods, who did not want to continue working for themselves. Human beings were, therefore, created to be slaves to the gods.[18] Interestingly, the work of supervising human slaves was given to some human beings who became representatives of the gods and were thus kings of the human communities. In effect, therefore, all other human beings became slaves to their kings, who branded themselves as divine representatives. This may explain the rise of the class of kings who considered themselves "semi-gods." Nonruling individuals were expected to work every day for the benefit and enjoyment of the gods and their representatives, the ruling class.

One of the central demands placed on slaves by the empires of old was that they surrender their bodies to the empire,[19] a demand which subsists to date only that it is presented differently under the concepts of patriotism, and love of the motherland. The body of the slave belonged to the master, who could use it in any way he may decide. Slaves had no control over their bodies, the masters did, that is why slaves did not even have control over their offspring because they belonged to the master. The master was the nucleus manifestation of empire in the lives of ordinary human beings. Ancient empires would not have accomplished a lot were it not for the control of the bodies of the slaves they had. According to Isaac Mendelsohn,

> The economic advantages derived by the state from this practice were obvious enough to make all conquerors follow the example set at the dawn of history. The great projects of military fortifications, of road, irrigation, and temple constructions, accomplished by the state would have been almost impossible without the help of the war prisoners, many of whom were skilled craftsmen.[20]

In cases where individuals have been taught to reject their bodies as a way of achieving higher degrees of spirituality, people could willingly submit themselves to exploitation as a way of getting control over their bodies. Empire was the beneficiary to all that.

Immediately after independence in Zimbabwe, there was an institution called the Youth Brigade that was deployed to drive community development projects. These groups had very efficient fitness programs that saw them marching and jogging early in the morning and they were singing during their drills. While they had many songs, their jogging song remains clear in my mind:

Simudza gumbo, ha, simudza gumbo ha,
Harizi rako, ha, harizi rako, ha
Nderemusangano, ha, nderemusangano ha,
  (NderavaMugabe ha, nderavaMugabe ha)
Kana rikatyoka, ha,
Tinoisa rimwe![21]
(Raise your legs / They are not yours / they belong to the Party [They
  belong to Prime Minister Mugabe] / If it breaks, we will replace it!)

This is what empire seeks: the rejection of the body, and individuals willing to break their bones for the benefit of the empire. Empire thrives when ordinary people are willing to sacrifice themselves for the goals and desires of the ruling class. Similar ideas can be discovered in the way so-called suicide bombers are nurtured by their masters to see their greatest and most noble contribution to be to sacrifice their own bodies for the good of the masters. They do not have to be poor or uneducated, they only have to be taught what is the greatest sacrifice one can make for their country and people, which in most cases is empire itself.[22]

The same can be seen in the way the doctrine of patriotism has been peddled by most modern states, where the defense of the motherland/fatherland is more important than anything else and where one's body is to be submitted for service to the motherland. This is particularly the case with the so-called "blind patriotism. Blind patriots adopt a stance of unquestioning endorsement of their country—denying the value of critique and analysis and generally emphasizing allegiance and symbolic behaviors."[23] War veterans are, therefore, highly celebrated by the empire they served even as they are sometimes discarded once they are injured or have aged that they can no longer serve the empire. The same war veterans are looked upon as war criminals by the empires they fought against; such is the situation in a world of multiple empires. With empire, so intent on controlling the human body and using it to its own ends, it is not surprising that religions that teach the rejection of the body may be (in)directly playing into the game of the empire.

An aspect of the human body that has been greatly feared and, therefore, attracted the greatest attention from both empire and religions is human sexuality. The potential of the human body to achieve pleasure has been thoroughly curtailed hence religions sought to present sexual pleasure as evil and sexual intercourse for procreation as a necessary evil that must be contained. The rejection of the body's desire for sexual pleasure was seen as a way of preparing the soul for eternal rest, while empire legislated against sexual pleasure and promoted procreation.[24] The promotion of procreation by empire was presented as abiding by God's command to multiply; the multiplication envisaged by empire was for strengthening the work and programs of empire. The fear created in religious circles effectively played into the hands of empire. It is in this context that the family unit, defined and understood as the marriage of man and woman (several women, in ancient empires), was constructed to provide a controlled use of sexual intercourse.

If, as some religions teach, the body is our enemy, can we ever stand up in defense of the body against the designs of empire to exploit that same body for profit and pleasure? Are we not supposed to thank those that exploit our bodies since our bodies are always endangering our standing in the eyes of God? While religion teaches that the desires of the body are inherently opposed to what God has planned for us, empire teaches us that the desires of the body are opposed to the patriotism demanded of us by empire. Either way, a rejection of the body is entailed but for whose ends? My contention is that the rejection of the body is not God's plan for human beings but largely the design of empire to control the body and to direct it to move in a particular direction in the interest of the empire.

GEN 1–3: BASES FOR BODY-AFFIRMING FAITH

Are our bodies our enemies? Is pleasure the enemy of salvation? Must we renounce our bodies for God to grant us salvation and eternal life? These questions are central in this section. Making use of two texts from the Bible, I state that there are texts in the Bible that could be basis of a body-affirming theology that will challenge the shame of sexual intercourse among human beings.

For most African communities, sex remains the act that we do secretly, spoken of in predefined fora using euphemisms. Christianity and traditional religion combined to produce a strong fear of sexuality among Africans, such that sins are graded, with sexually connected sins as the most feared. Generally speaking, therefore, our bodies are the greatest obstacle to our attainment of salvation. "The bias against the body as impure, sinful and distracting from the spiritual, is upsetting, and to attach primary importance to rational thinking, disturbing."[25] To fear our bodies as an impediment to our spirituality and salvation appears to me to be irrational and theologically unsound. I think there is every reason for Christians and people in general to affirm their bodies.

I revisit the creation etiologies of Gen 1–3, whose significance lies in the attempt to explain the complex beginnings of life on earth. We are doomed if we read these etiologies as history. Instead, I approach them as hypothetical reconstructions of what might have happened in the beginning of time. I agree with Dorham that "the precise starting point of these reflections is the two-fold creation account found in the opening chapters of Genesis (cf. Gen 1:27, 2:18–25). These two accounts converge in the revelation of man as a creature who is created in the image and likeness of God. In addition, God's image in man [sic] is not purely spiritual, but is manifested in the body."[26] This is a critical realization that however we were brought into this world, there cannot be a discussion of humanness that excludes the body, such that we cannot be too certain that the image of God language can make any sense at all if we also exclude the body from such talk. Due to our physical differences, as human beings, we have sometimes tried to spiritualize the image of God because we have thought that the image of God cannot be represented in our bodies with all these differences. Based on the Gen 1–3 etiologies, we can confidently assert here that there has never been and there will never be human beings without the human body—this we believe is God's will. How can God will us that which is impure and distracting? This is the first and possibly most important reason for the affirmation of the body in our lives—because God willed us these bodies.

In Gen 1:28, God blesses the embodied human beings to multiply. The growth of the human race is not possible outside of the bodies that God willed for humans. Even with all the technological advancement of our times, there is no substitute to the human body when it comes to procreation. We, therefore, are called upon to celebrate the bodies that make it possible for the human race to continue. This perception would have been more acute in ancient times when the body was not aided by technological advancement. To suggest, as some early Christians did, that God intended for another way of procreation that did not include carnal knowledge is stretching the argument. The fact is that we were created with bodies because the body was an indispensable component of what it meant and means to be human. On the basis of this creation etiology, we are called upon to affirm our bodies. In affirming the role of the body in procreation, we must be quick to realize the danger of making procreation the *sin qua non* function of the body and sexuality. Procreation allows for the human race to persist but that does not mean all created persons will actively contribute to this one function; a minority will not, irrespective of whether s/he is in hetero- or homosexual relationships. Therefore, we affirm not only the bodies that will procreate but all bodies because they have been willed by God.

There is yet another basis for affirming the human body, based on Gen 2:18–25. This is an etiology more interested in explaining the hierarchy of persons than their origins, as is the case with Gen 1:26–28. This second account brings to the fore the fact that as embodied creatures we also desire companionship. There is more to our bodies than procreating; our bodies are fit for the expression of companionship without which we cannot be a community. The kind of companionship that we yearn for is not simply sexual but also emotional, social, and intimate. This kind of companionship is such that we can only share it with a selected individual(s), but it is limited to our bodily lives; it cannot go beyond the grave when we lose our bodies. While some bodies may not be fit for procreation, all bodies are fit for companionship. We, therefore, are called upon to affirm our bodies for it is only through our bodies that we can share in companionship with other persons and become members of the human family. We all had friends and relatives with whom we once shared so much of our lives, some of them we would have wanted to be here with us, but because they lost their bodies to death, they can no longer be our companions because they no longer possess the prerequisite for companionship, that is, their bodies. With this understanding of the human body, there is room for many forms of companionship in the house of God.

In these forms of companionship, sexuality or sexual expression is a small component. This brings us to that which, as Christians, we have been most afraid of, pleasure and pleasuring the body. Even though the continued existence of the human race is dependent upon the ability of the majority to procreate, procreation is not the only use of the human body and human sexuality. One of the reasons why sexual pleasure has not been trusted is the ancient understanding of sexual intercourse as an act which is performed by one on another thereby making it inadequate to express the reciprocity expected in relationships of companionship.[27] We have moved from understanding our bodies as child-making machines; sexual intercourse is now an activity of self-giving to the other in ways that allow our bodies to reach heightened levels of pleasure, which in no way undermines our spirituality. A recent study by scientists from Duke University, North Carolina, made interesting observations on the connection between sexual intercourse (pleasure) and human spirituality:

> Hormones released while having sex can increase spirituality and belief in God, scientists have claimed. According to the research, the release of oxytocin not only promotes social bonding and helps childbirth in women, but also stimulates increased feelings of religiousness.[28]

A study of this nature supports the view that our bodies play an important role in bringing us into greater communion with God as well as improves our role as companions to fellow human beings with whom we choose to share our bodies. Pleasuring the body or allowing the body to experience sexual pleasure may not be mutually exclusive with our quest to attain higher spirituality. The body and all its desires are not inherently evil even though it is possible that some activities may end up crossing the line. There is, therefore, no rational reason for the fear of the body, for only through our bodies can we enjoy companionship with other human beings as well as be in communion with God. When properly pleasured, the body is in good condition to serve God in the manner of Luke 10:27 where Christ calls for us to serve God with the totality of our bodies and humanity.

What greater incentive do we have for the affirmation of the body than the realization of the mystery of Christ? This challenges the traditional Christian view of the body as something to overcome in order to receive the joys of heaven, but it affirms the most important article of the Christian faith, namely that God became human, with a body, in Jesus.[29] That God had to take up a body is a most important reason for us to affirm the human body. Affirming the human body entails defending the human body from the designs of empire, which exploits it for the advancement of its own interests and which are frequently opposed to the interests of God.

"I AM MY BODY"

The history of Christianity can rightly be regarded as a history of wrestling with the human body. This is the case because the body has always been central to the life, aspirations, and fears of Christians who realize that they had to live with their bodies, which were also highly attracted to many things of this world, some of which appear to oppose the will of God. The desire to be with God in heaven led early Christians to design a path that largely involved renouncing the body and its desires. In so doing, Christians over the centuries end up aiding empire, that in renouncing the body Christians disengage from the world of the empire and allow empire to do as it pleased (while Christians focus on their heaven-bound quest). We allow empire to exploit our disengagement from the governance of this world making empire unaccountable to anybody and even worse, we allow empire to exploit our bodies for profit.

By affirming our bodies, we acknowledge the interconnectedness of humanity (the totality of our outer and inner persons) and Christianity. We could not agree more with the succinct explanation of Sölle and Cloyes:

> My body tells me that I am in pain, hungry, have sexual needs. It is through my body that I know it is not so very good here on earth. The wrong way to relieve this tension is to deny and to suppress the body and its needs in favour of affirming an idealistic spirituality cleansed of all bodily desires.[30]

Our self-realization is not possible without an affirmation of our bodies and as indicated in this study, this recognition of the centrality and importance of our bodies is indispensable to our lives as Christians. In an era characterized by the excesses of the overbearing nature of empire, we are called upon to wrestle our bodies from being instruments of the empire and to affirm them as willed by God and, therefore, to be used as instruments in the propagation of the will of God. We are our bodies and our bodies are the vehicles through which we can serve God by promoting justice in this world as opposed to promoting profit in the service of the empire.

NOTES

1. Description of Stephen Garner (ed.), *Theology and the Body* (Hindmarsh: ATF Theology, 2011) on *booktopia*: https://www.booktopia.com.au/theology-and-the-body-stephen-garner/prod9781921817229.html.

2. Gail Hawkes, "The Problem of Pleasure and the Making of Sexual Sin in Early Christianity," presentation at *The Society for the Scientific Study of Sexuality, in Cooperation with The Kinsey Institute 50th Anniversary: Honoring Our Past and Envisioning Our Future* (Nov 7–11 at Hyatt Regency, Indianapolis, IN), 2.

3. Pieter Van Niekerk, "Towards a Theology of the Body. A Spirituality of Imperfection," *Towards a Theology of the Body* 53.3 & 4 (2012): 369.

4. April D. DeConick, "The Great Mystery of Marriage: Sex and Conception in Ancient Valentinian Traditions," *Vigiliae Christianae* 57.3 (2003): 307–342.

5. Hawkes, "The Problem of Pleasure," 3.

6. E. Tolle, *The Power of Now. A Guide to Spiritual Enlightenment* (London: Hodder & Stoughton, 2005), 95.

7. Hawkes, "The Problem of Pleasure," 6–7.

8. Ibid., 5.

9. Cormac Burke, "Saint Augustine and Conjugal Sexuality," *Church History Information Centre* (http://www.churchinhistory.org/pages/booklets/augustine.pdf accessed May 15, 2017), 1.

10. Hawkes, "The Problem of Pleasure," 5.

11. DeConick, "The Great Mystery of Marriage," 315.

12. Hawkes, "The Problem of Pleasure," 3.

13. F. H. Sandbach, *The Stoics* (London: Gerald Duckworth, 1989), 163.

14. Burke, "Saint Augustine and Conjugal Sexuality," 1.

15. DeConick, "The Great Mystery of Marriage," 316.

16. Hawkes, "The Problem of Pleasure," 4.

17. Ibid., 5.

18. Joshua Mark, "Enuma Elish—The Babylonian Epic of Creation," *Ancient History Encyclopedia* (http://www.ancient.eu/article/225/ accessed May 15, 2017).

19. Obvious Vengeyi, *Aluta Continua Biblical Hermeneutics for Liberation: Interpreting Biblical Texts on Slavery for Liberation of Zimbabwean Underclasses* (Bamberg: University of Bamberg Press, 2013), 48.

20. Isaac Mendelsohn, *Slavery in the Ancient Near East* (West Port, CT: Greenwood Press, 1898), 2.

21. This song was sung in the early years of Independence and captures how the bodies of individuals were understood as effectively belonging to the state (empire) that attempts at protecting the body by an individual were construed as sabotage and unpatriotic behavior.

22. Massimo Introvigne, "Of Cultists and Martyrs: The Study of New Religious Movements and Suicide Terrorism in Conversation," in *Dying for Faith: Religiously Motivated Violence in the Contemporary World*, ed. Madawi al Rasheed and Marat Shterin (London: I. B. Tauris, 2009), 43–48.

23. Joseph Kahne and Ellen Middaugh, "Is Patriotism Good for Democracy? A Study of High School Seniors' Patriotic Commitments," *Phi Delta Kappan* 87.8 (2006): 600–607.

24. Jim Stacey, *Liberating Jesus from Christianity: Healing from the Fear and Shame of Religious Dogma* (New York: Page Publishing, 2015), 209–214.

25. Van Niekerk, "Towards a Theology of the Body," 371.

26. Elliot T. Dorham, "A Brief Consideration of Human Sexuality through the Lens of the Theology of the Body," *NDGS-Spring* (2015), 4.

27. David M. Halpern, *One Hundred Years of Homosexuality and Other Essays on Greek Love* (New York: Routledge, 1990), 114.

28. Harry Cockburn, "Having Sex Increases Spirituality and 'Makes People Likely to Believe in God,'" *Independent* (September 26) (http://www.independent. co.uk/life-style/health-and-families/health-news/having-sex-believe-in-god-resear ch-religion-duke-university-patty-van-cappallen-a7330076.html accessed January 1, 2017).

29. Lisa Isherwood and E. Stuart, *Introducing Body Theology* (Sheffield: Sheffield Academic Press, 1998), 15.

30. Dorothee Sölle and Shirley A. Cloyes, *To Work and to Love: A Theology of Creation* (Philadelphia: Fortress, 1984), 29.

Chapter 5

Utopian Couplings

When Bem Viver *Meets Mary*

Nienke Pruiksma

There are various kinds of Bem Viver. Bem Viver, for example, in my Kain-gang community is to have a bit of our forest, of the fish, of the river. I say, we indigenous of this state [Rio Grande do Sul, in the very south of Brazil], we try to preserve a bit of what is left over. We defend the little we have to maintain our culture. If there is no forest, I cannot live my culture. If I do not have land, I cannot have my rituals. If I do not have the forest, I do not have my source of good water to drink. So, I have to defend the forest in order to have Bem Viver for future generations.

So Francisco Rokán dos Santos described *bem viver*, "the good life."[1] Now, centuries of colonization, genocide, forced relocations, agro-business, evangelization, prohibitions of languages, and schooling have destroyed vast amounts of lands, indigenous knowledge, and ways of living, or have forced them to go underground. But still and yet, they are there and they are speaking up, struggling for land as the primary source of life and a way of life. One of the examples of how they are speaking up and challenging nonindigenous societies, ways of life and thinking, is through what in the colonial tongue Portuguese is called *bem viver* (for the Quechua *sumac kawsay*, the Aymara *suma qamaña*, or the Guarani *nhandereko*).[2] *Bem viver* "with its proposal of harmony with Nature, reciprocity, relationality, complementarity, and solidarity between individuals and communities, and with its opposition against the concept of perpetual accumulation"[3] offers alternative visions on life, founded in Andian and Amazonian indigenous ways of life. This proposal of *bem viver* is the vanguard of decolonial thinking from the side of marginalized, othered, and subaltern peoples in the Latin American context.[4] Alberto Acosta, an economist, philosopher, and politician from Ecuador, remarks that *bem viver* finds like-minded communities struggling for a different world order in other parts of the world such as the ecological, feminist, coop, Marxist, and humanist movements,[5] and that it needs to complement and amplify itself with other proposals rooted in different realities that are spiritually kin to *bem viver*.[6]

Could this call for coalition of people struggling to find a way out of the present neocolonial, neoliberal, ecological, and humanitarian mess we live globally mean that *bem viver* could dialogue also with theologies that reflect on sexuality, human identity, and bodies? This question is critical because these theologies and the communities that they represent also seek a *bem viver* for people who frequently do not fit in, or who are marginalized and discriminated against (not in the least in religious contexts). How could *bem viver* impact the way those theologies look at biblical narratives? What happens when *bem* viver meets Mary (as she is narrated in the Gospel of Luke)?[7] And what happens when *bem viver* meets Mary, not the biblical woman who bore Jesus but the gay man affectionately or cheekily addressed as Mary by his (gay) friends?

Discourses around sexuality and gender do not necessarily sit comfortably with *bem viver*, within theology, or within Christian circles. So why propose this "marriage of inconvenience" (or "ménage a trois")? I argue *bem viver* and critical thinking about sexuality and bodies meet in the critique of hegemonic knowledge and power structures that the existence, expression, and resistance of different/othered communities (in casu resisting/persisting indigenous communities and LGBTQI communities) offer. My aim here is to see how the critique *bem viver* offers to hegemonic traditions could amplify what it means to be human, body, flesh, sexual. What could the impact be on the reading and interpretative practices of biblical texts?

Before I continue, some background information to these questions. Over the last few years, I (a native of The Netherlands) have been living in Brazil, working for a church-related NGO that works for and with indigenous people and their rights.[8] My part, as foreigner, is working in the educational projects targeted at nonindigenous peoples: thinking together on issues such as prejudice, multi- and interculturality, and dialogue. Living and working abroad, to me, has meant gaining dimensions in the way I view the world, not leaving things behind. I have experienced enormous privilege by the coincidental of geography, timing of birth, skin color, and social background—and I know that others have paid the price for those in the past and the present, and that I will never be able to account for those.

Writing about my context in Brazil is not about forgetting where I come from, nor is it my intention to appropriate knowledge that is not mine. Rather, it is primarily about listening, about asking questions, dialoguing, and looking for different ways and alliances. It is also about following up on requests that people have made: to share what is happening in Brazil, to tell (my) people about the people in Brazil and about their lives, to show that the people of Brazil have a lot of knowledge that is denigrated and stolen. And, it is, in a tertiary move, about trying to bring the lessons that I have learnt from people I have met and books I have read to bear on my theological thinking, in the hope that it contributes to destabilizing interpretations that underpin empire, racism, patriarchy, heteronormativity, and neocolonial, neoliberal exploitation of the earth and the lives in and on it.

A caveat: this essay is not based on fieldwork in the direct, enormously diverse, and complicated realities of daily life of indigenous communities. Rather, I use *bem viver* to bring some of the values of traditional indigenous ways of life to bear on nonindigenous thinking and living. A certain amount of generalization is inevitable in this exercise looking at macro relations.[9] I bring stories and questions together in this essay, which is very much a work in process: it's a patchwork, a mosaic. It isn't meant to make a pretty whole of what is interconnected but intends to show the seams, the fissures, to tell stories and rethink; it attempts to be communal, in dialogue, even when it's done at the writing desk.

STORY 1: OF RAINBOWS AND MONKEYS

The Gavião people of Rondônia state tell the following story of how corn was given to them. The main character in the story is a woman who became pregnant without having relations, without using a man. The story begins with a fruit, Xum Xum-ra, which grows from a great and beautiful tree special to the Gavião people. A group of women go to harvest the fruit but find only a little of it lying on the ground:

> When they came back, the pregnant woman asked: "And? Was there a lot of fruit?" "No," they responded, "we only found a bit." So she went and said: "I am going to go and see if I find at least a bit for me to eat."
> So when she arrived there, she sat down, opened her legs and from her vagina came the rainbow. It went up there into the trees, swung around and the fruits fell. It was a lot of fruit. She gathered them and filled her basket. She returned to the communal house with a full basket. She went to her house in the village and upon entering, the women were shocked: "Damn, woman, where did you pick all those fruits?" "Ah, I found them just there and gathered them," she answered.

The women were suspicious when this happened again and again, so they determined to follow her the next time she went out.

> So they saw the rainbow come out from within her when she opened her legs. They ran to inform the men, who then also went to have a look to see that the

women were telling the truth. They took a big knife and cut the rainbow close to the women, about 70 centimeters. So, a smaller piece ran back inside her and the other fled up into the sky. The bit that remained inside her became human, a boy. What went up in the sky is now the rainbow that we see until today.

The boy was born, grew, became human. The one that went up communicated with the woman: "How is our son?" "Ah, he's already big," she answered. "I will make a field here for my son," said the father. "There will be lots of corn, and only you will know of it. When I went there the other day, the corn was already high." And it really was corn.[10]

The story continues that the woman went to harvest some corn, to take back home. A black monkey came and stole some of her corn, and ran away screaming. On the monkey's path was a man, who took the corn and asked the monkey, "Who belongs this corn to?" The woman replied, "The corn is mine!" The man then gave the corn back to the woman and asked where she had harvested it. She answered, "There is a field." And she showed the field to the people.

Disposable People(s)

The survival of this narrative is testimony to the resilience of indigenous communities such as the Gavião people. In the sixty-odd years since intensive contact in the Amazon region, life for the many indigenous peoples of the region has changed in ways unimaginable. Yet, the stories continue to be told, despite the strong impact of money, loss of land, logging, and (recently) neo-Pentecostal condemnation of indigenous worldviews. Many of the stories and the rituals of indigenous peoples in Brazil have been reduced—due to the reduction or loss of land and thus of way of life—or have become part of the "secrets" of that people. Committing such stories to paper is an act of sharing beyond the people, of dialogue, but often primarily an intentional act of committing memory to paper, so that the stories will not pass away with the elder generations who carry these stories written in their bodies and minds.

Spirits impregnating girls, girls having rainbows exiting from their vulvas, rainbows coming and going from a belly and then turning into helpmates, fathers, and babies are not narrative elements that missionaries were or are keen on. These narratives are too fleshy, too, to borrow a word, indecent.

The rainbow for the Gavião people is connected to the subaquatic plane, and the people (to the Gavião the beings populating other realms are not spirits but people) from that plane manifest through phenomena connected to water. Whenever corn was harvested, the Gavião had a feast with dancing and music[11] and offered people from the subaquatic realm some of the corn in thanks.[12] Shamans from "our" cosmological plane can travel to the other planes, whereas during feasts—such as the harvest of corn—beings from other planes visit ours to participate in the feast.[13] There is no separation between the realms or between human beings, animals, and nature. Nature and gifts of the spirits/other realms sustain human beings; human beings do not occupy the center of creation.

Bem viver reconciles various aspects of life "such as knowledge, codes of ethical and spiritual conduct towards the environment, human values, the vision for the future, among others."[14] As such, it has communitarian roots and is "socio-biocentric."[15]

Its point of departure is the different ways to view life and its relation to *Pacha Mama*. Relationality and complementarity are considered the joining axes between all living beings—human and non-human. It is forged on the principles of interculturality. It lives in economic and solidary practices. And, because it is immersed in the search for and construction of alternatives for common and marginalised groups, it needs to be constructed primarily from below towards the centre with a democratic logic of communitarian roots.[16]

Bem viver is a proposal for a holistic way of life, a way of living that seeks balance and well-being in and for life as a whole, not just "living better" for a small group of human beings at the center of power, with other groups considered disposable: black and brown, gender and nonconforming sexual bodies are marginal, just as the land and its resources are considered disposable after use.

A Brazilian politician managed to formulate this worldview most succinctly by stating publicly that "Quilombola's, indians, gays and lesbians are good for nothing."[17] For completeness, other categories should be included: transsexuals, transvestites, prostitutes, garbage collectors, landless farmers, to name a few. Expendable, negligible lives. And lost lives are plenty among these groups: Victor Kaingang, a toddler stabbed in the neck while nursing on the street in a southern Brazilian town; the burnt body of a nameless transsexual youth in a wasteland in greater Porto Alegre; the long long list of indigenous leaders, landless farmers, and their allies killed and persecuted in the struggle for land and human rights. Contemporary crucifixions and pietas. These no-good or, to apply Judith Butler's terminology, non-grievable lives lay bare the power structures a particular frame applied to life and living.[18] And it is in those black, brown, queer and nonhuman lives cast aside as "no good" that we find alternatives rooted both in ancient traditions, reinventions of community, and in contemporary challenges.

Bem Viver is not about romanticizing a past that has disappeared, and not about idealizing indigenous cultures, nor about proposing a homogenous view of indigenous cultures and spiritualties. It is about pursuing dialogue and transformation to ensure a future for our planet. As a proposal coming from the margins of Latin American societies, *bem viver* wants to upend the logic sustaining our present relations and reconceive of relations beyond develop-ment and progress (concepts which both capitalists and socialist thinkers hold dear).[19] Though the thinking is about global systems, it is rooted in the lived realities and spiritualities of indigenous peoples and other marginalized groups. When asked about the principles of *bem viver*, the Bolivian politician and phi-losopher David Choquehancua outlined twenty-five postulates that undergird *bem viver* as it was included in the Bolivian constitution. They include the fol-lowing: prioritize life, reach consensual agreements, respect and accept differ-ences, balance with nature, respect seeds, listen to the elderly, as well as know how to eat, to drink, to dance, and to work.[20] Complementarity and reciprocity are two of the key terms to structure relations. The approach given to gender by indigenous women is exemplary and significant in this context:

> a relationship that is respectful, sincere, equitative, balanced, in equilibrium—what in the west would be equality—of respect and harmony in which both men and women have the opportunity. . . . Only this way can one be well spiritually, with one's own being human, with the earth, with the heaven and the elements of nature that give us oxygen. . . . For us, talking with a focus on gender sup-poses referring to the concept of Duality maintained from the perspective of the indigenous cosmovision in which everything in the universe is governed in terms of Duality, the heaven and the earth, happiness and sadness, the day and the night complement one another: one can not exist without the other. If we had ten days of only sun, we would die; we would not be able to support that. Everything is structured in terms of Duality, undoubtedly, man and woman.[21]

Complementarity in *bem viver* should not be confused with heteronormativ-ity.[22] Complementarity, for example, is frequently thought along different exogamic groups within a people:

> Tikuna women, in contrast, defend homo-affective relationship as consistent with clan rules of exogamy. They defend homo-affective ties as strengthen-ing the rule of nations, as belonging to Tikuna ancestrality. For them, there is little doubt that sexual diversity is intrinsically Indigenous whereas sexual discrimination was brought in by a vogue of evangelical religions. The arrival of neopentacostal churches changed marriage expectations in Tikuna society. Homo-affective unions became a form of sin, abominable in the eyes of God, clandestine. Churches introduced lesbianism as a forbidden love, permeating Tikuna cosmovision with exogenous moralities that signal the power of religion over Indigenous peoples. For Tikuna women what is detrimental to their culture is the foreign imposition of religions by non-Indigenous missionaries.[23]

Also, care needs to be taken with identifying female with women and male with men: both men and women have female and male aspects in varying measures and these complement one another—bodies are but one aspect.[24] Other criteria such as age and clan affiliation within a group order the relations between people. The same logic of duality is frequently applied to nature: plants and animals carry characteristics that make them belong to a certain group due to their appearance. The relations that structure life are not limited to human society.

As such, the question on grievable life is stretched beyond Butler's categories of human life. One of the most impacting videos I have seen on YouTube in the last couple of years is the video of a woman of the Krenak people who live beside the Rio Doce, in central-eastern Brazil.[25] When a dam collapsed and a reservoir containing poisonous residues from mining activities spilled its contents in November 2015, killing all that lived in and from the river for 500 kilometers, she stood among her community beside the river lamenting not just the human lives and their livelihoods but the animal and plant life as well.[26] The human lives are not more or less grievable than the lives they share creation with. In another, more recent reflection on the disaster,[27] the Krenak people commented that the Rio Doce has been silenced and that the *Uatu*, the spirit of the river that sustained and conversed with the people, is now silent too: "Every bother that has come to us, the white man has been in the middle of."

Complementarity and relationality are not limited to human community. It is in these notions of relational and complementary living, the seeking of the good for all life, that a shift happens: human beings shift from the center or pinnacle of life and take their place in the circle of interconnected life that *bem viver* proposes. *Bem viver* thus offers an alternative epistemological framework through the ways of life and knowing the world of the indigenous peoples of the continent: one that is fundamentally communal, consensual, spiritual, in solidarity, reciprocity, complementarity, and interdependence.[28] As such it also proposes to decolonize the production of knowledge and opens up to intercultural and intersectional dialogue.[29] In this intercultural and intersectional dialogue, indigenous communities too are challenged to reflect critically upon their heritage, their way of life today, and what *bem viver* could mean—avoiding a romantic and stagnant idealization of indigenous cultures.[30]

STORY TWO: OF ANGELS AND VIRGINS

Considering that the aforesaid story of how corn came to the Gavião people is a "marginal myth," the coincidences with a familiar story in Christian contexts are striking. The annunciation of the birth of another boy without the interference of a man, but merely the promise of "the Holy Spirit coming upon her and the power of the Most High overshadowing her" (Luke 1:35), is quite interesting. The contrapuntal reading of these two stories may offer new insights into Luke 1.

For a Protestant from The Netherlands, Mary never figured large in my religious imagination, and neither was obedience or virginity a major theme in my relatively liberal surroundings. Even though virginity was not a big deal, girls were taught to be safe within consensual monogamous relationships (whether with a man or a woman was of no consequence). The disappearance of Mary as a religious example of womanhood for women in the Reformed tradition served to further erase women from the religious sphere, reducing their choices in life to the role of wife and mother. Without the image of Mary there wasn't another "anchor" for women (except maybe the good wife in Proverbs?).[31]

Yet the impact of centuries of projecting onto women an image of Mary as the unfallen Eve, untouched and pure, hardly flesh and blood, and certainly not a woman enjoying sex, intimacy, and eroticism cannot be erased. We may emphasize the "ok, I'll do it" and thus her agency in the Lucan version of the story—at least on a narrative level. Considering the "paternity" of Jesus and the supposed absence of heterosexual penetrative intercourse in the conception, opens up new visions: we can think beyond the traditional nuclear family and the exclusivity of matrimonial relationships. And, if God is not necessarily male, then Jesus for sure was a different conception.[32] However, hermeneutical suspicion kicks in when we widen the frame a couple of inches and move away from the narrative and zoom in on the context of the text and its writers, or the interpretative traditions. Can we move beyond the inherent patriarchy of the context in which women's bodies as procreative potential are owned by men—be they their fathers, heavenly Father, or church fathers? Reflecting on Hannah, the blueprint for the Lucan Mary, Deryn Guest writes:

> The sentiments of such hymns of praise has sometimes been highlighted by feminists, who latch on to the spirit of liberation thought to pervade them. However, this fails to recognize the problematic nature of the songs: their rewarding of obedience, of dutiful adherence to the heterosexual imperative, their endorsement of the sex-gender economy. Women like Hannah are scripted characters in a male play. Operating as the male director's puppets. These women never speak or act with their own genuine voices and the image of these women longing for motherhood needs to be resisted.[33]

In European Mariology, the character of Mary has been purified sexually beyond the resemblance of flesh and blood women—who are reminded of that fact every couple of weeks—and she has also been whitewashed: she was the ideal of purity, not just sexual purity but also purity of the race.[34]

The occupiers of what is now called the Americas wanted to create lands in their own image—and the brownish people they met here, conveniently died in masses. Interestingly, I think for repopulation of the Latin American continent, there was a double standard: white men were encouraged to marry dark women to whiten the population of the continent. Less so, for white women (due to the lack of women as the majority of European immigrants were male as well as the fact that white women were kept to the domestic realm). White women's virtue was linked to their production of perfectly white children.

Rather than sitting on the ground with the fragments of the stories we hold dear as Christians broken in our hands, we may try to "take back the word,"[35] even if we don't care much for the historical settings. Can we be like the monkey in the Gavião story, taking the corn and running with it, changing the course of the plans, and creating a community that shares for the good of all, rather than for one's own benefit? It is after all the trickster that turns things upside down.

Marcella Althaus-Reid offered one of the most thorough deconstructions of the Virgin Mary in her groundbreaking *Indecent Theology*. She argues that the Virgin of Guadeloupe and her veneration are symbols of colonialism, patriarchy, and heteronormativity superimposed on women and the indigenous culture of Mexico:

> Mary is the colonial spirit of servitude to patriarchalism incarnated to such an extreme that she could not be represented as a common human being. She is a patriarchal gender performance going solo. . . . The indecenting of the Virgin Mary needs to accept that the Mary is not a historical figure, which does not mean that some Mary mother of Jesus did not exist historically. She may have, but that person is not relevant theologically. The Mary of Christianity is something else; her real existence is the religious alien Virgin symbol. . . . A religious myth can become a mystification supporting an elite in power and hegemonic control instead of bringing symbolic elements of liberation to the community. Mariology is sexually stagnant. Only a rupture at the level of theological imagination can liberate her and the communities that worship her.[36]

Althaus-Reid invites us to look at the messiness and plurality of lived realities that are foundational for our religious symbols:

> Therefore, let us consider that Mary is not the woman who conceived by inhaling the smell of Fatherly semen. Let us think that she is the woman who has had "seven times seven" clitoral pleasure. Let us say that she may have conceived by pleasure in her clitoris; by self-given pleasure, perhaps. In this way, lust and love may then be re-linked together in the same way that love and solidarity for justice, in Patriarchal Liberation Theology, has been reconnected effectively.[37]

Can this be a starting point to reimagine Mary from the full reality of women's lives, and not from a "thin" image of official doctrine? Finding myself at the other side of our shared colonial history, these texts challenge me to consider that our bodies and sexuality, our physicality, are part of power relations inherent in our social relations, and as such are reflected in our theologies. Those images reflect our colonial relations in which white women, myself included, are privileged, are often blind to the multiplicity of realities, are complicit in making "others" invisible, and who want to speak on their behalf. The images of women as portrayed in the Bible and/or in tradition may actually need more hermeneutic of suspicion and a stronger postcolonial questioning than I may have warranted.[38]

The same goes for the taboo sphere of their and our bodiedness and sexualities: how and why have these been hidden when we talk Mary/theology? How does that affect those who are living with bodies and sexualities (and as a consequence representing different communities and ways of life) outside "the norm"? How does the silencing of those aspects of human lives, both biblical and contemporary, collude with racism and heteronormativity? How can the idea of bodies and how they are supposed to look, act, and feel be "indecented"? How does that impact on our view of incarnation? Lisa Isherwood writes about embodiment and incarnation:

> Once we locate ourselves in our divine bodies we are challenged to find alternatives to the way things are, to engage in an obstinate way with the patriarchal world and declare another set of values. Of course, this location while in our bodies is an enactment that goes far beyond the edges of the skin. It is a counter cultural enactment for and with other, our protest is not just about those things which oppress us, our redemption is tied up with that of all. There is a sense in which we may assert that the grounded reality of our lives also gives us a transcendent quality, it is the radical nature of our incarnation that moves us into a place that may be called transcendent. This does not imply a moving beyond but rather a broadening of vision and joining in the struggle with those we do not know and cannot see.[39]

Isherwood proposes (with Carter Hayward and Rita Brock) that the erotic is the power that impulses us to open up to the other, to deepen relationality, and open up the self:

> As erotic suggests, this process involves a fully embodied engagement with the world and those in it. However, the emphasis is not on the erotic in the narrow sense of genital sexuality but rather points to an alive and embodied connection with all aspects of life.[40]

The perspectives of Althaus-Reid and Isherwood on embodiment, incarnation sexuality, and the erotic may offer new dimensions to Mary and the song she sings: not the isolated, venerated, sanitized version of a woman and mother but fully human and connected in all her dimensions, with the critical notions of the song she most probably never sang restored to her.

STRANGE BEDFELLOWS AND/ OR UTOPIAN COUPLINGS?

Thinking *bem viver* with theologies that reflect on bodies and sexuality challenges me to think differently about my body, my sexuality, my doing theology: not as isolated and individualized but as fundamentally relational and political. My body is allowed to be present with all its faults and failures, its loves, likes, and lusts, in how it relates to other bodies—human bodies, animal bodies, plant bodies, the body of the earth, bodies of texts and traditions, divine/spiritual bodies. As such, questions about racism, gender, and sexuality are brought to the fore. And beyond the deconstruction, both queer theologies and *bem viver* offer proposals for transformation of power relations and lived realities—not as a blueprint for each and every context but as a start to dialogue and change.

These stories, and the realities they represent keep asking questions about how we treat "other" bodies, how we *are* other bodies, how center and margin relate, how we live day in and day out, how social structures and institutions are created and proliferated, how sexuality is viewed, used, and exploited, in the same way that it allows the earth and our environment to be exploited. How then do we read these two stories contrapuntally?[41] How do Mary and *bem viver* meet? How does this contrapuntal reading of hegemonic stories with non-hegemonic ones contribute to the *bem viver* of all and not just a few? Could Mary be reimagined in the plurality of expressions of *bem viver* that does not shove her back in the closet? Could Mary be imagined as a black, brown, indigenous person without colonial co-optation? This offering is a start and leaves more open than answered (which is how I like it anyhow), especially methodologically. But here some notions run in various directions like a monkey with a cob of corn.

Much of the deconstruction offered by Althaus-Reid coincides with the thinking behind *bem viver* on the present social, political, and economic system that sows poison and reaps poverty and death. However, *bem viver* is not a proposal for revolution, because revolutions are fixed in the logic of human progress and development rather than dialogue and reciprocity. *Bem viver* is based in the slow processes of life, of communitarianism, of looking for consensual ways forward, of care. It says that neither human beings nor Mother Earth are for invading, exploitation and profit. It's not about offering a "quick fix," satisfying our needs for change immediately, which may actually be revolutionary. It wants to change, decolonize, the way we live just as much as the way we think. Also, I argue, it is never a neatly wrapped-up story: the rips and fissures of life, the complicated power relations do not allow us, and should make us suspicious of, wrapping things up nicely.

Reflecting on the twenty-five points given as essential to *bem viver*, maybe we could add knowing how to dance: and knowing how to make love with an other, with oneself, with the earth. Because making love is about care, about mutuality, about reciprocity, about celebration, it is life-giving, life-sustaining, and life-creating (far beyond the procreative sense). There it connects with the power of the erotic as it relates not just to bodies but also to the land and all that it brings forth. Not for the sole purpose of production and the immediate fulfillment of a desire, but, as Nancy Cardoso Pereira argues as a way of tending to the earth in which "the 'body' of the place is known, its places of vulnerability respected, its capacity to give and receive pleasure is recognized and stimulated. . . . But without any pretension to know and dominate all the processes and all the possibilities."[42] It is the hard graft, the protecting of the seeds and the ways of lives in which these practices continue as opposed to the "for sale" logic behind large scale agriculture and agricultural businesses.[43]

If we continue limiting life to certain forms of life, denying the plurality of incarnation beyond the human body—complicated as that may be as we are so used to thinking human-divine relations—our frame will remain too narrow. It will profit those who do not lament the death of a river, and in the same move will exclude those whose bodies and lives they consider "no good." It sanctifies domination, exploitation, and discarding of supposedly non-grievable life.[44] Could the woman that stood beside the dead river become Mary: not the untouched one but the deeply touched one? A Mary who cries for precious life damaged and lost with no chance of resurrection on the third day? Then the river may become Mary and speak for herself. I imagine Mary to be more than a virgin, more than a mother, beyond a human being. Maybe *then* her song becomes her own, because it is life bursting forth, resisting and flourishing. I reimagine Mary as

The woman who holds her child, part of her, lost to violence, because her body was brown, was transsexual, was different.

The community that decides to open an urban garden, work together to plant, care, and harvest and that shares the vegetables and flowers with each other and with those who need them.

The woman who enjoys touching and being touched, herself and/or others, who cherishes the intimacy that comes with touch, sexual and nonsexual.

The river that sings with life, with abundance of life, birds dipping in and out, fish hunting for bugs dancing on her surface, children launching themselves into her.

A gay man out on the town for a night of dancing, laughter, friendship, and sex.

The little green point of a newborn plant that breaks the earth.

The elderly men and women teaching the young their way of life.

The woman who sings her own words, be they lullabies, songs of freedom, and resistance or songs that reply to the birds and the trees.

The lush forest unthreatened by deforestation, birdsong bouncing between the trees, moist foliage, earth fecund, home to the richest variety of life.

The indigenous community that—even amid fields with poison-addicted monocultures—plants their seeds and guards them with care.

The woman who gestates a rainbow that ebbs and flows from her vulva and that sustains her, not a pale modest Mary greeting an angel with a rainbow in the back of the painting as a sign of the new covenant through another man.

The undulating hills of Mato Grosso do Sul again full of trees, the seeds hidden in her sprouting, the poison slowly seeping out of her. The soil that once only grew transgenic soy resurrected.

The women, men, and children, who from their bicycles seed-bomb urban wastelands to turn them into a sea of flowers.

The men, women, and those not identifying as either, of all colors, sizes, and shapes who know that dancing in the street while Abba's "Dancing Queen" is loudly playing from a truck is liberation. Not only because we're here and we're queer but because dancing and singing connect our bodies to life, to that unstoppable force that connects all of creation.

NOTES

1. Francisco Rokán dos Santos, "Viver com a natureza," in *O Bem Viver na Criação*, ed. Cledes Markus and Renate Gierus (São Leopoldo: Oikos, 2013), 69–70.

2. Cf. Alberto Acosta, *O Bem Viver. Uma Oportunidade para Imaginar Outros Mundos* (São Paulo: Editora Elefant, 2016), 23.

3. Ibid., 33.

4. Breny Mendoza, "La epistemologia del sur, la colonialidad del género y el feminism latinoamericano," 2015, 19–20 (https://simposioestudosfeministasct.fil es.wordpress.com/2015/03/mendoza_la_epistemologia_del_sur.pdf accessed April 26, 2017).

5. Acosta, *O Bem Viver*, 34.

6. Ibid., 66.

7. Cf. https://wordofthegay.wordpress.com/2008/03/02/1-mary/ accessed April 25, 2017.

8. See also Povos Indígenas no Brasil, "Quadro Geral dos Povos" (https://pib.so cioambiental.org/pt/c/quadro-geral accessed April 25, 2017).

9. Terminology is tricky. Because, for example, the question who is and who isn't indigenous is not easy to answer in many Latin-American contexts. In Brazil, the

discussion of who is "real indigenous" is at times dividing indigenous communities. Neither can it be claimed that indigenous communities speak with one mouth and have one agenda. There are isolated communities, ones that live inside urban parameters, ones that are almost completely neo-Pentecostal, ones that trade wood, and so on. Neither are they defined by one characteristic or are politically united. The same, obviously, goes for nonindigenous societies. As such, any identifier, such as "North," occidental, European, "South," and so on, brings along a slew of problems. Yet, we have to use words, imprecise though they may be.

10. Cited in Ivaneide Bandeira Cardozo, Israel Correa Vale Júnior, eds., *Diagnóstico etnoambiental participativo, etnozoneamento e plano de gestão Terra Indígena Igarapé Lourdes* (Porto Velho, RO: Kanindé, 2012), 22–23.

11. The feasts are not celebrated regularly anymore due to the conversion of the people to Christianity. Elements of the cosmology and the rituals have been joined with Christian feasts and worship. Cf. Lediane Fani Felzke, *Dança e imortalidade. Igreja, festa e xamanismo entre os Ikólóéhj Gavião de Rondônia* (http://repositorio. unb.br/handle/10482/22959 accessed April 16, 2017).

12. Ibid., 198.

13. See Ibid., 156–216.

14. Acosta, *O Bem Viver*, 71.

15. Ibid., 72.

16. Ibid., 74.

17. Globo, "Em vídeo, deputado diz que índios, gays e quilombolas 'não prestam'" (http://g1.globo.com/rs/rio-grande-do-sul/noticia/2014/02/em-video-deputado -diz-que-indios-gays-e-quilombos-nao-prestam.html accessed March 16, 2017).

18. Judith Butler, *Frames of War. When is Life Grievable?* (London: Verso 2009), 1.

19. Acosta, *O Bem Viver*, 73.

20. David Choquehancua, "Viver bem: Chanceler explica experiência da Bolívia" (http://www.cut.org.br/imprimir/news/2b718747c195879070e9c28f90336587/ accessed April 18, 2017). Alas, the reality of politics and economics are such that cohesion between laws and lived reality is frequently absent. Despite the inclusion of *bem viver* in the constitution, projects that destroy the earth and indigenous territories are implemented. Cf. the highway that is being constructed through the TIPNIS territory (https://www.theguardian.com/environment/2017/aug/15/bolivia-appr oves-highway-in-amazon-biodiversity-hotspot-as-big-as-jamaica accessed August 29, 2017).

21. Cited in R. Aída Hernandez Castillo, "Confrontando la Utopía Desarrollista: El *Buen Vivir y la Comunalidad* en las luchas de Mijeres Indígenas," in *Feminismo y Buen Vivir. Utopias Decoloniales*, ed. Soledad Varea and Sofía Zaragocin (Cuenca: Pydlos Ediciones, 2017), 40, 26–43.

22. Gender relations in indigenous cultures are more complex than I am able to address in this essay. It is one of the most complicated and confounding discussions: gender and power relations for me as a Dutch woman is quite different from how indigenous women perceive and live them. There is a wide gap between our worlds and interpretations. There is, also, a difference between traditional ideas and

the daily, lived reality. The ideal of complementarity does not erase the existence machismo or violence against women in daily life. That "respect women" is one of Choquehancua's twenty-five points of *bem viver* is quite telling. But the fact that there are other systems of organizing social relations, such as age or exogamy, points to another social location of gender relations. Cf. Mendoza, "La epistemologia del sur Mendoza," 22–23.

23. Manuela Levinas Picq and Josi Tikuna "Sexual Modernity in Amazonia" (http://www.e-ir.info/2015/07/02/sexual-modernity-in-amazonia/ accessed March 30, 2017).

24. Compare with the male and female energies in Andean spiritualties such as that of chacha-warmi in Amawtica philosophy in Bolivia. See Wara Wara, "Pedagogía Ancestral Amawtica" (https://mujermedicina.wordpress.com/2016/04/18/pedagogia-ancestral-amawtica/ accessed April 24, 2017).

25. https://www.facebook.com/yrerewa.kerenak/videos/800440790102395/ accessed March 30, 2017.

26. Compare Adam Taylor, "There Are Now 3 Rivers That Legally Have the Same Rights as Humans" (https://www.washingtonpost.com/news/worldviews/wp/2017/03/21/there-are-now-3-rivers-that-legally-have-the-same-rights-as-humans/?utm_term=.c4b660838ebd accessed April 28, 2017).

27. Fred Bottrel and Larissa Kümpel, *Agora o Rio corre calado* (https://www.em.com.br/app/noticia/gerais/2017/11/05/interna_gerais,914115/agora-o-rio-cor re-calado-barragem-de-mariana-destruiu-a-fe-do-povo.shtml accessed November 5, 2017).

28. Castillo, "Confrontando la Utopía Desarrollista," 36–40.

29. Zaragocin refers to intercultural epistemology as the point of meeting between decolonial feminism and *buen vivir*. Sofía Zaragocin, "Feminismo Decolonial y Buen Vivir," in *Feminismo y Buen Vivir. Utopias Decoloniales*, ed. Soledad Varea and Sofía Zaragocin (Cuenca: Pydlos Ediciones, 2017), 12.

30. Castillo, "Confrontando la Utopía Desarrollista, 36.

31. Cf. Wanda Deifelt, "Teologia Feminista: Uma História Construída em Mutirão," in *História, Saúde e Direitos. Sabores e Saberes do IV Congresso Latino-Americano de Gênero e Religião*, ed. André S. Musskopf and Marcia Blasi (São Leopoldo: CEBI, 2016), 21, 17–26.

32. Marcella Althaus-Reid, *Indecent Theology: Theological Perversions in Sex, Gender and Politics* (London: Routledge, 2000), 55.

33. Deryn Guest, *When Deborah Met Jael. Lesbian Biblical Hermeneutics* (London: SCM, 2005), 131–132.

34. Wietske de Jong, "How Do You Solve a Problem Like Maria?" in *Onder de Regenboog: De Bijbel Queer Gelezen*, ed. Adriaan van Klinken and Nienke Pruiksma (Vught: Skandalon, 2010), 75.

35. Robert E. Goss and Mona West (eds.), *Take Back the Word. A Queer Reading of the Bible* (Cleveland: Pilgrim, 2000).

36. Althaus-Reid, *Indecent Theology*, 72.

37. Ibid., 73.

38. Cf. Musa Dube, *A Postcolonial Feminist Hermeneutics of the Bible* (St. Louis: Chalice, 2000), 121–123, 199–201.

39. Lisa Isherwood, "Sex and Body Politics: Issues for Feminist Theology," in *The Good News of the Body: Sexual Theology and Feminism*, ed. Lisa Isherwood (New York: New York University Press, 2000), 32–33.

40. Lisa Isherwood, "Erotic Celibacy: Claiming Empowered Space," in *The Good News of the Body: Sexual Theology and Feminism*, ed. Lisa Isherwood (New York: New York University Press, 2000), 158.

41. Edward Said, *Culture and Imperialism* (New York: Vintage Books, 1994), 51.

42. Nancy Cardoso Pereira, "Da Agropornografia à Agroecologia: Uma Aproximação Queer Contra as Elites Vegetais . . . Em Comunicação com o Solo," in *História, Saúde e Direitos. Sabores e Saberes do IV Congresso Latino-Americano de Gênero e Religião*, ed. André S. Musskopf and Marcia Blasi (São Leopoldo: CEBI, 2016), 40.

43. Ibid., 40–41.

44. J. Michael Clark, *Beyond Our Ghettos. Gay Theology in Ecological Perspective* (Cleveland: Pilgrim, 1993), 47–48.

Chapter 6

Eve's Serpent (Gen 3:1–9) Meets Sina's Tuna at *Fāgogo*

Brian F. Kolia

In ancient times, there was a beautiful *taupou*[1] named Sina from the Samoan village of Matāvai. Words of her beauty traveled far, and it attracted a young man from one of the neighboring islands. This young man was so attracted of Sina's beauty that he wanted to be with her every day.[2]

Knowing that she often comes to the village rock pool to bathe, the young man turned into a *tuna* (eel) and lived there so that he could see her every time she comes to bathe. Sina became familiar with the *tuna*, and as a result she did not fear the *tuna*. Sina met with him every time she went into the pool.

As the *tuna* grew fonder of Sina, she began to fear him, and was overwhelmed by his obsession. The *tuna* continually tried to seduce Sina to live with him, but Sina found the request impossible and left him. Hurt by Sina's absence, the *tuna* became depressed and sought death as his only option. Before his death, he gave his final request to Sina—that upon his death, he wanted Sina to bury his head. From his head a tree will grow, the fruits of which Sina will feed herself and her children. It was his dying act of love for Sina.

Sina granted the request, and the tree that grew up from the head of the *tuna* was the coconut tree. When one husks a coconut, one finds a "face" (with two eyes and a mouth) on the coconut. This is said to be the face of the *tuna*, whose heart was broken by the love of his life.

FĀGOGO AND *TALANOA*

Picture this: It is night time, the owls are hooting from a distance, and you are sitting in a traditional Samoan *fale*—an open house consisting of a thatched roof held up by strong wooden poles, allowing the cool oceanic breeze to

pass through. You have just finished supper and now you are relaxing, awaiting a story. An elder tells a story, while you and other listeners, young and
old, congregate and listen intently. If you have watched the animated movie
Moana, at the beginning of which the old lady was telling the children the
story of Maui and the heart of Tefiti, you could easily see the scenery. You
are in the *fale*, and the event of telling enhances the atmosphere and makes
you want to enter into the mystical world of the story. This kind of event is
known as *fāgogo*.

Samoans enjoy *fāgogo*. Similar to the English fable, it is the art of Samoan
storytelling that involves mythical encounters between mortal heroes/hero-
ines and immortal legends, existing in a space where the impossible becomes
possible. A space where spirits roam and animals possess humanlike quali-
ties, where animals speak and have conversations with humans, and in some
cases, animals have relations with humans.

There are many types of *fāgogo* with different agendas. Some seek to
explain the origins of a village, an honorific, an important name, or an element of the cosmos. Some explain relationships between villages and ancestral lines. And most, if not all, emphasize moralistic and pedagogical agendas.
The emphasis on moralistic and pedagogical agendas reflects the cultural and
wisdom significance of *fāgogo*, which Sueala Kolone-Collins highlights in
her thorough research into the pedagogical significance of *fāgogo*:

> The *fāgogo* and *fāgogo* telling point to the significance of *matua-tausi* and
> *tama'ita'i matua* as the keepers, distributors and carer of cultural knowledge
> and traditions that any culture must keep and respect.[3]

Matua-tausi (the elderly) and the *tama'ita'i matua* (eldest woman, like the
grandmother in the movie *Moana*) embody the association between elders
and wisdom. The word *matua* has an extensive range of meanings associated with "age," which suggests that the *matua* has experience, maturity, and
wisdom. *Matua* also refers to ancestors and parents, who are associated with
nurturing and pedagogy. It is through *matua* that wisdom is brought about and
given out. Kolose-Collins therefore argue that *matua* has a prominent place
in *fāgogo* as storytellers who knew the correct message. Ironically, a theme
or main message to a story is also known as *matua*.

This *matua* element of *fāgogo* and *fāgogo* telling is not evident in the biblical narrative. In this essay, therefore, I insert the *matua* element into the Genesis story. The biblical narrative may have different agendas and priorities
depending on who reads it, and for too long, island natives have had to read
with Western and colonial perspectives. From a methodological perspective,
the biblical narrative, like *fāgogo*, should acknowledge the *matua* (message)
of the story and the *matua* (pedagogy) of the storyteller. This is important

because of two things: first, as Smith vouches, Western modes of reading need to be decolonized in order to center native concerns and worldviews in approaching the biblical narrative.[4] And second, old age for island natives "is associated with more knowledge and wisdom known as *tofa mamao and loloto* (long and deep view)."[5] These reasons provide an alternative view to the pedagogical understanding behind the Genesis story.

Fāgogo springs to life through *talanoa. Talanoa* is a common term in Pasefika, which denotes conversation. Yet it is more than conversation as Jione Havea states:

> Talanoa is the confluence of three things: story, telling, and conversation. Talanoa is not story without telling and conversation, telling without story and conversation, or conversation without telling and story. Talanoa is all three—story, telling, conversation—as one.[6]

Talanoa and *fāgogo* go together. Because *fāgogo* emanates the art of *talanoa*, as the storyteller is intentional in his/her use of language to weave together a magical description of the world of the story, not only to tell the story but to be persuasive in doing so. But in *talanoa*, the storyteller can also be unintentional. The word *talanoa* combines the words *tala* and *noa*. In *talanoa*, the word *tala* means "story," "talking," or "conversation," and *noa* as a suffix implies "no limits" or "without boundaries." Accordingly, *talanoa* is a story, conversation or talk without boundaries. It allows the storyteller opportunities to take the tale or conversation where s/he desires. This is how *talanoa* is unintentional. In this sense, *talanoa* is postcolonial for it allows island natives to tell their stories in macroscopic fashion. *Talanoa* also gives island natives the platform to cross borders, while carrying on the conversation and story beyond those borders.

In the reading of biblical texts, I propose (in *talanoa* fashion) to read the text as *fāgogo* so that it does not lose the magic of storytelling, and see the story for what it was written. In other words, to understand that stories are *telling* truths as opposed to telling *the* truth. Stories communicate values and morals. We must then assume the role of the listener, and *faalogo* (hear) the story as though one of our elders (*matua*) was recounting it. *Fāgogo* and *talanoa* will thus act as the hermeneutical frameworks for my rereading the story of Eve and the serpent in Gen 3:1–19. To provide an alternative reading that sees the tale in Gen 3:1–19 as a love story, I read it in light of the well-known Samoan tale of Sina and the *tuna* (from here on, I refer to this tale as the Sina *fāgogo*) recounted earlier. The purpose of this *fāgogo* reading is to enhance the reading experience, while also shedding further light on the relationship between Eve and the serpent from a Samoan perspective.

THE SINA *FĀGOGO*

A text (*tala*) like Gen 3:1–19 has multiple layers that need to be opened (*tala*) up! Upon opening it up, one cannot ignore the encounter between Eve and the serpent. Such an encounter is intriguing from a Samoan perspective because it echoes the Sina *fāgogo*. The story of Sina and the *tuna* is a love story. The beautiful Samoan girl Sina had been seduced by a friendly *tuna*.

There are many versions of the tale, not only across the isles of Polynesia but also in Samoa.[7] I recounted earlier the version from the village of Matāvai on the Samoan island of Savaii, where it is claimed that the first encounter between Sina and the *tuna* occurred at the rock pool known as *Mata o le Alelo* (Eye of the Demon). The main agenda of the Sina *fāgogo* is etiological, told to explain the origins of the coconut tree. Yet it is also a love *fāgogo*; a rendezvous between two lovers from different worlds; a forbidden love.

This is what we hear when we *tala* (open) the *fāgogo*, etiological *fāgogo* as well as a *fāgogo* of love. In the same vein, I seek to *tala* the Genesis story of Eve and the serpent in order that we could hear the Genesis story in more ways than one.

HEARING THE *FĀGOGO*

Is there an oral aspect to Gen 3:1–19? Can we "hear" it? In order to hear anything, we need something to be said or read aloud. We need to hear the storyteller telling the *fāgogo*, to connect us as hearers to the world of the story. This is important because it focuses on the narrative and pedagogical aspect of the story of Eve and the serpent; this is an aspect that has been lost to obsessions with historical questions, authorial intentions, and ideological musings.

To hear in Samoan is *faalogo*, and I use this term to explain the process of hearing for native Samoans. The word *faalogo* is derived from the word *logo*, which means "to alert" (as in to alert someone of a news item). The prefix *faa-* intensifies the action. So upon the deliverance of such news to a person, the act of alerting is intensified through hearing or *faalogo*. It is a causative verb which implies that the alerting of the news is so emphatic and intense it cannot escape all ears.

The retrieval of the message can be drawn out through storytelling, which Samoans have been able to do through *fāgogo*. This also is an attempt to restore the fantasy associated with the so-called myths of Genesis, as such stories are told and retold to generations after generations. While historians may be preoccupied with the scientific aspects of the story and questions of objectivity, it must not be forgotten that there is pedagogy involved, to teach lessons and *truths* without worrying about whether those are real or not.

It should be apparent that *fāgogo* belongs to indigenous Samoan people. I say this because as Linda Tuhiwai Smith argues, Western methodologies do not apply all that well to indigenous communities. The historical and philosophical questions promoted by Western methodology do not resonate with indigenous beliefs and understandings.[8] For Samoans and neighboring Pasefika people, and for some indigenous people worldwide, this is a significant point, because the biblical text, particularly through colonial times, has been read through Western eyes and propagated with Western ideologies. So much so that Samoan children today easily accept the appearance of Jesus as Caucasian, with long smooth hair and blue eyes, a far cry from what Palestinian and Jewish men resemble. This is the product of Western propaganda permeated through the teachings of European missionaries.

I do not intend to make a similar ruse of recasting the characters of Gen 3 with Samoan characters; rather, my aim is to decolonize Western methodologies as Smith modeled.[9] So that the story in Gen 3 can find resonance with Samoan listeners, and find room for other indigenous readers and their stories to find resonance with the biblical stories. I thus draw upon the Sina *fāgogo* to hear the story of Eve's rendezvous with the serpent. This is critical given that tourists see Pasefika as a paradise getaway. They see Pasefika as an exotic nirvana with romantic scenery, heightened by the sight of the ocean waves washing up on its utopian beaches. However, in all the romanticized perceptions of the islands of Pasefika, tourists forget that the land (*fanua, fonua, vanua,* or *whenua*) is not as romantic as it may seem. Behind the exotic beaches and tropical beachfront hotels lie the realities of rising sea levels where Kiribati, Tuvalu, Tokelau, and the Marshall Islands face the extinction of the very land they live on. *Fāgogo* thus connects the world of fantasy to a reality that lies beneath.

This quest to hear the story of Eve and the serpent as *fāgogo* connects the story of Eve and the serpent to a certain reality. This certain reality is weaved into the story, much like how Pasefika realities are weaved into *fāgogo*. They are magical stories, they are epic, they speak grandeur, but beneath, they entail the emotion and reality of the land and its people.

Fāgogo implies that the text is a *tala*. The word *tala* in its verbal sense means "to open" or "to unpack" as though the text needs unpacking. So when a *fāgogo* is told, it is a package layered with meanings that need to be *tala*, to unpack, to unfold. The process of *tala* does not mean discarding the packaging, but like the presentation of an *ie toga* (a traditional Samoan fine mat), *tala* denotes the action of opening up, that is, to open so that the whole *ie* (mat) can be seen in its complete state. The packaging, therefore, is part of the final product. The *tala* gives the opportunity for the audience to hear the whole story. Thus conceived, *fāgogo* gives indigenous readers the opportunity to read the story in light of their own context; to highlight oppressive and colonizing voices, and thus raise their own questions of the text. *Fāgogo* is postcolonial. It gives indigenous readers the opening to (re)locate (thus liberating) the message in the text.[10]

This process of *tala* guides *fāgogo*. It is the process by which the hearers can approach the biblical text with intent to see and hear the whole *tala*, as it unfolds.[11] Through this process of *tala*, we are mindful of other possibilities for interpretation, as directed by the elements of the *fāgogo*. This may seem simple but as Tui Atua Tupua Tamasese Efi stresses, it is not "because its value to the Samoan Culture is deep. Because it is the process of weaning, of nurturing, of sharing stories, values, rituals, beliefs, practices and language. It helped sustain and could still sustain a nation."[12] This is the essence of *fāgogo*, for it is, as Efi says, a process. I approach the story of Eve and the serpent in this manner, to unfold the story as a whole, and to see the final package. This may *tala* opportunities for new meaning, while attempting to recover the magic of the Genesis story. As such, I explore the themes from the Sina *fāgogo* which could be heard in the Genesis story. I wish to highlight seduction, the equal status between species, virginity, and the significance of fruit.

EVE AND THE SERPENT AS *FĀGOGO*

Seduction

Seeing seduction in Gen 3 is not new.[13] The goal behind the serpent's seduction is commonly associated with the fruit. However, I find that like the *tuna*, the serpent is interested in the woman, more specifically, the woman's nudity. In 3:1, the Hebrew word used to describe the serpent is *arum* which means "shrewd," yet it sounds very similar to *erom*, the word for naked.[14] Ironically, this is how Adam and Eve end up, as Gordon Wenham writes: "They will seek themselves to be shrewd (cf. 3:6) but will discover that they are 'nude' (3:7, 10)."[15]

The question that arises from the Sina *fāgogo* is why the young man turned into a *tuna* (eel)? The *tuna* in Samoan mythology is a phallic symbol, so its sexual connotations are obvious. Similarly, J. Harold Ellens claims that serpents were also a phallic symbol.[16] However, taking the form of an eel meant that there was room for exploitation (or more appropriately, *sex*ploitation). Knowing that Sina would come down to the rock pool, it was the perfect place to admire Sina in full scope.

For the serpent in Eve's *fāgogo*, who was the shrewdest of the animal kingdom, he was able to move about freely and admire Eve. His movements and his access to Eve dictate this, for Eve was nude, and the serpent had known that all along. But Eve may have been mesmerized by the serpent's seduction, just as Sina had been dazzled by the eel. Yet when her eyes were opened (3:7), she realized she was nude. I hear echoes of the Sina *fāgogo* when Eve realizes her nakedness. It is the unraveling of the serpent's request to Eve. The serpent tells Eve in 3:5 that she and her husband will become like gods. As seduction, it was an invitation for Eve to come to his world: the world of knowing good from evil, knowing right from wrong, the world of gods. And Eve was seduced to the point that not only did she eat the fruit but she also seduced Adam into eating it also. It is this seduction which proved too much for Sina, and that caused Eve's downfall. In both cases, the seduction was overwhelming, and in both cases, they cover up: Sina leaves the rock pool never to return, while Eve sews fig leaves together to hide her nakedness.

Virginity

Both Eve and Sina, as far as their two stories imply, were virgins. Eve's virginity is a whisper in the story and not entirely obvious. Yet the perception of virginity in *fāgogo* is not primarily a matter of sexuality but a title associated with the high chief. In addition to being a virgin, she is also a woman of nobility; *taupou* is an honorable title given to the virgin daughter of the high chief. In the Genesis *fāgogo*, Eve is a *taupou*. She is the daughter of the high chief (YHWH) and she is perfect, and also a virgin.

This is significant, because Eve has often been portrayed as the culprit in the fall.[17] Yet as *taupou*, she is given stature as a leader. She may not have made the best decision, but she did *make* the decision. The onus and the pressure of being a decision maker is usually afforded to men in the biblical narrative. Eve, the *taupou*, turns the tide against such misogynist attitudes, as she becomes the commander of her destiny. Eve is a virgin, and a powerful virgin at that; a *taupou*.

The Fruit

The whispers of the Sina *fāgogo* are heard in Gen 3 when Eve eats the fruit. This brings to mind the coconut in Sina's *fāgogo*. The image of Sina drinking from the coconut is rather sexual, when considering the image of the coconut. The etiology of the coconut, as suggested by the Sina *fāgogo*, presents the coconut as the head of the eel, with its two eyes and mouth.

When Sina's lips are planted on the coconut for a drink, it is as though Sina kisses the eel and enjoyingly tastes its juices. Coconut drinking ensures *Tuna* is kissed by his love. It is not known what sort of fruit Eve ate, but the image of Sina drinking the coconut may add an element of sensuality to Eve's eating of the fruit, for Samoan (and islander) readers, or other coconut lovers.

The seduction by the serpent was sure to have an effect on Eve's senses and as a result, she enjoyed the fruit so much that she seduced her husband into eating it also.

Crossing Borders: Wisdom

The crossing of borders in this story is obvious. The serpent crosses into the human world as it converses with the first humans while the humans cross into the world of *'elohîm* (3:5) when they eat the fruit from the tree in the middle of the garden. The world of the story itself crosses from the scale of the heavens and the earth to the smaller scale of interaction between species.

The perspectives that emanate from these border-crossings are intriguing. I pay particular attention to the perspective of the serpent. Animal perspectives are not common in the biblical narrative, as they are in *fāgogo*. In fact, in *fāgogo* the interactions between animals and humans are framed by *faaaloalo* (respect). For instance, Efi, a former Head of State for Samoa and a well-respected custodian of Samoan mythology and indigenous knowledge, explains the significance of the fish species through a story from the village of Fagafau. One of its head fishermen in ancient times was a man named Pupu Luki, who went one afternoon to fish for *naiufi* (a type of shark). Efi tells that

> the village would get excited at the prospect of a good catch. Prayer vigils would be held by his family during the night to ask the gods for protection over Pupu and his companion. Fishing was not perceived as an exercise in luring, trapping and killing mercilessly, but of inviting the fish to honour the village chief's mana by being an equal adversary and then ultimately by gifting himself to the chief to help bolster or sustain the chief's status. It is believed that the *naiufi* are a special gift, a direct endowment from Tagaloa [the creator god of the Samoans]. This is evidenced in the honorific term for sacred fish, which is *tamasoaalii* (*tama soa* meaning aide to; *ali'i* meaning chief): God Tagaloa's gift was for these sacred fish to become aide to the chief.[18]

Naiufi and fish were not primarily food in indigenous understanding. Rather, they were gods, adversaries, chiefs. They were respected as equals, and were considered sacred. This is evidenced by the name given to the turtle, which is *i'a sā* (*i'a* meaning fish, and *sā* meaning sacred or holy).[19]

For the Genesis story, the perspective of the serpent when read as *fāgogo* highlights other elements in the conversation. In 3:5, the verb ידע (to know) is stated twice, referring to God "knowing" and that if the humans eat the fruit, they too will "know." It is implied that the serpent too also "knows." It is not what they know that is significant, but the fact that they *do* "know." This invites the question: Why is it that, at the beginning, the serpent "knows" but the humans do not? This question frames my discussion of border-crossing in Gen 3. God puts a boundary between humans and the divine. The serpent wants Eve to join him in crossing this boundary, to become an equal as the *naiufi* were with the chiefs. The serpent was the *tamasoaalii*, an aide of the divine world, who sought humans to become a part of the divine world of "knowing." We also see the serpent as *matua*, because in terms of the creation order, the serpent existed first, and he "knew" Eve first. And as the *matua*-serpent knew first, it becomes the source of knowledge and wisdom for the first humans.

CONCLUSION

Echoes of the Sina *Fāgogo* ripple into and through Gen 3, and as a *fāgogo* it is a form of storytelling for islander natives and for other readers who love storytelling: the story of Eve and the serpent from an islander perspective may thus be read and heard as *fāgogo*. From a *fāgogo* perspective, the Genesis story is macroscopic and liberating in the following ways:

First, islanders are connected by the ocean which, as Epeli Hau'ofa theorizes, is a bridge-way instead of a boundary between islands. Hau'ofa argues that our island ancestors "did not conceive of their world in microscopic proportions. Their universe comprised not only land surfaces but the surrounding ocean as far as they could traverse and exploit it."[20]

The world in *fāgogo* is macroscopic in scope. Colonial attitudes have long caused islanders to believe in their tiny existence, as just a "dot on the map." Yet *fāgogo* manifests Hau'ofa's contention, and this is my contention also. As I mentioned earlier, *fāgogo* is postcolonial because *fāgogo* liberates islanders from colonial attitudes that diminish our identity. So when reading Gen 3 from a *fāgogo* perspective, the garden narrative is macroscopic in the sense that as an alternative to it being a story that takes place in a garden, the encounter between Eve and the serpent can also be seen as a crossing of boundaries. The serpent, a representative of the "chaos battle myth"[21] and a possible allusion to the Leviathan of the "battle myths" (Job 26:13; Isa 27:1), crosses into the world of the first humans. In this crossing, the serpent invites Eve into his world, to the world of those who "know," and thus to become like gods.

Second, *fāgogo* is liberating. It is liberating for women, and as an islander male, I am sympathetic to islander women and their constant struggle in the face of domestic violence and misogynist attitudes. This is the reality that lies beneath the *fāgogo*, the reality of islander women's struggle. When I speak of islander women, I am speaking of my mother, my sisters, my wife, and all islander women who are significant in my life. I don't speak for them, but I vouch for them. And in *fāgogo*, women are liberated; they are women of power, and women of stature. Sina was a woman of stature, a *taupou*. Eve, from an islander perspective, is also a *taupou*, and therefore, she is a woman of stature. Through *fāgogo*, Eve is not the culprit; she is the master of her fate, the mother of all humanity. This is the call of indigenous readers who see women being reduced to culprits and scapegoats, for women to be given the respect and status they deserve.

Finally, to *tala* (open) up stories enables us to see the *tala* in all its complexity, and as we see with the story of Eve and the serpent, there is more to it than just an etiology explaining "how the first human couple came to be alienated from the eirenic conditions of the Garden of Eden."[22] What we see, and hear, are the ripples of *fāgogo* illuminating other layers of the Genesis narrative that tend to be discarded. The efforts of this *fāgogo* reading and hearing are toward reclaiming those layers to discover alternative readings of the *tala* (story). These readings *tala* (open up) the world of the text to macroscopic proportions, which can be both liberating and magical but, at the same time, tragic.

NOTES

1. *Taupou* is the name given to the high chief's daughter, whom Samoan traditionalists expect to be a virgin.

2. I acknowledge with gratitude a grant from the University of Divinity, Melbourne, that enabled me to present an earlier version of this essay at the SBL Annual Meeting in Denver, Colorado (November 18, 2018).

3. Su'eala Kolone-Collins, "Fagogo: Ua Molimea Manusina": A Qualitative Study of the Pedagogical Significance of Fagogo-Samoan Stories at Night-For the Education of Samoan Children" (Masters Th., Auckland University of Technology, Auckland, NZ, 2010), 93.

4. Linda Tuhiwai Smith, *Decolonizing Methodologies: Research and Indigenous Peoples*, 2nd Ed (London and New York: Zed Books, 2012), 39.

5. Kolone-Collins, "Fagogo," 94.

6. Jione Havea, "Bare Feet Welcome: Redeemer Xs Moses @ Enaim," In *Bible, Borders, Belonging(s): Engaging Readings from Oceania*, ed. Jione Havea, David J. Neville and Elaine M. Wainwright (Atlanta: SBL, 2014), 210.

7. There is an expression in Samoa, "e tala lasi Samoa" which translates as "there are many versions in Samoa." The point of this expression is that the stories and legends of Samoa have some connection to particular villages, and depending on which village you consult you are bound to receive a different version. No one village can claim ownership to a legend because it is already connected to multiple villages.

8. Smith, *Decolonizing Methodologies*, 1.

9. Ibid., 39.

10. Cf. George Aichele, et al., *The Postmodern Bible: The Bible and Culture Collective*, ed. Elizabeth A. Castelli, et al. (New Haven: Yale University, 1995), 284.

11. I use the term "hearing" interchangeably with "reading" to account for the indigenous reader who, as is common in indigenous communities, may not be able to read the written text.

12. Tui Atua Tupua Tamasese Efi, "More on Nuance, Meaning and Metaphor" (Keynote Speech at the Pacific Fono, Moving Ahead Together, Pataka Museum, Porirua, NZ, 2002).

13. Cf. J. Harold Ellens, *Sex in the Bible: A New Consideration* (London: Praeger, 2006), 55.

14. Wenham, Gordon J., *Genesis 1–15*, vol. 1 of *Word Biblical Commentary*, ed. Bruce Metzger et al. (Dallas: Word Books, 1987), 72.

15. Ibid., 72.

16. Ellens, *Sex in the Bible*, 55.

17. Carol Bakhos, "Genesis, the Qur'ān and Islamic Interpretation," in *The Book of Genesis: Composition, Reception, and Interpretation*, ed. Craig A. Evans, et al. (Leiden and Boston: Brill, 2012), 615.

18. Efi, "Whispers and Vanities," in *Whispers and Vanities in Samoan Indigenous Religious Culture*, ed. Tamasailau M. Suaalii-Sauni, et al. (Wellington, NZ: Huia Publishers, 2014), 46.

19. In Samoan folklore, the turtle was deemed *sā* (sacred) because of its power in saving fishermen who were lost at sea. In modern times, the fishing of the *i'a sā* is forbidden, as most villages in tandem with the Samoan government have conservation projects for the turtle.

20. Epeli Hau'ofa, *We Are the Ocean: Selected Works* (Honolulu: University of Hawaii Press, 2008), 31.

21. Tryggve N. D. Mettinger, *The Eden Narrative: A Literary and Religio-Historical Study of Genesis 2–3* (Winona Lake: Eisenbrauns, 2007), 83.

22. Mark G. Brett, *Genesis: Procreation and the Politics of Identity* (London and New York: Routledge), 32.

Chapter 7

Rape Matters

Dinah (Genesis 34) Meets Asifa Bano

Monica J. Melanchthon

To my daughter I will say,
"when the men come, set yourself on fire"

—Warshan Shire[1]

In this essay I reflect on the functioning of gender and violence within empires—empires of sex, caste, class, religion, language, ethnicity—all of which are explosive within the Asian context. I am interested in addressing the manner in which texts of various kinds—written, oral, visual—oppress and/or liberate women. How might we read those texts for the sake of women, for their empowerment and their flourishing? I pose this question with the words of Virginia Wolff in mind:

> if you insist upon fighting to protect me, or "our" country, let it be understood, soberly and rationally between us, that you are fighting to gratify a sex instinct which I cannot share; to procure benefits which I have not shared and probably will not share; but not to gratify my instincts, or to protect either myself or my country. For, the outsider will say, "in fact, as a woman, I have no country. As a woman I want no country. As a woman my country is the whole world."[2]

CONTEXT: RAPE STORIES

Documentaries and news stories containing footages smuggled out of Myanmar on the 2017–2018 Rohingya crisis show many women and girls fleeing with horrific accounts of (alleged) rape, sexual assault, torture, and murder at the hands of government forces in what has been called "clearance operations." Evidence is mounting to back allegations that Myanmar's autonomous military (*Tamadaw*) uses sexual violence as part of a coordinated campaign of ethnic cleansing. Attacks against women and girls by security forces are not a new phenomenon. For twenty years, there have been reports of the military using rape and sexual assault in its armed conflict against ethnic minorities in several states—Rakhine, Kachin, Karen, and Shan among others.

Across the border, India has witnessed in recent years a disturbingly high volume of sex crimes—so much so, that when the rape and murder of Asifa Bano, an eight-year-old girl from a Muslim nomadic community in Kathua, in the restive Jammu and Kashmir province, came to light, it was not a major news story right away. Asifa's family was *too poor to matter*.

Asifa belonged to the Bakarwal community, a nomadic tribe that is predominantly Sunni Muslim although they have kept alive a strand of Hindu belief in their identity.[3] She lived in a village 72 kilometers from the nearest city. Asifa loved horses. One of her favorite pastimes was to take the community's horses grazing in the fields. So when Asifa's mother asked her to collect the horses from the meadows on January 10, 2018, the young girl complied happily. Later that day, the horses returned to the village but Asifa did not.

Two days later, Asifa's parents filed a complaint to the police and they were quickly dismissed—told that the young (eight-year-old) girl most likely ran away with a boy. Five days later, Asifa's body was found. She had been sedated, abducted, raped over the course of four days, and then murdered by a group of men. Her innocent body was then dumped in the forest near the temple where she was sexually assaulted.

Of the men involved in the rape and murder of Asifa, one was a retired government official Sanji Ram, and his juvenile nephew. The third man was special police officer Deepak Khajuria, who was part of the investigation into Asifa's abduction. It has also been reported that another three police officers tampered with evidence to prevent the police officer, the retired government official, and his nephew, from being linked to the crime.

What is our response to such violence? The answers are complex because definitions of female sexuality vary from culture to culture. In India, women's sexuality is inbuilt into the hierarchical structure of caste—a colonial sense of preserving power, brutal power, for maintaining order. The structures and systems of colonialism, initially external but now internal, and the Hindu systems of caste, dominance, and patriarchy join forces to keep women in their place, to teach them how to behave and how to act. The complexities that underlie female existence in such circumstances need to be situated in and reflected upon in relation to the control and exercise of the colonizing power of gender, caste, religion, and economics.

FROM KHATUA TO SHECHEM

The story of Dinah, the daughter of Leah and Jacob, comes to mind. While in Shechem with her family, Dinah visits the daughters of the land. Shechem, the son of Hamor and the prince of the land, sees her, "seizes her and lays with her by force." He violates her sexually, and then he falls in love with her. He asks his father Hamor to meet Jacob, the father of Dinah, to request her hand in marriage. The matter is reported to Jacob and he stays silent, awaiting the return of his sons, who were out herding cattle. Just as they return, Hamor arrives to present his son's desire to marry Dinah—"The heart of my son Shechem longs for your daughter: please give her to him in marriage. Make marriages with us; give your daughters to us, and take our daughters yourselves, and the land shall be open to you; live and trade in it and get property in it" (vv. 8–10). Shechem adds, "Put the marriage present and gifts as high as you like, and I will give whatever you ask me; only give me the girl to be my wife" (v. 12).

The brothers are outraged that their sister has been defiled. They agree to the request and long-term proposal on the condition that all Hivite men undergo circumcision. Hamor and his son convince the men of Shechem to accept this condition. On the third day while they were still in pain and recuperating, Dinah's brothers Simeon and Levi attack and kill all the men including Shechem and Hamor, and they take their sister Dinah out of the house. The rest of the brothers come and loot the city of Shechem of its wealth. They take their flocks and their herds, their donkeys, and whatever was in the city and in the field. All their wealth, all their little ones and their wives, all that were in the houses, they captured and made their prey (v. 29). Jacob's thoughts get verbalized—"you have brought trouble on me by making me odious to the inhabitants of the land, the Canaanites and the Perizzites: my numbers are few" (v. 30). In response to his concern, the sons reply, "Should our sister be treated as a whore?" (v. 31).

Dinah the daughter of Leah and Jacob never expresses her thoughts or feelings to Shechem or Hamor, her father or her brothers. In fact, we do not hear her voice in the text or anything about her ever again in the Hebrew Bible.

JUXTAPOSING ASIFA WITH DINAH

What might the stories of Dinah, Asifa, and the Rohingya women say to each other? In what follows, I highlight the suffering that women endure when caught in the "contact zone" and amid the "fault lines" of diverse communities, religions, and ethnicities. I seek to discern with this reading how we might use these texts, violent as they are, to shape the survival of women and foster solidarity among women and their communities across ethnic or religious ties.

Reading Gen 34 alongside the stories of Asifa and the Rohingya women literalizes the rape and assault of women. Such literalizing is vital in a context where rape, abuse, assault, and humiliation are spoken of in undertones, or concealed. As I began writing this paper, there were reports of Rohingya women in refugee camps in Bangladesh giving birth to babies as a consequence of being raped by Myanmar soldiers. Theorizing of rape as is often done within the academy is helpful, but it is essential that we demystify rape and literalize it for the purposes of engaging with it and recognizing the complex ways in which it lays its cost on women and men.[4] By doing so, we safeguard the victim from disappearing in death or silence. In this way, we may hear the *silent scream* of the character Dinah in *The Red Tent:*

> All the way back up the hillside to the tents of Jacob, I screamed in silence. Oh gods. Oh heaven. Oh mother. Why do I still live?[5]

The ability to hear silent screams is crucial within the Asian scene, where rape is ubiquitous (in fact, in India, on an average 108 women are raped every day, which is approximately, one woman raped every 13 minutes).[6]

Age and Consent

While the name Dinah means "judgment," Asifa in Arabic means "organizer, virtuous, pure, spotless, upright." We know that Asifa was eight years old, but the Genesis text gives no clues of Dinah's age. Was Dinah old enough to give consent? The relationship between age and the capacity to act autonomously, and act with discretion, is insufficiently considered in current scholarship. Most assume she was old enough without any speculation. Luther renders her twelve or thirteen years old and this suits my reading. Luther refers to her as an infant/child stressing the Hebrew term *yāl'dāh* ("she bore") used in the text. The "daughter of Leah" goes out to meet the "daughters of the land." She was young and innocent, "free from care and without any fear of any injury and much less of defilement, since, indeed she was not yet marriageable."[7]

Her curiosity got the better of her. She threw caution to the wind to meet her new neighbors; like any normal child, she was desirous of meeting girls her own age. The text is troubling in that Dinah's consent is never sought in the follow-up to her violation. The text reinforces the notion that whether virgin or not, consent resides in the guardians of her sexuality—her father, and brothers. While it is true that a woman's opinion was not sought because she did not matter in ancient Israel, neither Dinah's nor her father's and brothers' consent was sought by Shechem before he claims Dinah's sexuality. He renders her as "used goods," and dishonors the family. Moreover, Dinah's family did not seek her consent when they planned action against the Shechemites. Was it because she was too young to understand? The issue of age is significant in that consent is only possible were she is old enough to make such a decision. The rape of little girls is particularly awful because they are still at that age where they are unable to give consent and are in most cases coerced, forced or manipulated.

Rape

There is no doubt that Asifa was gang-raped by no fewer than three men. On the other hand, it is not clear (and biblical scholars are divided on) whether Dinah is a victim or complicit in the act.[8] The ambiguity is created by two factors: first, the verb *yatsa'* ("went out") in Hebrew and cognate languages connotes promiscuous behavior or whoring, especially when it is used with respect to a woman.[9] Second, Shechem's surprising actions in verse 3—"And his soul was drawn to Dinah daughter of Jacob; he loved the girl, and spoke tenderly to her"—suggests consensual sex. In the eyes of her family, that defiled her.[10] And the language used to describe what Shechem did to Dinah points to rape.[11]

The narrator informs us that Shechem saw her and "took" (*laqach*) her. According to Gunkel, she is abducted or kidnapped,[12] that is, taken aggressively and violently to a location convenient for Shechem. He laid (*shachav*, a verb commonly used to denote sexual contact) with her. He was after all the prince of the land; he took her, had sexual intercourse with her, and "defiled" *'anah*) her—the language connotes physical force or moral defilement (JB— "raped and so defiled"; KJV—"humbled her"). This expression in this particular context denotes that Shechem seized or snatched Dinah by force and took her before he actually had violent sexual intercourse with her.[13] Daniel Hankore argues that it was a form of "abductive marriage."[14] This position does not lessen or soften the aggressive nature of taking a woman. I am in agreement with Suzanne Scholz who is suspicious of Shechem. As a feminist reader, Scholz privileges Dinah as victim and translates verses 2 and 3 as follows:

> [2]And he took her and he laid and he raped her. [3]And he stayed with/kept Dinah, the daughter of Jacob and he lusted after the young woman and he tried to quiet the young woman.[15]

Scholz reads a form of "acquaintance rape," and she rightly insists that the focus should be on Shechem's action rather than on Dinah's intentions for going out.[16] Shechem needed to hide his violent act and he attempts to soothe

Dinah because she did not give her consent.[17] From the point of view of Dinah's experience as well as from the mental representation of the event by the narrator and his public representation of the same in that social context, all signs point to rape.

Violence in the Realm of the "Everyday"

Communalism in India and Asia has usually been linked to violence.[18] However, *spectacular* moments of strife, be they riots over cow protection or over music near mosques, they do not tell us the full story of communal antagonisms. Conflicts are more often generated from the frictions of everyday life and practices—reading, talking, walking, and cooking.[19] The circumstances of daily existence—at work, at home, and at play—and exploring social history in its experimental and subjective dimensions cannot be ignored. Everyday life reproduces social currents; it reflects the socialization of nature and the degree and manner of its humanization. Larger public arenas tend to be more impersonal or national; the everyday is more personal, interactive, and pervasive. Larger collectives are also easier to disparage and protest against because of their visibility, whereas daily individual interaction is more hidden and muted and thus more difficult to control.

The realm of the everyday is more crucial in a gender perspective, for women play a more central role in this arena. To engage with this history of everyday life as a history of gender is to inquire into the meanings of sexual affiliations, and the repeated exchanges between women and men, as well as castes, religions, ethnicities, and communities.

One cannot miss the "everydayness" of the acts of these two young girls— one (Dinah) went out to perhaps find a playmate and the other (Asifa) went out to bring home the horses. At least one (Asifa) was not doing it for the first time. And yet, it was this routine act of the everyday that gave an opportunity to the rapists to plan and execute.

Asifa and Dinah fell victims to the fractures and fault lines that characterize the everyday living of a woman—her body, whether naked or fully clothed, whether in the day or in the night, whether accompanied or not, becomes susceptible and vulnerable to being violated once it has been targeted by the male gaze. Even a woman who behaves with modesty may become an occasion of disgrace by provoking the volatile desire of men. Little stops the resolute male from attacking a victim, whether indoors or out, rendering nonexistent a place that can be "safe" for women.

The stories of Dinah and Asifa are examples of the androcentric preoccupation with the power of female sexuality when not totally confined "within" the house (domestic sphere). Their identities as Bakarwal or non-Canaanite, as part of the colonizing or colonized community, are located within fractures created by caste, religion, ethnicity—all of which increase their vulnerability. It is in this broken landscape that the postcolonial feminist framework invites dialogue, storytelling, and the birthing of relationships of liberating interdependence from and among women, who are wounded by both patriarchal and colonial structures of oppression (both external and internal) and domination.

Ethnic Clearance

The gruesome rape and murder of the eight-year-old Bakarwal girl had a chilling message embedded in it for her community. The incident and what followed have revealed much about the communal divide that exists in the valley. The Bakarwals are recognized by the long journey they take with their cattle every summer to Kashmir and Ladakh and back to Jammu in the winters. The Bakarwal community is a Muslim nomadic tribe, some of whom have settled in the Hindu-dominated Rasana village in Kathua, Jammu. Hindus in this region see themselves as an Indian nationalist bulwark against what they consider Pakistan-backed Muslim separatists. According to the charge sheet, the motive behind the rape and the murder was to instill fear and dislodge the nomadic tribe from the forest areas of the Jammu province. The minor girl's horrific rape and murder is part of the larger social engineering to terrorize the Bakarwal community to an extent that they are forced to leave the area. This is also the reason for the rape of the Rohingya women and girls—a form of ethnic cleansing and genocide, a strategy used as part of "clearance operations."

Was there another motive behind Shechem's rape of Dinah? Most readers assume that lust was the motive and that Dinah was the victim of a determined male. He probably knew she was a member of the Israelite community that camped on their land. Were there frictions between the two communities in the everydayness of life? Did tensions arise out of the material circumstances of daily existence? Since the story is told from the perspective of the Israelites, we are unaware of the impact the Israelite settlement had on the local people. Was the rape an attempt to oust the Israelite family? My questions arise out of the fact that the rape was not condemned by anyone from within the Shechemite community including Hamor the father. In the Asifa case, it was surprising how many from within the Hindu community came out in support of the perpetrators, protesting their arrest and condemning the Hindu lawyers representing Asifa's family. In the case of Myanmar, I am perturbed by the lack of comment from Myanmar Christian communities.

Shechem does not show remorse although he tries to woo and console her. Hamor does not preface his request for Dinah's hand with any statement of confession, repentance, or expression of guilt on behalf of his son. Neither does he apologize or offer to discipline or punish his son. He is straightforward in his request and makes a liberal promise:

Make marriages with us; give to us your daughters and take our daughters for
yourselves and the land shall be open to you; live and trade in it and get property
in it. (Gen 34:8–10)

Shechem requests a listening heart on the part of the brothers and the father,
but he does not confess to any wrongdoing. Instead, he offers a gift over and
beyond the bride price. He declares that if he is given Dinah as wife, he will
do anything.

The brothers do not demand an apology from Shechem or his father. Deceit
plays a key role in their participation in this story. The lack of repentance gives
rise to a deceitful response by the brothers. Without consulting their father, they
request the circumcision of the entire adult male population of Shechem for
they can only give their sister to a circumcised man. The brothers also promise,
"we will give our daughters to you and we will take your daughters to ourselves
and we will dwell with you and become one people" (v. 16). A blatant lie.

It is plausible that Shechem raped Dinah to oust the Israelites from the
land or to frighten them into submission. In their address to the rest of the
Shechemites, Hamor and Shechem do not explain that the request for circumcision arose in response to the rape and Shechem's desire to marry Dinah.
Instead, they stress the friendly nature of the Jacob family and suggest that
the land is large enough to accommodate the Jacob family. They entice the
people further by asking, "Will not their cattle, their property, and all their
beasts be ours? Only let us agree with them, and they will dwell with us" (v.
23). They mislead the people and their agenda was to eventually lord over
the tribe of Jacob and oppress them. Were these the dreams of traditional
owners and dwellers of the land? Were these in resistance and opposition to
the colonial agenda of the Israelites? I do not think either party is innocent of
such dreams. Their offer to the Israelites was not genuine and rested on such
colonizing dreams. The pathology of imagining the dominant self as weak
under threat from minorities/foreigners, and hence engaging in violence, is
part of majoritarian chauvinist thinking and this is apparent in the stories to
which this essay draws attention.

Land and Colonizing Dreams

The Jacob brothers were equally deceitful. The brothers were suspicious of
Hamor's motives and such suspicions suggest that there were already tensions between the communities—tensions that arose out of differences in
culture, religion, and ethnicity, and the fact that they were nomads sojourn-
ing on another's land. The brothers demand circumcision of all Shechemite
males. With circumcision, the Shechemites were rendered incapable of resisting and protecting themselves from the onslaught that followed. Simeon and
Levi were violent, they "took" (same Hebrew verb used in v. 2) their sister

and massacred the Shechemite males. Then, joined by the rest of the brothers, they plundered the city and took away the flocks, the wealth, the women, the children and all that were in the houses.

The gang rape of Asifa follows the ongoing tussle between the community members and the BJP-PDP[20] government's land eviction drives in the region. In the recent past, a BJP (a right-wing Hindu nationalist party) leader in that region promised the retrieval of hundreds of forestlands, a move that the Bakarwals believe would take away their traditional rights on the forests. Reportedly, since the Bakarwal Gujjars are Muslims, the BJP is feeding into communal fears by propagating the idea among the Hindu population that the Bakarwals are skewing the area's demography and that they are responsible for the encroachment of large sections of forest areas.

Turning back to Dinah's story, I follow Musa Dube who rightly points out that the book of Genesis weaves and constructs the colonial dreams and desires of the Israelites—which stretches into the rest of the Pentateuch.[21] God will make them a great nation, give them land that is already occupied by the Hivites among others, and make them a blessing to the world. The rape gave them opportunity, reinforced the negative constructions of the Shechemites, and set in motion the colonizing dreams of the Jacob family. The rape provided justification for their invasion and conquest of Shechemite land. There is much to be said for connections between women, rape and land. If Genesis was edited for an exilic audience, what we have in this text is not a rejection of imperial oppression as an unacceptable evil but rather, imperialism on the part of the Israelites and dimensions of that imperializing ideology also extant among the Shechemites.

Both Asifa and Dinah are children/women in the contact zone.[22] As a girl child in the contact zone, Dinah becomes victim to these colonizing dreams. It is the land that they are interested in and hence are willing to sacrifice the future and life of their sister as a pawn in this enterprise. The rape of Dinah, even if an illicit interaction, justifies Jacob's colonization of the land. Along with her, the wives and children of the Shechemites also become victims by being in the contact zone. Rape and sexual violation of women is both cause and effect of male struggles for power over land, and colonization. Asifa was killed and the Bakarwals do not have the wherewithal to challenge the strong and politically backed Hindu majority in the region. The Bakarwals are counting on a conscientious task force and the public to come to their aid in seeking justice for their dead daughter. Similar is the plight of the Rohingya community awaiting international intervention and negotiation to help them return to their homes. Consistent with the dynamic tension of the contact zone colonial ideology, the Shechemite desire to have and to hold the body of the woman of the colonial Israelites and oust them from their land is denied. The *Tamadaw* of Myanmar have been a little more successful.

Circumcision as Instrument of Genocide?

I have suggested that rape is an effective tool in situations of conflict to send a message to the other community, to shame the women and men in the opposing community. What of circumcision? When Israel enters Canaan, Joshua circumcises all the males of Israel (Josh 5:2–9). Both the circumcision and the Passover celebrations that follow are meant to affirm Israelite identity as a unique people bound by covenant to YHWH through the performance of rites which mark beginnings but stress continuity with the past.

Violence has been committed against Dinah, an Israelite woman, and the response is demand for circumcision followed by violence to justify and to ensure that the imperial, divine, and surrogate powers are intact.[23] Among the reasons for why circumcision was practiced is the explanation that circumcision was an act of initiation into membership in the tribe or nation or into the duties of manhood, a kind of tribal mark, an act of initiation into the covenant people.[24] Circumcision was suggested as a rite of initiation of the Shechemites into the Israelite fold. There are two ways of understanding this—circumcision as an instrument of cooption or inclusion, or circumcision as an instrument of genocide. Circumcision, an Israelite mark of identity, is forced on the men of Shechem under the pretext that their sister cannot be married to a man who is uncircumcised. Perhaps the Shechemites assumed that this was not a big ask and agreed. For Brueggemann, "Insistence on circumcision was posed not for purposes of faithfulness, but for purposes of social control and exploitation."[25] It is a means to an end and hence "this most precious symbol of faith has now become a tool of inhumanity."[26] The chapter calls to mind Saul's request for foreskins of the Philistines in exchange for his daughter (1 Sam 18:24), and here the brothers too were asking for foreskins in exchange for their sister. The Shechemites played into their hands, driven by their own colonizing dreams. Circumcision led to their decimation. The brothers in this genocide of the Shechemites effectively used circumcision. Either way, one cannot overlook the colonizing potential of circumcision and its impact on the "other" on whom is placed this demand of circumcision. Even if seen as cooption or inclusion, it comes with possible erasure of one's own religious and cultural identity. Or literally, death!

VIOLENCE AND VIOLENT TEXTS

As a story that is often skipped over and neglected by scholars, churches, and lectionaries, the Dinah story begs attention. I am intrigued by the fact that the female protagonist is named by her mother and yet the name is not explained, as is the case when her brothers are named.

The name perhaps does not need an explanation. Instead, it is an invitation to readers to judge this incident and this experience of Dinah. Judge, not in the sense of finding fault with her (as most classical commentators seem to do) but judge in the sense of feeling the pain, the suffering, the vulnerability, of Dinah, to evoke rage that would lead to hearing, feeling, and eventually to justice for her and for other women and children in her situation. The story calls us to be cognizant of, to identify and to wrestle with the fault lines of our own interpretations. Some of those fault lines work to our own individual or communal advantage. Action will become particularly difficult if our readings and interpretations reinforce the incentives to settle for the status quo.

The "monopoly of violence" has historically been men's domain. Patriarchy is not an autonomous oppression system but a system deeply rooted in imperialism, racism, and capitalism. Masculinity, as one of the manifestations of patriarchy, is a social construction built upon ideas of virility, honor, and power strength.[27] This story is an invitation for all, men and women, to judge patriarchy, colonialism, and violence against women.

Ending violence is enmeshed in narratives of violence. In the end, destroying violence becomes a story of oppression and the never-ending, vicious, additional layers of violence. In this regard, Gen 34 can be instrumental in understanding and mitigating the forces and systems of power that threaten women's lives today. I agree with Jenkins:

> Without these tales of slaughter and ethnic cleansing, later generations would not have developed the kind of religious consciousness that allowed them to look back in horror on earlier acts of bloodletting, whoever the victims might be. The moral dilemma later believers face in dealing with the violent scriptures results precisely from the success of those same texts in achieving their cultural and moral goals.[28]

It is not enough to point out the violence committed against women that needs eradicating, rather, one must have the courage to observe that the violence in this story has its genesis in religion (faith, God) which perpetuates such violence by aligning with the chosen and the powerful. Often embedded in such narratives is an undercurrent narrative that feeds the vices, and which generates violence.

The experience of Dinah is embodied by thousands of women the world over. It is not just a memory; it is a body full of images of horror and destruction, where physical wounds and mourning cannot be separated, leading to death as the unyielding end. The story as judgment is an invitation to recognize all the images and pain that she carries in her body. The memory never goes away and as Shire suggests, "her memory hardens into a tumor." Our inattention or apathetic response to such stories, as Warsan Shire reminds us, "Apathy is the same as war, it all kills you, slow like cancer in the breast or fast like a machete in the neck."[29] Our humanity, our future, and our faith rest in addressing and countering the violence that women today experience.

Women are aware of the fault lines that impinge on their lives. And yet, they have a passion for life and this is what saves Dinah from a literal death. So that she does not disappear from the pages of the story, she needs to be reclaimed as a subject of violation and as a survivor. Her story provides the opportunity to confront ideologies of the colonizer, of patriarchal culture and the violence that sustains it.

WHERE IS GOD?

God is not named or mentioned in this chapter. Perhaps this is what makes theologizing difficult when it comes to this story. It raises too many uncomfortable questions. Do we need to include God where God does not want to be? Or where the author perhaps intentionally did not include God as character? This has not stopped some from bringing God into the picture. Luther suggests that God causes the rape to test Jacob, and that the violence against the Shechemites was justified.[30] If God would punish the Shechemites for acting contrary to the law of nature, would God require the Jacob brothers to act contrary to the same law in murdering men, women, and children that never did them injury? Would God in such a case choose a people prone to violence as the Shechemites themselves? We need to question the orthodox justification for the slaughter of the Shechemites. Who might take seriously a claim that the Israelites were executing justice when the killers themselves profit so enormously from the act? The Shechemites are sinful, but our only evidence for that comes from the people who wiped them out, and who thus stood to benefit from offering such an explanation.

Dinah does not receive any support from any one and she is also silent or is silenced. I imagine that God too has been struck dumb by the actions of both the Shechemites and the Jacob brothers. God chooses to be silent in solidarity with Dinah. If God speaks, God speaks through the disturbing and unsettling questions that the text raises.[31] "The presence of God is associated with disquiet regarding the prevailing situation."[32] God continues to be silent as long as we do not wrestle with these disturbing questions. It is in the questioning that our consciousness will be troubled enough to not reject or explain away the chapter.

NOTES

1. Warshan Shire, "In Love and in War," in *Teaching My Mother How to Give Birth* (London: Flipped Eye Publishing, 2011) (https://www.goodreads.com/work/quotes/18606097-teaching-my-mother-how-to-give-birth).

2. Virginia Woolf, *Three Guineas* (London: The Hogarth Press, 1986), 138.

3. The Bakarwals are part of the larger ethnic group known as Gujjars who dominate large parts of Northern India, Pakistan, and Afghanistan. Found among both the Hindus and the Muslims, the Bakarwals are listed as a scheduled tribe, who have retained large parts of the Hindu belief system as other Gujjars across the country. "They have a common history, culture, ethnic affinities beliefs and languages with the Hindu, Sikhs and Muslim Gujjars of the Indian plains," writes Professor K. Warikoo in "Tribal Gujjars of Jammu and Kashmir," *Journal of Himalayan Research and Cultural Foundation* 4.1 (January–March 2000): 7–8. But keeping alive a Hindu belief system in their identity has not prohibited the group from following Islam as well. The fluidity in Bakarwal religion, however, has often resulted in the alienation of the community, particularly when their tribal identity has come into conflict with their religious identity. In recent years, the community has been facing the wrath of Hindutva forces, especially the cow-protecting groups who target their mode of living that is dependent on cattle.

4. Rajeshwari Sunder Rajan, *Real and Imagined Woman: Gender, Culture and Postcolonialism* (London, NY: Routledge, 1999), 67.

5. Anita Diamant, *The Red Tent* (London: Pan McMillan, 2002), 205.

6. According to the statistics published by the National Crime Records Bureau (NCRB), a total of 38,947 cases of rape were reported in 2016, and there were many unreported cases (http://ncrb.gov.in/StatPublications/CII/CII2016/Press%20release-Crime%20in%20India%202016.pdf).

7. Martin Luther, "Lectures on Genesis: Chapters 31–37," in *Luther's Works*, Vol 6, ed. Jaroslav Pelikan (Saint Louis: Concordia, 1970), 190.

8. Yair Zakovitch suggests that the story is multilayered by multiple authors. He maintains that the Dinah and Shechem story was actually a love story disapproved by the brothers. Dinah's rape was a later addition to justify the murder of the Shechemites by the Jacob brothers. Yair Zakovitch, "Assimilation in Biblical Narratives," in *Empirical Models for Biblical Criticism*, ed. Jeffrey H. Tigay (Philadelphia: University of Philadelphia, 1985), 175–196.

9. Shaul Bar, *A Nation Is Born: The Jacob Story* (Eugene, OR: WIPF and Stock, 2016), 97.

10. Cf. Danna Fewell and David Gunn, "Tipping the Balance: Steinberg's Reader and the Rape of Dinah," *JBL* 110 (1991): 193–211; Mark Brett, *Genesis: Procreation and the Politics of Identity* (London: Routledge, 2000); Claudia V Camp, *Wise, Strange and Holy: The Strange Woman and the Making of the Bible* JSOTS 320 (Sheffield: Academic Press, 2000).

11. Gen 34:2—"When Shechem son of Hamor the Hivite, prince of the region, *saw* her, he *seized* her and *lay* with her *by force*" (NRSV; my italics); "And Shechem

the son of Hamor, the Hivite, the prince of the land, *saw* her, and he *took* her, *lay* with her, and *violated her*" (JPS; my italics).

12. Herman Gunkel, *Genesis.* Trans. Mark E. Biddle, 3rd ed. (Macon, GA: Mercer University Press, 1997), 358.

13. Carolyne Blythe, *Terrible Silence, Eternal Silence: A Consideration of Dinah's Voicelessness in the Text and Interpretive Traditions of Genesis 34* (PhD Diss., University of Edinburgh, 2008), 48–51 (http://www.era'lib.ed.ac.uk/handle /1842/2593).

14. Based on a Jubilees rendering which says, "they carried off Dinah," Hankore maintains that Shechem did not rape Dinah but attempted "abductive marriage"— that is, marriage by abduction. Danile Hankore, *The Abduction of Dinah: Genesis 28:10–35:15 as a Votive Narrative* (Cambridge, UK: James Clarke & Co, 2013), 145.

15. Suzanne Scholz, *Sacred Witness: Rape in the Hebrew Bible* (Minneapolis: Fortress, 2010), 30.

16. Ibid.

17. Ibid., 35–38. See also Blythe, *Terrible Silence,* who offers convincing arguments in favour of Dinah as victim of rape.

18. In South Asia "communalism" refers to attempts to incite strife between communities because of their different religious or ethnic identities.

19. Michael de Certeau, *The Practice of Everyday Life*, trans. Steven F. Rendall (Berkeley: University of California Press, 1984), xi–xxiv.

20. The alliance between two political parties, the Bharathiya Janata Party (BJP) and the People's Democratic Party (PDP) in Jammu and Kashmir.

21. Musa Dube, "Dinah (Genesis 34) at the Contact Zone: Shall Our Sister Become a Whore?" in *Feminist Frameworks and the Bible: Power Ambiguity and Intersectionality*, ed. Juliana Classens and Carolyn Sharp (London: Bloomsbury T & T Clark, 2017), 39–49.

22. Contact zones are social spaces where cultures meet, clash and grapple with each other, often in contexts of highly asymmetric relations of power, such as colonialism, slavery, or their aftermaths as they are lived out in many parts of the world today. See Mary Louis Pratt, "Arts of the Contact Zone," *Profession* 91 (1991): 33–40.

23. Cf. Robert S. Warfula, "The Exodus Story as a Foundation of the God of the Father," in *The Postcolonial Commentary and the Old Testament*, ed. Hemchand Gossai (London: T & T Clark, 2019), 10–26.

24. J. P. Hyatt, "Circumcision," in *The Interpreters Dictionary of the Bible*, Vol 1, ed. Keith R. Crim and George A. Buttrick (Nashville: Abingdon, 1962), 630.

25. Walter Brueggemann, *Genesis. Interpretation* (Atlanta: John Knox Press, 1982), 278. Mark Brett also writes, "Jacob's sons have inappropriately transferred warfare legislation on to a case where it did not apply and have deceitfully adopted a circumcision rite that H considers to be an acceptable strategy for social inclusion" in his article "The Priestly Dissemination of Abraham," *Hebrew Bible and Ancient Israel* 3 (2014): 104–105.

26. Brueggemann, *Genesis*, 278.

27. Michael S. Kimmel, "Masculinity as Homophobia: Fear, Shame and Silence in the Construction of Gender identity," in *Theorizing Masculinities*, ed. Harry Brod and Michael Kauffman (London: Sage Publishing Press, 1994), 119–141.

28. Philip Jenkins, *Laying Down the Sword: Why We Can't Ignore the Bible's Violent Verses* (New York: HarperOne, 2011), 240.

29. Shire, *Teaching My Mother How to Give Birth.*

30. Martin Luther, "Lectures on Genesis," 192.

31. Felix Wilfred, *Margins: Site of Asian Theology* (Delhi: ISPCK, 2008), xii.

32. Ibid.

Part II

DARE TO (RE)IMAGINE

Chapter 8

Bodies, Identities, and Empire

Wanda Deifelt

Christianity often falls short in proclaiming and living out its liberating message, and nothing illustrates this more clearly than the gradual move from a persecuted sect of Judaism to become an official religion of the Roman Empire. Slowly but surely, Christianity became the stronghold of elite, male, Eurocentric, and heteronormative ideals. Human bodies were at the receiving end of these concepts. Defenders of imperialistic mentalities assumed Christianity to support natural law, that is, a divine ordering of the world that justified the social, political, economic, and culturally ascribed positions of power and privilege. As a result, some were acclaimed citizens and others deemed barbarians, outcasts, slaves, or savages—in sum, non-citizens—who were nevertheless instrumental in ensuring the power and privilege of Rome. This political ideology required the subjection of local communities in service of imperial self-interests by means of social and economic exploitation.[1]

THE CONTEXT OF EMPIRE

The coercive power of the Roman Empire was often enforced through indirect rule, that is, by utilizing provincial kings and religious leaders to carry out imperial orders and comply with its expectations. In ancient Palestine, for instance, Judean, Samarian, and Galilean people were subjected to a Roman-style reign of terror through the appointment of Herodian rulers. Any resistance was crushed. Under Herod, the high priests of Jerusalem served as religious legitimation for oppressive and exploitative authority. Herod's expensive building projects, uncovered through archaeological evidence, suggest the increasing wealth that resulted from the close collaboration with the Roman elite.[2] While the affluent high-priestly families and Herodian rulers inhabited extravagant dwelling places, the common people were exploited through tithes, taxes, and tributes.

Protests were not unusual. Richard A. Horsley argues that Galilean and Judean peasant communities were particularly prone to revolt against the Herodian client-kings and Jerusalem's high priests. In his opinion, this resulted from "the prominence of resistance to oppressive alien rule in Israelite tradition" which originated from the narrative of God's liberation from pharaoh's bondage as told in the exodus and celebrated in Passover.[3] Uprisings of peasant communities were met with violence. But not everybody was as willing to protest, particularly those who were dependent on the temple apparatus in Jerusalem. The vested interest in and loyalty to ruling institutions, added to economic dependence on the temple itself, rendered the liberating message of the exodus less pressing or urgent.

Such was the context of Jesus's ministry. Many resistance movements—prophetic and messianic—rose before, during, and after his lifetime. The purpose of these movements was to attain freedom from the Roman and Herodian rule while also establishing a more egalitarian social and economic order. This greatly explains Jesus's own perspective, as a member of an oppressed community advocating for the socially, politically, and economically disenfranchised. In his ministry, Jesus focused on the sick, impoverished, and outcast. Much of his time and attention were spent on feeding and healing those around him, and to encouraging his followers to do likewise. In his ethics of care, Jesus invited disciples who would also care for the well-being of others. Jesus proclaimed the renewal of Israel through his depictions of the Reign of God. Through it, he condemned oppressive rulers and promoted resistance to all forms of oppression. His crucifixion at the hands of the Roman Empire can be interpreted as an attempt to suppress resistance, in the same way as the Roman Empire crucified many other political insurgents.

Through slaughter and enslavement, the Roman Empire maintained its dominance and ensured peace. The *Pax Romana* was, of course, a synonym for the security of Roman geopolitics and not the well-being or safety of individuals and peoples. The brutal execution practice of crucifixion was one of the many ways to instill fear and quell any resistance to the imperial hegemonic power. "The ancient Romans believed that to ensure their own national security they had to conquer other peoples with their superior military force in order to extract *fides/pistis* = 'loyalty' (i.e., submission and deference) from subjected people."[4] Torture of bodies was both a way to punish and to entertain, as seen in the spectacles conducted at the Colosseum.[5]

ATTITUDES TOWARD THE BODY:
GRECO-ROMAN BACKGROUND

Christianity proposed a new understanding of the relationship between humanity and God that resulted in newfound respect for bodies because of the belief in divine incarnation (the Word becomes flesh). However, in its development, Christian attitudes toward the body were deeply influenced by the historical contexts in which they developed. Christianity emerged in the late classical world, composed largely of Greek and Roman components with a few Eastern influences.[6] Religion in the Roman Empire was generally syncretistic and open, although it was connected with the Roman government and became intolerant when state security was perceived to be involved. Prehistoric understandings of life and death were still present. Early Roman gods were also remembered, although syncretism occurred between Roman gods and the gods of other cultures. Magic and rituals were also key aspects of religion, including ritual instructions, charms, and taboos, used especially to exclude strangers or the profane. Despite governmental efforts, the mystical and emotional influences of Eastern religions pervaded Roman religion.

The more educated Romans preferred Greek philosophy to this syncretistic religion because it was instrumental in their pursuit of virtue.[7] Virtue implied control over the body and its desire for pleasure. Greek philosophers, especially Aristotle and Plato, taught that political participation, intellectual activity, and ethics were key aspects of life. During the first century CE in Athens, the Epicureans and Stoics strongly influenced the thinking of the upper classes. The Epicureans believed in reason and free will, teaching that gods were nonexistent. In order to attain *atarazia*, a state of peace and tranquility, dedicated Epicureans would avoid public politics, passion, and marriage to lead a separated and contemplative life. However, when these principles combined with the materialism and excesses of Rome, some people interpreted Epicureanism as promoting self-indulgence. Stoicism was based on a strong belief in eternal order. The law of reason that was thought to govern the universe was also applied to human life by teaching that humans should follow a divine purpose. When Stoicism entered Rome, it retained its association with duty, self-discipline, and the suppression of emotions. The teachings of Pythagoras were also present in this context, which included promoting asceticism as a way to prepare for the transmigration of one's soul to the next life. In Rome, Panaetius's combination of these beliefs with the Platonic-Aristotelian teaching of soul-body dualism was promoted by Posidonius. According to Warde Fowler, in these dualistic teachings, "it is the soul that gains and the body that loses."[8] The results of this teaching are especially evident in the conclusion of *The Republic*, in which the character the Younger Scipio is told that his mortal body is a prison he must escape, but that his soul is his true self.

Not all Romans abided by these ideas. Horace and Catallus, for instance, advised that men immerse themselves in the enjoyment of things like conversation, wine, and women. During the peak of the Roman Empire, nearly every other day was a holiday filled with entertainment for the masses.[9] This entertainment included chariot races accompanied by crucifixion and other brutalities, theater focused on an individual actor that included themes of violence and sex, and gladiatorial shows at the Colosseum. The gladiatorial shows at the Colosseum involved the bloody killings of large numbers of both humans and animals. Frank Bottomley believes that the Romans' apparent enjoyment of this entertainment demonstrates that their society had destroyed their natural feelings and instincts toward human bodies. Decadent Roman attitudes toward the body were also shown in other excesses, including banquets with vomitoria, orgies, and prostitution. Messalina, the wife of the Emperor Claudius, is a well-known example of how prostitution had become widely acceptable. Respect for the bodies of slaves was also nearly nonexistent, and the killing of slaves was not banned until the reign of Hadrian, in 117-38 CE.

Nevertheless, the Romans also demonstrated care for the body, particularly the body of the citizen. "The body that the citizen put on display should be clothed, scrubbed and under control. Nature—that is, anything to do with procreation or defecation—had to be concealed."[10] This care for the body, referred to as *cultus*, involved eating adequately and keeping hair and beard trimmed. To suspend one's body *cultus* was to abandon one's culture, that is, one's capacity to keep the body under control by sinking into squalor or giving in to passion. The effect of passion was debilitating, since it caused the soul to lose its grip over the body and gave the body free reign to follow its animal nature.

The soul had influence over the body, and the body had influence over the soul. Hence, *mens sana in corpore sano* (healthy mind in a healthy body).[11] In addition, the well-being of the body was ensured by the practice of bathing. The Roman baths had special water supplies and low or free entrance fees. The baths also served as places for social gatherings and recreation. Some of the city baths were particularly ornate and included statues of gods of health and hygiene, providing massage, depilation, food, and in some cases also prostitution. In summarizing this era's attitude toward the body, Bottomley observes, "The thoughtful found meaning either in service of the state or life of the mind, while the thoughtless lost themselves in others' torments or their own physical satiety."[12]

PAUL AND THE BODY

In spite of Jesus's positive tenor regarding human bodies, his followers were not always able to keep his teachings. In fact, Christianity has always had an ambiguous relationship with embodiment. On the one hand, the very core of Christian teachings affirms the care for and well-being of bodies, but there is a counter-surge that renders this message moot. Paul is a good example of the tension between the liberating and nondomineering message of Jesus and the need to comply with the societal norms of the Roman Empire. Paul navigates both worlds: he is both a Roman and a Jewish citizen. His reference and acclamation of the household codes (Ephesians 5:21–6:9, Colossians 3:18–4:1, and 1 Peter 2:18–3:7) are evidence of the domestication of Jesus's radical message. The submissiveness of women and slaves are not part of Jesus's teaching, and yet they become hallmarks of Christian teachings in centuries to come. In other texts (such as 1 Timothy), unknown authors pretend to be Paul in order to have their teachings carry more weight. Paul himself, it could be argued, struggles with the dual approaches to embodiment: God's good creation or a path to damnation. In 1 Cor 6:12–20, the tension is evident. There are usually two approaches to this text. One group uses this passage to justify what they deem to be morally acceptable to God: virginity and celibacy, no sex before marriage, sex only for the purpose of reproduction, opposition to same-gender relations, in sum, moral and religious disapproval of what they perceive to be fornication. Another constituency highlights the positive tone about the human body as a temple, an indwelling of the divine in the material world—similar to God's incarnation. This second group argues that the human body and sexuality are gifts to be used as long as this practice does no harm and is ethically consequent. The text and its interpretations exemplify why Christianity has so many ambiguities regarding embodiment and human sexuality. How can the same text lead to such opposing views? Biblical scholars have used adjectives ranging from "disjointed" to "incoherent" to describe this passage. It contains many well-known lessons: we glorify God with our bodies (with the way we act and carry ourselves), there are many things that are legal but not always good (because something is allowed does not mean that it should be done), or that sin is a bodily affair that can be committed against one's own or against other people's bodies (like violence, starvation, deprivation of health care or murder).

The text also reveals an ambiguity that has burdened Christianity for nearly two thousand years: how do Christians deal with embodiment, with their own bodies, and with the bodies of those around them? This ambiguity is found in Paul himself. As somebody who spouses both the Jewish and the Greco-Roman way of thinking, Paul is torn. In the Jewish, Semitic tradition, the body is a good creation, made by God. This is stated in Genesis, when God creates male and female as divine image and gifts them with sexuality.[13] There is no guilt or condemnation in the enjoyment of bodily pleasure if the body is treated with the respect that it requires. Having been made by God, the body is good. Body and sexuality are gifts to be enjoyed (albeit within certain limitations).

On the other hand, Paul is also influenced by a Greco-Roman antagonism to the material and bodily world. In the Platonic view, to pay attention to the body is to yield to inferior desires. It distracts from higher goals. In this perspective, the human body is but a carcass, a prison to the soul that yearns to be freed. The quicker one moves through this life, the quicker one achieves eternal bliss.

This tension is so obvious in Paul that he even employs two different words to describe physicality: when the body is a good creation, he uses the word *soma* (body). When he wants to talk about the human predicament, the fallen body and all of its temptations, he uses the word *sarx* (flesh). As Hannah Hunt explains, Paul's interpretation of the Jesus event provides a "theological grammar" for subsequent generations.[14]

> Applied to the human person, *soma* means the physical aspect of the person. Man [*sic*] as a body represents part of God's creation, working in accordance with nature. This is in contrast to *sarx* which can convey the same sense of the entire human person, but standing in hostility to God's purposes.[15]

This ambiguity is exemplified with the term *porneia*—prostitute—in Paul's letter to the Corinthians. Biblical commentaries state that "pagan temples were the restaurants of antiquity where prostitutes were frequently on offer."[16] Although it is not clear whether Paul is debating secular or religious prostitution in this particular passage (most authors lean toward a more generic description due to the use of the term *porneia*, as opposed to the term *ierodulos*, which means cultic prostitution), Paul, nevertheless, makes use of theological language to engage it. Prostitution is a sin against God. It compromises the human body, the temple of the Holy Spirit. A sin against God's creation, the body, is a sin against the creator. But what is at the receiving end of Paul's vehement critique? Is it sexual immorality in general, incest, sacred or secular prostitution, idolatry, personal vices, adultery? Is he addressing particular men in the church of Corinth who are going to prostitutes? Is their misconduct happening during bacchanals and feasts at pagan temples, when sexual play was a regular part of the meal? Nobody knows exactly.

Because Christianity often embraced a dualistic mentality, focusing more on the afterlife than the here and now, the kinds of sins described by Paul were reduced to a few moralizing teachings about sexuality. What many Christians have taken away from this passage is the verse "anyone united to the Lord becomes one spirit with him" (1 Cor 6:17). This spiritual connection with God is overemphasized so that membership in the body of Christ is a matter of the soul, not of the body. This blatant assumption is already present in the text itself, as Paul did not think of the body of the prostitute as a temple of the Holy Spirit. Nobody asks about the circumstances or conditions of her life, the defamations, entrapments, and abuses that prostitution affords.

Paul's silence reveals that some bodies are more valuable than others, and this double standard sets the stage for the violence carried out in the name of Christianity in the following centuries: crusades, genocide of indigenous populations, slavery, the rape of women, and holy wars. Christianity lost track of the key tenet that the body—including sexuality—is God's good creation. It lost track of the centrality of incarnation, that God became flesh to live in our midst. The care for bodies, the welfare of the neighbor, and the concern for the well-being of God's creation are overlooked and the Christian message reduced to a few moralistic rules.

Perhaps, the most important point to take away from this text is not its critique of any specific sin, but of all sins that defile human and bodily integrity. This requires a more complex reading of the text because it curbs the tendency to list particular vices or transgressions and deeming them as sinful. Rather, this interpretation would require us to engage in ethical deliberation. Instead of reducing the message to a list of do's and don'ts, we are invited to think about the causes and consequences of our acts. For instance, if *porne* were not reduced to prostitution (paying money for sex) but extended to systemic and structural sins as well, we could not dismiss it as a personal choice judged by moralistic values. Paul conceives of sins against the body as sins of religious allegiance—and these sins include everything that prevents human flourishing: hunger, illness, violence, destitution—in sum, everything that diminishes the body and robs it from its dignity.[17] In this sense, the Christian message would lead us to critique and overcome a pornographic culture.

Porne is at the root of the word "pornography." Pornography is the use of the bodies of others for one's own immediate gratification; it is a denial of the power of mutuality. In the words of Audre Lorde, "pornography emphasizes sensation without feeling."[18] It offers selfish pleasure without relationality or accountability. Ours is a culture of immediate rewards, self-centeredness, objectification of others and self, where the measure of everything is personal indulgence, and satisfaction is measured by possessions and social status. This pornographic culture objectifies bodies for the sake of consumerism. We treat our bodies and the bodies of others as objects, for our benefit, entertainment, or profit. We might not pay for sex with money, but the way our culture perceives bodies—as exposed flesh for consumption in the way of advertisement, sports, cheap labor, sweatshops, or human trafficking—makes a compelling argument that our culture is indeed pornographic.

CHURCH TEACHINGS REGARDING THE BODY

While the well-being of bodies was at the center of Jesus's life and ministry, the reduction of Christianity as a religion to save souls instead of bodies gradually led to its demise. This negative attitude toward bodies becomes more evident as the Christian church ceased to be a minority movement and became the official religion of the Roman Empire. The combination between a Greek way of thinking (the dichotomy between body and soul, material and immaterial, and so on) added to a Roman mode of administration (hierarchical and centralized) gave prominence to a celibate male clergy. Embodiment was reduced to sexuality, and sex was abhorred. Women were described as constantly tempting men, tools devised by the devil to deviate them from their chastity. It is ironic that celibate men would have so much to say about women and sex!

Early church fathers (such as Augustine, Jerome, Tertullian) had both an obsession with and aversion to sex, which was targeted primarily against women. The human body, physical pleasure, and procreation placed women as closer to nature. All these things distracted men from higher and more spiritual concerns. From the very beginning, they said, Eve was already tempting Adam with her sexual appeal. Man was created first as a spiritual idea, an image of the divine *Logos*. "Before the creation of Eve, the material or bodily component of Adam was under the control of his spiritual self. . . . With Eve's creation, Adam becomes seduced to his lower self through sexual desire."[19] As Philo stated, not only Eve's disobedience after her creation but her mere existence "is the beginning of iniquities and transgressions, and it is owing to this that men have exchanged their previously immortal and happy existence for one which is mortal and full of misfortune."[20]

Jerome had similar ideas, assuming that all that sustains physical life (sex, eating, reproduction) sustains the realm of death and needs to be ceased. That included flagellation, lack of sleep and very restricted food. Sexual continence was ideal: "It is hard for the human soul to avoid loving something, and our mind must of necessity give way to affection of one kind or another. The love of the flesh is overcome by the love of the spirit. Desire is quenched by desire. What is taken from the one increases the other."[21]

For ascetics, to be a Christian was to abandon the world with all its temptations, embrace a life that pursued only religious and spiritual goals, and abstain from any sort of pleasure (food, drink, sex, etc.). The body represented a prison for the human soul and a hindrance to a devout spiritual life. Procreation perpetuated the circle of sin and death. Taking control over the body was a symbol of Christ's victory over death and the corrupt human order (including sin). To control the body was to deny sexuality and the sinful desires of the flesh, not giving in to the flesh and its appetites. The practice of asceticism and the model of sexual renunciation were developed in the first five centuries of the Church. Continence, celibacy, and lifelong virginity—at first marginal spiritual practices—became the ideal for Christian life. Jerome, for instance, when comparing virginity, widowhood, and marriage, gave virginity a numerical value of 100, widowhood, 60, and marriage, 30. He said that virginity filled heaven, while marriage only populated the earth. Here is another statement by Jerome:

> In those days, as I have said, the virtue of continence was found only in men: Eve still continued to travail with children. But now that a virgin has conceived in the womb and has borne to us a child … now the chain of the curse is broken. Death came through Eve, but life has come through Mary. And thus the gift of virginity has been bestowed most richly upon women, seeing that it has had its beginning from a woman.[22]

Marriage was seen as a state morally inferior to virginity, and sexual intercourse could be justified only with the obligation to procreate. This offered only two alternatives for women: either the spiritual life of bodily renunciation or the physical life that reduces women to seductresses. Although the church fathers stated that sexual intercourse defiled both women and men, they emphasized women's corrupting influence on men instead of the other way around. Women are described as lustful and always moved by the desire to rule a man's household, to be able to spend his hard-earned money.

The ideal of sexual suppression (for men) and virginity (for women) stems from the early Christian teachings that yielding to the desires of the flesh is sinful. Jesus is described as a celibate and chaste man and Mary as a virgin before, during, and after his birth.[23] Both become models to emulate. If Eve had tempted Adam into eating the forbidden fruit (thus leading to the fall of humanity and introducing sin into the world), Mary represented an alternative. While Eve's seduction caused suffering and death, Mary's virginity and abstinence brings forth Jesus. Mary redeems Eve. Thus, women were presented with two options: to express their sexuality and be like Eve, the one who introduced suffering and death into the world, or be like Mary, the vessel through which the savior was born. Mary became the ideal woman, but by being both a virgin and a mother she also became an impossible model for women to aspire.[24] Either as virgins or mothers, women were always deemed guilty.

An opposing force to celibacy came from a former monk, Martin Luther, who in the sixteenth century challenged monasticism. He insisted that those who live chaste lives are no purer than others. "In this world we are bound by the needs of our bodily life, but we are not righteous because of them."[25] Luther's assertion that a Christian is both a saint and sinner means that nobody is better or worse than anybody else. Luther critiques the ascetic, monastic ideal: "Is it not true that money, property, body, spouse, child, friends, and the like are good things created and given by God Himself?"[26] In the mundane, bodily realities of life, believers testify to their faith not by judging each other but by caring for one another. Luther then concluded that God is also the God of bodies.

> I will say nothing of the other gifts and goods—also the physical ones—which He bestows on us, such as father and mother, government, order, temporal peace, and the like. How angry can God really be if He lets His sun rise for us every day, if He gives us good weather, if He lets all kinds of plants, fruits, and nourishment grow for us, if He favors us with healthy bodies and members? If we could look at these things properly, we would have to say: "He surely has given us great treasures—above all, peace and joy toward Him and, in addition, all kinds of physical benefactions on earth, visible and palpable evidence of His mercy and His willingness to help us." Therefore, we should learn not to be afraid or fainthearted before Him.[27]

The whole of creation provides opportunities for encountering God in gratitude. Material resources "are gifts of God put into practice not only in the spirit but also outside and toward people, for God is also the God of bodies. Therefore he provides us with bodily gifts, and he wants us to enjoy these gifts with gladness."[28] To squander, lose a sense of awe, or objectify the material world is sinful. Life is a gift, as is the whole creation. This theological approach allows us to see creation as a manifestation of divine grace, which we are invited to partake and share with one another. Our bodies and our sexuality are God's gifts to us, in which we are to take delight. God's creation of the material world is to be cared for and enjoyed.

CURRENT REFLECTIONS ON EMBODIMENT

Religion is connected to family, education, politics, economics, and the overall shaping of social and cultural mores. Religious communities offer answers to people's everyday problems and can offer meaning to their existence. While this power can have positive effects, it can also have problematic consequences when used to prevent human flourishing. An example of the latter is how religion deals with violence and sexuality, topics the churches have not always addressed in positive ways, by supporting healthy approaches to embodiment, sexuality, and relationships. As in other religions, Christianity offers mixed messages about the body.

Human sexuality is complex, established through the interaction of factors as diverse as cultural expectations, religious teachings, and gender norms. Gender constructs contribute to the formulation of human sexuality by promoting binary divisions (either as male or female) and by endorsing stereotypical roles for each category. As Judith Butler writes, "Gender is an identity tenuously constituted in time, instituted in an exterior space through a stylized repletion of acts."[29] As such, gender constructs influence and control people's sexual identities. In terms of attraction, men are supposed to be drawn to women and vice versa. What escapes this heteronormativity risks social disapproval. Because gender is part of one's identity, it is also accompanied by expectations, contingencies, and roles.

This is detrimental not only to women but also to men. The construction of masculinity has identified men with aggression and dominance. Masculinity is described as a reactive term that is ultimately a rejection of everything feminine (physical weakness, emotion, procreation, and the domestic sphere). Cultural stereotypes, including those promoted by the media, define masculinity as control of emotions, control of women's bodies, and control of social situations. It teaches that men need to be strong, stoic, and always refrain from expressing their feelings.[30] As it turns out, social constructions of masculinity tend to do more harm than good because it encourages domination and perpetuates patriarchal standards.

This patriarchal domination is often wielded through violence. It is prevalent in domestic abuse, whether it be physical or not. Masculinity expects women to be in a submissive role. These characteristics of manhood are described as oppositional traits to everything a woman must be. It is not surprising, therefore, that so much bullying happens precisely by characterizing young boys with feminine traits and that violence is the sole means of conflict resolution. This violence plays into other forms of domination as well, as spelled out through patriarchal ideals: destruction of the natural environment, subjugation of peoples and nations, dominion through class and caste systems, and so on.

The binary and hierarchical social constructs are pervasive through family structures, education, mass media, and everyday social encounters. Not conforming to gender stereotypes can lead to stigmatization and social rejection, frequently accompanied by physical and psychological violence.[31] The LGBTQ+ community has challenged the notion that human behavior conforms to one's biological sex, and, as a result, experienced multiple forms of violence. That is why queer[32] theory and theology have employed the term "gender identity" to describe how people feel and present themselves, as distinct from biological sex or sexual orientation.[33]

Often, in this binary construction of sexual identity, women turn violence against their own bodies (for instance, through cutting and eating disorders such as bulimia and anorexia) and men turn violence against others. The documentary *The Mask You Live In* highlights the damaging effect of socially constructed gender norms. Athletic ability, economic success, and sexuality are the main factors to judge manhood. By enforcing aggression as a form of competition, young men are taught that *winning* is synonym of masculinity (whether it is a sports match, a business transaction, or a girl).[34]

The documentary describes masculinity as a mask, a cover that hides the true humanity of men.

The central theme of this domination is the objectification of bodies, particularly women's bodies. Female bodies are treated as commodity, as objects of desire and means to sell products. Individuality, dignity, and assertion of one's personhood are disregarded when a person is reduced to a sexual object. Women are to be "sexually submissive, sexually suggestive, sexually available, and sexually willing."[35] The objectification of women's bodies plays an important role in gender inequality, and its effect becomes nefarious when women objectify themselves, seeing their self-worth hinged on compliance with their role as objects of male desire. Their bodies are not for their pleasure and enjoyment but for their male counterparts.

Religious teachings add further rules and expectations for regulating sexuality (mainly in gender-specific ways). Religious teachings present an additional layer to perceptions of embodiment and sexuality because they invoke an ultimate authority, namely God, to justify these teachings. Thus, for instance, if the cultural expectation for women is to be beautiful, submissive, and pure, this gains another connotation when women are regarded as subordinate and dependent on their male counterparts because women are seen as inherently sinful. Aruna Gnanadason examines this in the Indian context, juxtaposing biblical teachings and other religious epics that implicate women for the existence of sin in the world. She quotes Ambrose to illustrate women's shaming: "Adam was led to sin by Eve and not Eve by Adam. It is just and right that woman accepts as lord and master the one whom she led to sin."[36]

This type of rhetoric has far-reaching consequences, from condoning rape culture to describing violence against women as divinely ordained. A woman is expected to submit, patiently waiting for the right man, keeping herself pure so that he may "unwrap" her virginity like a present on their wedding night.[37] This gives men a sense of entitlement. Women exist to give pleasure to men but not to experience sexual pleasure themselves. In our culture, there are clearly double standards regarding male and female virginity. Whereas men are expected to be sexually experienced and always take the initiative, women are supposed to guard their virginity and keep pure.

WHAT CAN CHURCHES DO?

Patricia H. Davis, in *Beyond Nice: The Spiritual Wisdom of Adolescent Girls*, points out that churches have done, for the most part, a lousy job in addressing sexuality besides just quoting Proverbs 31. When the churches' default answer is "don't have sex until you are married" and refuses to address their natural curiosity, it leaves women and young adults vulnerable to violence. If the churches cannot answer real-life questions regarding human sexuality, they give the impression that everything related to embodiment is sinful and ugly. Churches have perpetuated societal ideals instead of changing them. As a result, they preserve the same abjection toward human bodies that has been the hallmark of colonial power and empire mentality. Churches miss out on the opportunity to preach and teach about healthy, body-affirming, and pleasurable sexuality.

Among the shortcomings of churches regarding embodiment and sexuality is the reduction of women's roles solely as wives and mothers. While these ambitions are acceptable and noble, they become problematic when they are not an option but an obligation. It does not allow women to be sexual and sensual beings without having their identities defined by their relationship to others. To reduce women's vocation to that of good Christian wives and good Christian mothers plays into the entrapments of heteronormativity, along with pressure to conform to sexual norms and gender expectations.

There is lack of safe spaces to talk about sexuality and the experiences that often pain church members. One such case is sexual violence. Because women are more often victims of violence, the churches' silence regarding sexuality and sexual violence ends up condoning it. A push for marriage and the stigmatization of divorce that still prevails in many parts of the world end up leaving little space to move out of violent relationships. The sanctity of marriage is protected over the sanctity of women's lives and their physical and emotional integrity. Churches feel less obliged to talk about consent than sexual purity and obedience. Inadvertently, churches perpetuate rape culture by silencing women, deeming them as objects, and preventing them to voice their own desires and expectations in a relationship. Women's agency regarding their own bodies and sexuality is seen as a threat. If the churches want to make a difference in people's lives, they must talk about the violence that people face, look for its root causes, and identify alternatives. Church leaders are called to speak against violence and support survivors.

Churches must reclaim a positive view of embodiment and sexuality to convey the divine beyond the typical standards established in both church and society. As Isherwood and Stuart explain, "It is therefore inevitable in a society which devalues the body that the body should become a site of resistance."[38] In spite of abusive teachings and practices, the body is recognized as a beautiful and noble creation of God. To reclaim this means to denounce the absurdity of classical teachings (some are mentioned earlier) and to look for life-affirming, participatory, and justice-filled teachings instead. This resistance must include the body as God's good creation and worthy of the love and care that Jesus also extended to us.

NOTES

1. "The Romans sought more from war than the heady but fleeting enjoyment of proving themselves the better fighters. Victory had to be final; plunder was not enough. Rome's policy of annexation and conquest turned enemy peoples into perpetually vanquished tribute-payers, at least until they gained the right to Roman citizenship"—Florence Dupont, *Daily Life in Ancient Rome* (Oxford, UK and Cambridge, US: Blackwell, 1989), 53.

2. Richard A. Horsley, *Jesus and Empire: The Kingdom of God and the New World Disorder* (Minneapolis: Fortress Press, 2003), 32–33.

3. Ibid., 37.

4. Ibid., 27.

5. Brian K. Harvey, *Daily Life in Ancient Rome: A Sourcebook* (Indianapolis, IN: Hackett Publishing, 2016), 314–323.

6. Frank Bottomley, *Attitudes to the Body in Western Christendom* (London: Lepus Books, 1979), vii.

7. Behavior among citizens was governed by a list of virtues grounded on gender roles. As defined by the aristocracy, men's virtues fell in the realm of public life, whereas women's virtues focused on home, husband, and childbearing. In his *Happy Life,* Seneca contrasts virtue with pleasure. Self-control and adherence to duty are described as a man's major virtues. In addition, also *virtus* (manly courage in the battlefield), *fortitudo* (bravery), *pietas* (devotion to the gods), *moderatio* (moderation), *clementia* (better treatment of people than they deserve), *severitas* (severity and the punishment of crime as it deserves), *iustitia* (justice), and *sapientia* (wisdom). See Harvey, *Daily Life in Ancient Rome*, 2.

8. Bottomley *Attitudes to the Body*, 5.

9. As pointed out by Brian K. Harvey (*Daily Life in Ancient Rome*, 294), public entertainment in Rome began as a component of religious holidays but evolved into a variety of forms ranging from chariot races, theatrical performances, and amphitheatrical games. Putting on games was expensive because they required professional entertainers. At first, the aristocracy had the duty to pay for games (although a financial burden, it could also be politically advantageous in order to win votes for election to public offices). After the creation of the empire, the emperor assumed the costs of holding games within the city of Rome, but, outside of the city, it remained the responsibility of the aristocracy.

10. Dupont, *Daily Life in Ancient Rome*, 241.

11. Ibid., 242: "In their eyes a sick body was often the result of a corrupt soul. Greed induced pallor and effeminacy; avarice made a man hard, dry and constipated; debauchery made people's bodies and breath stink. Satirical poets lavished a wealth of details on the nauseating spectacle of spiritual corruption."

12. Bottomley, *Attitudes to the Body*, 15.

13. For further reflection on the goodness of sexuality in Gen 1:1–2:4 creation account, see Wanda Deifelt, "And G*d Saw That it Was Good—*Imago Dei* and Its Challenge to Climate Justice," in *Planetary Solidarity: Global Women's Voices on Christian Doctrine and Climate Justice*, ed. Grace Ji-Sun Kim and Hilda P. Koster (Minneapolis: Fortress Press, 2017), 119–132.

14. "Paul's understanding of the new law given by Christ was grasped by Christians in their attempt to live as part of the body of Christ, and explained how Christ's death and resurrection ensured salvation for those who chose to share in His sufferings. So the word 'body' can mean a corporate sense of identity, an organism or means of maintaining a community as well as the physical aspect of the human being . . . The Christ that is thus depicted is constituted in various unities; he inextricably combines the dual natures of divine and human"—Hannah Hunt, *Clothed in the Body: Asceticism, the Body and the Spiritual in the Late Antique Era* (Burlington, VT: Farnham, 2012), 31.

15. Ibid., 41–42.

16. Brian Rosner, "Temple Prostitution in 1 Corinthians 6:12–20," *Novum Testamentum* 40 (1998): 337.

17. "Sin always has a personal as well as a systemic side. But it is never just 'individual'; there is no evil that is not relational. Sin exists precisely in the distortion of relationality, including relation to oneself"—Rosemary Radford Ruether, *Sexism and God-Talk: Toward a Feminist Theology* (Boston: Beacon Press, 1983), 181.

18. Audre Lorde, "The Power of the Erotic," in *Sister Outsider: Essays and Speeches* (New York: Crossing Press, 1984), 54.

19. Ruether, *Sexism and God-Talk*, 169.

20. Philo. "Commentary on Genesis," in *The Works of Philo Judaeus*, Vol. 1. Trans. D. Younge, ed. Charles Yonge (London: Henry G. Bohn, 1854), 53.

21. Jerome, "Letter XXII to Eustochium," in *The Principal Works of St. Jerome*, trans. W. H. Fremantle (New York: Parker, 1893), par. 17, 28.

22. Ibid., par. 21, 30.

23. "The goal of virginity is to see God. Virginity is a means to restore the self to its original nature as image of God that can grow through voluntary obedience into the 'likeness of God,' the increasing approximation of the divine nature. Through virginity, as the renunciation of all ensnarements of the soul by bodily lusts and its increasing purification in union with God, the human being, while still in the mortal body, approximates the redeemed life that will be completed through the joining of the soul to the resurrected body"—Rosemary Radford Ruether, *Women and Redemption: A Theological History* (Minneapolis: Fortress Press, 1998), 67–68.

24. In Latin America, for instance, there is a dual set of mores for women and men. While *machismo* sets the cultural expectations for men, *marianismo* (following in the footsteps of Mary) is the pattern for women. See Wanda Deifelt, "Beyond Compulsory Motherhood," in *Good Sex: Feminist Perspectives from the World's Religions*, ed. Patricia Jung, Mary Hunt, and Radhika Balakrishnan (New Brunswick: Rutgers University Press, 2001), 96–112.

25. Martin Luther, "The Freedom of a Christian," in *Martin Luther: Selections from His Writings*, ed. John Dillenberger (New York: Anchor, 1962), 81.

26. Martin Luther, "The Magnificat," in *Luther's Works*, Vol. 21, ed. Jaroslav Pelikan (Saint Louis: Concordia Publishing House, 1956), 334.

27. Martin Luther, "Sermons on the Gospel of St. John: Chapters 14–16," in *Luther's Works*, Vol. 24, ed. Jaroslav Pelikan and Daniel E. Poellot (Saint Louis: Concordia Publishing House, 1961), 180.

28. Martin Luther, "Lectures on Genesis: Chapters 21–25," in *Luther's Works*, Vol. 4, ed. Jaroslav Pelikan (Saint Louis: Concordia Publishing House, 1964), 273.

29. Judith Butler, *Gender Trouble: Feminism and the Subversion of Identity* (New York: Routledge, 2015), 179.

30. The expectations of masculinity are oppressive and reworking them must include not being ashamed of expressing emotions and learning how to solve problems without violence. This would not only reduce gender violence but also make men happier and capable of leading more fulfilling lives.

31. "Growing numbers of young people describe themselves as 'non-binary'. Others say gender is a spectrum, or that they have no gender at all. Facebook offers users a list of over 70 gender identities, from 'agender' to 'two-spirit,' as well as the option to write in their own"—"Transgender Identity: Found in Transition," *The Economist* (November 18, 2017), 51.

32. "Queer" is used as an umbrella term for all variations of sexual orientations and gender identities that encompass the LGBTQ+ community. The + sign is used to indicate that these identities are not limited to the letters represented in the acronym: lesbian, gay, bisexual, transgender, and queer.

33. Cathy J. Cohen, "Punks, Bulldaggers, and Welfare Queens: The Radical Potential of Queer Politics?" in *Feminist Theory Reader: Local and Global Perspectives*, ed. Carole R. McCann and Seung-Kyung Kim (New York and London: Routledge, 2017), 419–435.

34. Robert Connell, *Masculinidades* (Mexico: UNAM/PUEG, 2003).

35. Donna Freitas, *Sex and the Soul: America's College Students Speak Out about Hookups, Romance, and Religion on Campus* (New York: Oxford, 2008), 6.

36. Aruna Gnanadason, "Women's Oppression: A Sinful Situation," in *With Passion and Compassion: Third World Women Doing Theology*, ed. Virginia Fabella and Mercy Amba Oduyoye (Maryknoll: Orbis, 1988), 69–76.

37. Freitas, *Sex and the Soul*, 81.

38. Lisa Isherwood and Elizabeth Stuart, *Introducing Body Theology* (Cleveland: Pilgrim Press, 1998), 100.

Chapter 9

In the Face of Empire

Black Liberation Theology, M. L. King Jr., and the Jesus Story

Dwight N. Hopkins

Black liberation theology began in the 1960s in the United States.[1] It was a time of ascendency of the United States, post–World War II, into a global empire over against the Union of Soviet Socialist Republics. Today, black liberation theology must reclaim its tradition, which springs from the Old and New Testament and the history of black church tradition. *To be true to itself and its intertwined relationships within the African American church, black liberation theology has to sharpen its focus on the black working class, those lacking material wealth in the USA.*[2]

In fact, the "liberation" part of black liberation theology means that the Jesus story focuses on liberating and healing the poor, working people, and all who suffer emotionally and spiritually. And "theology" asks the question, how do people apply this Jesus story today and in every contemporary situation? The "black" aspect asks the question, how does that Jesus story and that theology show themselves in African American or black American culture? So "liberation" goes back to what was the purpose of the founder of the story. "Theology" applies that purpose in new situations. And "black" looks at black or African American culture to see where, in that culture, it can find examples of this liberation and theology.

The origin of black liberation theology began July 31, 1966, culminated in a March 1969 book, and arose from three factors. The first factor was the Martin Luther King Jr.'s civil rights movement. On December 1, 1955, in Montgomery, Alabama, white policemen arrested Mrs. Rosa Parks (a working-class seamstress) for refusing to give up her bus seat to a white man passenger. Rev. Martin Luther King Jr. (1955 PhD in systematic theology from Boston University School of Theology) was elected to head the opposition against segregation in Montgomery. King believed that Christianity not only dealt with spiritual things but also earthly matters, especially related to jobs and income. The civil rights efforts began with King and the Montgomery, Alabama, bus boycott on December 5, 1955. From King and civil rights organizing, black liberation theology took the new definition of the church as a group of people who were concerned about people on earth, especially the material needs of people; of course, continuing to recognize spiritual and emotional challenges.

On June 16, 1966, the youth wing of the civil rights movement became impatient with the slow progress of civil rights efforts of the King generation. So, the young people broke away from King and on that date called for black power. These youths had been community organizers among black poor rural workers in Mississippi. Because of that real work with people on the land, the actual first meaning of black power was for black poor workers and peasants to own the land, the water, and tools for working the land. It also meant that these same citizens should control all the elected offices where they lived locally. In addition, the youth wanted blacks to be proud of Africa and their cultural identity.[3]

Black liberation theology took its second emphasis from the black power movement. Explaining the foundation of the process called "Black Power," Stokely Carmichael and Charles V. Hamilton write the following in their classic 1967 book *Black Power: The Politics of Liberation in America*:[4]

> Black Power means, for example, that in Lowndes County, Alabama, a black sheriff can end police brutality. A black tax assessor and tax collector and county board of revenue can lay, collect, and channel tax monies for the building of better roads and schools serving black people. In such areas as Lowndes, where black people have majority, they will attempt to use power to exercise control. This is what we seek: control. When black people lack a majority, Black Power means proper representation and sharing of control.

The third factor influencing black liberation theology was the international situation, especially the post–World War II anticolonial and national liberation struggles in Africa, Asia, and South America. Of course, at that time, with the rise of African consciousness in the minds of the young people, they were particularly excited about the new nations from Africa.[5] Black liberation theology learned from these "Third World" new nations and began to connect domestic U.S. theology with African, Asian, and South American "liberation." These newly formed countries focused on owning their own earth, air, and water to serve the needs of the indigenous citizens.

We remember that when the youth shouted "Black Power" on June 16, 1966 (in Greenwood, Mississippi), the youth wing of King's civil rights movement broke away from the older religious leaders. Because of the existence of two proposals that highlighted a way forward for Negro/black peoples (and, indeed, for all of the United States)—(1) the M. L. King civil rights direction and (2) the new black power alternative—many African American pastors of churches and leaders of local communities were caught in a dilemma. Should they continue following King and the old Negro way or the new rapidly growing black power direction?

On July 31, 1966 (a little over a month after the cry of black power), a group of forty-eight black religious leaders and pastors (forty-seven men and one woman) wrote a full-page religious response to the cry of black power and published it in the *New York Times*. In that statement, the 47 + 1 said there is no contradiction between black power and a good moral consciousness. Power goes along with racial reconciliation. Morality and power go together. In addition, they saw the Jesus story containing power and material resources for the poor on earth, even as he dealt with physical, emotional, and spiritual healing.[6]

Though black liberation theology begins with a group of 47 + 1 pastors and religious leaders (and not professors or academics; in fact, some believe black liberation theology is the only theology in the United States not started by professors and not coming from the academy), the first scholarly liberation theology book on the topic was written by James H. Cone (published in 1969).[7] We can see how the 1966 "Black Power Statement" to the 1969 Cone book reveals African American pastors being one of the first creators of global liberation theology.

From 1969 to 2019, black liberation theology has become a recognized academic discipline. It covers all of the usual theological topics—history, scriptures, ethics, comparative religions, practical applications, theology, and so on. Various types of black theology have even emerged in South Africa, England, the Caribbean, and in the Pacific Islands. In fact, the awareness of black liberation theology can be found throughout Africa, Asia, South America, and, to a degree, different European graduate schools.

Black liberation theology is a subset of theology (mainly Christian theology), which is a subset of the larger study of world religions. Within this tradition, my writing and teaching has been on the accumulation of wealth, connecting to global developments, and preparing youth/young people for the future, a future partly influenced by empire.

EMPIRE AND WEALTH

Empire reduces citizens' access to earth, air, and water, the essential material wealth from which everything else is derived. Particularly hard hit are the working-class and poor citizens. Indeed, anyone unaware of poor and working-class people's desire to own wealth or things based on wealth probably aren't poor, never lived with the poor, or never organized the poor.

The 1950s to 1970s developments in the United States provide data for this conclusion. Over against empire, the U.S. civil rights and black power movements pulled communities together to realize such goals. For instance, the 1955–1956 Montgomery, Alabama, bus boycott started by Rosa Parks and led by Martin Luther King Jr. wanted more Negro bus drivers in Negro neighborhoods. Jobs were key.

The 1963 march on Washington demanded jobs or income. The official march slogan was "Jobs and Freedom." To that point, though most remember the "I have a dream" theme of King's speech at that march, actually the more powerful theme was the need for Negros to ask the U.S. federal government to cash a check to provide funds for Negro communities.

And King's 1968 Poor People's Campaign (his second march on Washington, D.C.) asserted that American poor and working-class people would not leave Washington, D.C., until the federal government passed meaningful legislation that lifted the load of poverty from the country's most economically vulnerable. King stated:

> We called our demonstration a campaign for jobs and income because we felt that the economic question was the most crucial that black people, and poor people generally, were confronting. There was a literal depression in the Negro community. When you have mass unemployment in the Negro community, it's called a social problem; when you have mass unemployment in the white community, it's called a depression.[8]

In addition to the Poor People's Campaign, King's last project (in the spring of 1968) was supporting black working-class garbage workers in Memphis, Tennessee, who wanted higher wages and better material working conditions.[9] Moreover, when Stokely Carmichael began the black power movement by shouting black power on June 16, 1966, in Greenwood, Mississippi, it bears reemphasizing the initial meaning of that slogan was that the black Mississippi rural working class should own the land on which they worked and they should occupy all the local to state political offices where they were the majority. The Nation of Islam (founded by Elijah Muhammed and led by Malcolm X) created businesses and jobs for black men and women so they could take care of their children. At one point, the Nation did international trade.[10]

Beginning in October 1966 in Oakland, California, the Black Panther Party provided free material goods and services for urban inner-city families—such as free medical checkups, education, food, clothing, transportation, and scholarships.[11] The Dodge Revolutionary Union Movement (the late 1970s black Detroit auto workers' organization—DRUM) desired better wages and working conditions.[12] The 1970s Boston black parents' efforts to improve their children's education first sought money and material resources to improve educational chances in the black neighborhoods in and around Boston. The 1970s African Liberation Support Committee raised funds, provided clothing, and boycotted tangible U.S. companies doing business with European and apartheid governments occupying Africa.[13]

Pan African groups attempted to set up real ongoing accountable black and African studies programs and departments on school campuses. These late 1960s and early 1970s projects included increasing black faculty hiring, black student enrollments, and African and black American educational programming.[14] Black churches have given money, jobs, food, housing, legal, and medical aid; offered classes, educational scholarships, psychological and marital counseling; and produced a host of other material benefits to its members.

From the beginning of U.S. slavery to the end of the U.S. Civil War (or War between the States), 1619–1865, enslaved Africans and black Americans wanted material resources for their children. Especially after slavery ended, the three priorities for the recently freed slaves were searching for family members who had been sold during slavery, acquiring land, and obtaining formal education. Actually, enough historical stories exist to back up the conclusion that, since August 1619 when the first group of seventeen men and three African women were sold as slaves to the British colony at Jamestown, Virginia, until today, fathers, grandfathers, mothers, and grandmothers have organized their lives to bring about a better and more comfortable life for their children, grandchildren, and great-grandchildren. To deepen the thread of material resources and wealth, an examination of Martin Luther King Jr.'s faith inspired work helps to distinguish between wealth and income and, consequently, focuses on the working class and the poor.

But first, we can define wealth as earth, air, and water. All that humans require emerge from and is linked to these three dimensions of life. Income is a derivative of wealth; it depends on who owns earth, air, and water. Take, for example, the 2008 Great Recession. This United States' 2007–2008 mortgage debt crisis impacted negatively the majority of Americans whose primary material ownership was their homes.[15] In contrast, the small group of wealthy Americans suffered little because they owned wealth such as global businesses of food, copper mines, technology, manufacturing, acres of land, transportation, bodies of water, air spaces, communication systems, and other tangible assets that made up the overwhelming majority of their investment portfolios. Restated, the removal of their personal homes from their possessions would produce, relatively speaking, negligible negative impact on their lives.

The majority of American homeowners experienced major disruption in their lives because the 2007–2008 housing mortgage crisis attacked the lifeline of U.S. citizens' families (i.e., those without wealth). Loss of ownership led to loss of capability to have a quality of life. The loss of homes or the rapid decrease in home values disrupted people's lives on a daily basis. Without a home or high home value, these group of Americans lost money. When one's monthly mortgage payments are more than the value of one's home, one is said to be "under water."

Actually, even in normal economic times, working-class homeowners don't own their homes as a form of wealth. Rather, financial institutions such as banks and investment funds own the home until all the mortgages are paid off. In this sense, for most American home ownership, such ownership is private ownership of "soft wealth." This wealth ownership is volatile and vulnerable. Larger global market forces decide the fate of such soft wealth possessions. In contrast, the small group of American families that own earth, air, and water own hard wealth—that is, wealth relatively unaffected by mortgage crises in housing markets.

If wealth means ownership of earth, air, and water, then working-class citizens are paid money for working for those who own earth, air, and water. If the latter three can also be called capital, then working-class citizens' lives depend on what income they can get from the owners of capital. Wealth or capital determines the income and lives of working-class families. Such income or lack of income influences fathers' and mothers' abilities to afford or not afford their children's educational, medical, recreational, and spiritual costs. Are they able to provide housing for their children? Do parents have enough money to give tithes or offerings to their local churches?

Put another way, if an American citizen lost his/her job and s/he was not able to find another job, would that loss disrupt his/her life? If a family owns earth, air, and water, the loss of an income-producing job could be insignificant. Why? Because their lives are sustained by the hotel chains, iron mines, manufacturing companies, downtown commercial land, and other forms of wealth possessions. There is a popular story that compares the realities of a working-class person and a member of the top wealth owners. In the story, both worked at a U.S. post office. When an economic crisis arrived, both were fired from their jobs. The working-class person had no income. The wealth owner began to decide which of his islands would become his home.

True wealth ownership means that several generations of family members never have to work. The working-class don't meet this criterion. Lack of wealth ownership and reliance on unpredictable jobs have profound impact on working-class people's spiritual well-being, emotional balance, healthy lifestyles, and parental duties. Martin Luther King Jr. was clear on the distinction between wealth and income, and he lived to help working-class and poor families.

MARTIN LUTHER KING JR. AND WEALTH

Some interpret King's "I Have a Dream" speech at the first march on Washington (August 28, 1963, in the U.S. national capital) as extraordinary oratory. And most remember the ending with its repeat of the powerful phrase "I have a dream." However, the thrust of his brilliant delivery lifted up the poverty of black working-class and poor people and the need to have wealth and money. For instance, at the beginning of his speech, King states, "the Negro lives on a lonely island of poverty in the midst of a vast ocean of material prosperity." And then immediately, he turns to his statement's core points of material compensation, underscoring a major purpose of this historic march:

> In a sense we've come to our nation's capital to cash a check. When the architects of our republic wrote the magnificent words of the Constitution and the Declaration of Independence, they were signing a promissory note to which every American was to fall heir. This note was the promise that all men, yes, black men as well as white men, would be guaranteed the unalienable rights of life, liberty, and the pursuit of happiness.
>
> It is obvious today that America has defaulted on this promissory note in so far as her citizens of color are concerned. Instead of honoring this sacred obligation, America has given the Negro people a bad check; a check which has come back marked "insufficient funds." We refuse to believe that there are insufficient funds in the great vaults of opportunity of the nation. And so we've come to cash this check, a check that will give us upon demand the riches of freedom and the security of justice.[16]

Also, when King refers to "life, liberty, and the pursuit of happiness," he restates the words that Thomas Jefferson inserted into the July 4, 1776, U.S. "Declaration of Independence" from England. Jefferson was paraphrasing the English philosopher and physician John Locke (1632–1704). Locke's original expression is, "Life, Liberty, and Property." Jefferson expanded this to mean that the pursuit of happiness was based on the possession of property.[17]

King's awareness of the working-class and propertyless citizens of the United States were evident in his first public speech. On December 5, 1955, King gave his presidential speech as head of the Montgomery Improvement Association, the group that led the successful bus boycott against segregation in Montgomery, Alabama (December 5, 1955, to December 20, 1956). The most thunderous applause occurred when he trumpeted these words:

> And you know, my friends, there comes a time when people get tired of being trampled over by the iron feet of oppression. [*thundering applause*] There comes a time, my friends, when people get tired of being plunged across the abyss of humiliation, where they experience the bleakness of nagging despair.

(*Keep talking*) There comes a time when people get tired of being pushed out of the glittering sunlight of life's July and left standing amid the piercing chill of an alpine November. (*That's right!*) [*applause*]. There comes a time. (*Yes sir, Teach*) [*applause continues*][18]

When King gave this historic speech written in less than fifteen minutes before this first mass meeting of the boycott, he was looking at the faces of many black women employed as domestics in the homes of white families. His eyes scanned the congregation and the thousands who listened outside of the church and saw black men who were domestics and laborers. And on the first day of the boycott (December 5, 1955), King drove the streets of Montgomery for an hour observing that Negroes were walking to work as an expression of solidarity with the bus boycott.[19] In other words, King spoke, preached, and organized his Christian message while seeing actual workers standing, sitting, and marching in front and around him. The theology of King arose out of his experiences with the black working classes of the South.

In addition to his December 5, 1955, and August 28, 1963, speeches, King's theology in support of black workers and all the world's poor continues to shine forth in another famous speech—"A Time to Break Silence." Delivered at the Riverside Church in the upper Westside of Manhattan, New York City (April 4, 1967, a year before his assassination), this speech marked his first major and unequivocal condemnation of the U.S. government's role in the war in Vietnam. Here too, King situates his opposition in the context of the pain of the American poor who lack material resources. The very first reason he opposes the war is the following:

> There is at the outset a very obvious and almost facile connection between the war in Vietnam and the struggle I and others have been waging in America. A few years ago there was a shining moment in that struggle. It seemed as if there was a real promise of hope for the poor—both black and white—through the poverty programs. . . . and I knew that America would never invest the necessary funds or energies in rehabilitation of its poor so long as adventures like Vietnam continued to draw men and skills and money like some demonic destructive suction tube.[20]

But the federal government redirected the material resources designated to lift the load of poverty from the backs of white and black workers to fund the U.S. war against Vietnam.

King's final speech on April 3, 1968 (the night before his assassination in Memphis, Tennessee), weaves themes of material wealth, the working class, and the poor. He urges members of the congregation to keep focused on the plight of black sanitation workers in Memphis. Raising these instructions to a general level for all church ministry, he proclaims:

> It's alright to talk about "long white robes over yonder," in all of its symbolism. But ultimately people want some suits and dresses and shoes to wear down here. It's alright to talk about "streets flowing with milk and honey," but God has commanded us to be concerned about the slums down here, and his children who can't eat three square meals a day. It's alright to talk about the new Jerusalem, but one day God's preacher must talk about the New York, the new Atlanta, the new Philadelphia, the new Los Angeles, the new Memphis, Tennessee. This is what we have to do.[21]

King gave these four major sermons/presentations in churches (i.e., 1955 Holt Street Baptist Church; 1963 Washington, D.C., where King seemed to perceive his audience as part of an outdoor church revival; 1967 Riverside Church; and 1968 [Church of God Christ] Bishop Charles Mason Temple). Thus, as a major forerunner and essential source for the rise of black liberation theology, he links together the need for material wealth and resources for the black and other working-class citizens of the United States at the heart of faith communities. Throughout his career, King mixed stories from the Christian sacred text into whatever contemporary issue he supported.[22] At root was the story of Jesus, one who was born in the poverty of a manger because his parents didn't have money to bribe an innkeeper for a room; one born literally in the midst of cow dung; one whose sole purpose on earth was to liberate the material poor and oppressed as his words are recorded in Luke 4:16–21; one who died between two criminals; one who was a Jew who drew on his prophetic tradition of Amos, Isaiah, and Jeremiah; one who gave criteria for helping the material poor and workers found in Matt 25:31–41; and the one who offered hope to all regardless of their circumstances.

SCRIPTURE, RESISTANCE, AND EMPIRE: PREPARATION, TEMPTATION, LIBERATION

In Luke 3:21–22, Jesus undergoes baptism as a conscious *preparation* to take on evil empire. Immediately, after his preparation, concentrated evil offers Jesus his personal rule over empire in Luke 4:1–13. But Jesus said no to these three *temptations*—(1) to personally own earth, air, and water—the ingredients of making bread; (2) to personally govern all the kingdoms of the worlds; and (3) to personally use the technology of the angels to fly. The reason Jesus denies these three offers is because they are presented to him for his personal rule. But in Luke 4:16–19, Jesus says the Spirit has anointed him for *liberation*—to resist empire temptation for the individual benefit of one person. Rather for the poor and the wounded, he is called to democratize ownership of earth, air, and water; to equalize participation in society; and to use technology so all people can soar in life.

In Luke, Jesus is tempted by Satan three times in the desert. Resisting the temptation helped to put Jesus on the path to becoming a teacher and liberator. What was so central about these three particular temptations? And what do they mean politically and ethically today?[23]

The desert temptation is actually the second part of a three-part movement in Jesus's public leadership. The first part is found in Luke 3:21–22 and depicts preparation, where Jesus is baptized in the water. The second is found in Luke 4:1–13, the Satan temptation story, which is Jesus's first major test. And the third (Luke 4:16–20) indicates liberation, which is Jesus's sole mission on earth. This movement toward the public mission of Jesus consists of tales of (1) his preparation through baptism, (2) fortification through temptations, and (3) liberation through service. Though all three play important roles for the life of Jesus, the temptation stories act as a key hinge. Without undergoing a trial (by or with fire, since the Satan character signifies fire), the reader would never know if Jesus's baptismal preparation had become effective. Likewise, if we don't have the temptation scene, then the reader would not take seriously Jesus's later claim that he is prepared for and able to bring about liberation through service. Because he overcomes the highest symbol of concentrated negative energy, which is basically the symbol of the Satan tales, then it follows that he is able to bring liberation to the oppressed in his earthly mission. Jesus undergoes preparation, which is fortified through temptations, which allows him to carry out his mission of liberation.

Baptism as Preparation

In part one of Jesus's journey to public leadership, which I am calling baptism as preparation, John the Baptist administers a full immersion of the man Jesus in to the river Jordan. John has been carrying out this ritual for many others prior to Jesus's arrival. In the new movement, of which John is the forerunner, one has to be baptized in water. In this part of baptism as preparation, Jesus opts to experience what ordinary men and women experience. He volunteers to identify with the common everyday people. It shows publicly (baptisms took place in an open space for all to witness) that the one who is to be followed, willingly undergoes the same preparation of those whom he has asked to follow him. Baptism here points to solidarity through participation in a threshold event toward new life. The one claiming new life demonstrates he too will endure full immersion in water with his followers in order that he can enjoy the process of new life with them.

And so, his act of submission to his own servant, who is John, proclaims a foretaste of his mission to come; that is to say, Jesus is being called not to be served but to experience everyday service with the ones he is called to serve. Here, in this aspect of baptism, we find a window into the full mission of Jesus that will be revealed in the third part of liberation for service in Luke 4. With this peek into his future mission, Jesus prepares his followers and the readers of this story to be on alert and get ready for the forthcoming full disclosure of his earthly goal—liberation through service.

Furthermore, the story of baptism as preparation indicates the nature of the new kingdom or new society that Jesus will later proclaim. During his full immersion in the river, a dove appears. The dove suggests peace, righteousness, and just relations among humans and with nature and the cosmos. Jesus comes to realize a novel way of building family, community, and global human interaction with all that has been, is, and is to be. The dove of peace brings this about with the foundational building block of righteousness and just relations. A righteous land reveals all humans having access to things required to be fully human. To achieve full humanity requires right relation to and with all that there is on earth and in the cosmos. Thus the dove symbolizes an additional window into the fullness of Jesus's earthly community which is to be unveiled later—a community where peace, righteousness, and just relations prevail for all on earth.

The symbols and dimensions of this baptism as preparation event contrast with the reality that all the people faced. Jesus is being prepared through baptism to take on the empire. The Roman emperor Tiberius had colonized Judea and Galilee (Luke 1:1). Similarly, Herod, the emperor's local representative, imprisoned John for preparing the way for one whom John called the true ruler of earth. It is no accident that the key to Jesus's baptism as preparation emerges from the heavens from an authority whom John and Jesus claimed was superior to all earthly empires. The dove symbolizes peace, righteousness, and how just relations become real on earth. This is in radical contrast to the Roman Empire colonizing the people who followed Jesus. And when John the Baptist baptized people in the name of Jesus, John was saying that Jesus was a higher authority than the Roman Empire. The symbols and rituals of baptism as preparation were a direct challenge to the politics and economics of the Roman Empire.

Perhaps the most striking part of the baptism as preparation is found in the voice announcing, "You are my son, the Beloved; with you I am well pleased" (Luke 3:21). Here too, the ultimate voice of authority comes out of the heavens, a place far above and superior to the claims of the Roman emperor. For the creators of these tales, God serves as the ultimate verification that, as a result of full immersion, Jesus is now prepared to go out into the world to take on the most seductive temptations.

Fortification through Temptation

If Jesus is truly prepared to take on his mission of liberation through service, then he must face the trials of temptations. Note the landscape of this tale in a desert. We imagine a barren place. Such a backdrop is quite apropos because it highlights the power possibilities to be offered by the Satan character. Restated, Satan displays his three tantalizing offers to Jesus by creating them out of a stark barren reality. In a sense, Satan's material creation-out-of-nothing temptations contrast with what God offers Jesus during his baptism. God only gives Jesus verbal affirmation. But the Satan character knows talk can be cheap, so Satan provides evidence of what he can do for Jesus. On the one side we see mere talk; for example, the symbolic nature of a dove of peace coupled with an absent father's voice of approval from the heavens. On the other side, we see material reality; for example, the physically present Satan and three concrete gifts/temptations of rulership for Jesus on earth. A voice or the reality? On the one hand, an invisible father with the promise of peace as Jesus baptizes in water, versus Satan, a potential alternative father who is actually visible, who presents tangible offerings. Not promise but material reality from Satan the ruler of fire. The three temptations, in other words, are taking place on a cosmic scale of the created elements of nature and the universe. Who is the true father? What should Jesus choose—water or fire? Which is the authentic path to new life on earth?[24]

Before the Satan figure offers the first temptation, the following sentence appears in Luke 4:1–2: "Jesus, full of the Holy Spirit, returned from the Jordan and was led by the Spirit in the wilderness, where he was for forty days tempted by the Devil." This shows that Jesus has been prepared by his baptism in the river Jordan. Full of the Holy Spirit means Jesus's baptism was a success. But the Spirit does not guide him directly to his mission of public leadership. Rather, the Spirit takes him into the wilderness or desert so that Jesus can be tempted by the Satan figure. The Satan character is concentrated negative energy that seduces by offering dimensions of empire. For instance, in the first temptation, the Satan figure proclaims to Jesus—"If you are the Son of God, command this stone to become a loaf of bread." Here Satan tempts Jesus to show his authority over the three basic elements of life, which are earth, air, and water. Bread is made from wheat (which comes out of the earth), water (a basic substance of life), and interaction with air (symbolic of energy). Anyone who can show control or ownership of these three fundamentals of life would be a person who commands the heights of a global empire. But Jesus refuses to display such power and control. He turns down the first temptation because he comes to serve the workers, the poor, and the oppressed of the world, not to rule empire over others.

In the second temptation, the Satan character makes it plain with no ambiguity. Satan, representative of concentrated evil energy, tempts Jesus by showing him all the kingdoms of the world and says to Jesus: "To you I will give this glory and all of this authority. . . . If you, then, will worship me, then it will be yours." The first temptation was sneaky and indirect. It talked about bread but tempting Jesus to show his power over earth, air, and water. In the second temptation, Satan is open and direct. He offers Jesus all of the empires as Jesus's personal possessions. But this temptation has a condition. Jesus can have global empire if he worships and serves Satan.

In the third and final temptation, the Satan figure sits Jesus high up on a rooftop and tells Jesus to throw himself down. Why? Because, if Jesus is the Son of God, then God will send angels to save Jesus from harm. I see this temptation linked to challenging Jesus to call on the technological know-how of the angels. In other words, the angels have knowledge of aerodynamics and flight in order for them to be able to save Jesus from death and harm.

But why does Jesus refuse these three temptations—the first is about economics (how to own earth, air, and water); the second is about politics (how to govern the governments of the world); and the third is about technology (how to use the most advanced wisdom known by humans). Jesus refuses these three because they are offered to him for his personal possession and for his individual use. I come to this conclusion based on the third part of Jesus's movement into his public leadership—liberation for service for others.

Liberation through Service

Now that he has been baptized for preparation, fortified through temptation, what is his mission on earth? Luke 4:16–20 is the primary place where Jesus states unambiguously his main reason for walking on earth. "The Spirit of the Lord is upon me, because he has anointed me to bring good news to the poor. He has sent me to proclaim release to the captives and recovery of sight to the blind, to let the oppressed go free, to proclaim the year of the Lord's favor."

Now we can begin to see why Jesus does not accept the three temptations. They were offered for his private possession and for his own personal use. To accept global economics, politics, and technology for one's own private ownership is to move into the realm of empire. Actually, Jesus does not have any problem using global economics, power, and technology. As long as it is for the poor, the oppressed, and the wounded. Why do we say this? Because the content of Jesus's primary mission on earth is to provide economic, political, and technological liberation for the materially poor, the oppressed, the wounded, and workers.

What do the global poor, oppressed, and wounded need in today's world? They need bread; that is to say, they need to collectively own earth, air, and water. This includes owning the businesses and jobs to properly use earth, air, and water. This is the economics of their liberation. They also need the power to make decisions about their lives and that of their families. This is the politics of their liberation. And they need the most advanced technology to help them realize the best opportunities for them and their children.

So the problem is not economics, politics, and technology in and of themselves. The question is how to get them in the hands of the poor, the oppressed, the wounded, and workers of this world.

LIFE AND LIBERTY FOR WEALTH

Let me end with a story of the South Side of Chicago, a typical black urban America that embodies elements from the King tradition and the Christian biblical witness and, consequently, a context of materiality where black liberation theology can thrive. The world knows about black people wounding and killing black people on the South Side. In fact, these shootings and killings appear regularly in Chinese, Russian, and other global newspapers. But there is a back story. Millions of black people came from the southern United States (1910–1940) for jobs when manufacturing was king in Chicagoland.[25] When the economy shifted more to information, technology, and service industries (in the 1970s forward), many black people who had migrated from the south and had several generations living in Chicago, were out of jobs.[26] Jobs gone.

Then public housing was torn down, particularly near and around the State Street corridor. No homes. Similarly, public education lost funding. In fact, five years ago, fifty public schools were closed. Now no schools.

What are people going to do in this situation? One possible option is to turn violence inward and to develop new forms of institutional community. This is partly where the new alignment of gangs comes into play. At the same time, others will find ways, often unproductive ways, with the lack of jobs, unfunded education, and dwindling housing by doing whatever is necessary to take care of their children and their families.

Let me give an example of how the three temptations of economics, politics, and technology can be used properly not for empire but to serve the materially poor, oppressed, and the wounded. A documentary called the "Streets Kill" included interviews with different gang members from Chicago. These young men asked for jobs, businesses, after school programs, more educational opportunities, the presence of black professional men in their neighborhoods, and more opportunities to have a productive life. All of these desires add up to collectively sharing the basic resources of what it means to be human. All of these possibilities add up to what Jesus came to earth to realize for the poor, the oppressed, and the wounded. All humans require bread—the essentials of earth, air, and water. All people long for the power to make decisions about their block, neighborhood, city, state, and country. And all want the most advanced knowledge to improve their lives. They want politics, economics, and technology not for personal empire but for healthy communities and healthy individuals in community.

In a word, the future of black liberation theology's relevance in families, churches, communities, and, indeed, the world depends on whether or not it will remain faithful to its own tradition and biblical stories. To take on the pressing questions of life, liberty, and the pursuit of happiness relies a great deal on helping working people and the poor have access to material sources. It is there where the spirit of harmony and balance of the Jesus stories is found. And wealth helps to make all the difference in the context of empire.

NOTES

1. See Dwight N. Hopkins, *Black Theology—Essays on Gender Perspectives* (Eugene, OR: Cascade Books, 2017); Dwight N. Hopkins, *Black Theology—Essays on Global Perspectives* (Eugene, OR: Cascade Books, 2017).

2. On empire, see Allan Aubrey Boesak, *Kairos, Crisis, and Global Apartheid: The Challenge of Prophetic Resistance* (New York: Palgrave Macmillan, 2015); Keri Day, *Religious Resistance to Neoliberalism: Womanist and Black Feminist Perspectives* (New York: Palgrave Macmillan, 2016); Cedric C. Johnson, *Race, Religion, and Resilience in the Neoliberal Age* (New York: Palgrave Macmillan, 2016); Anthony G. Reddie, *Black Theology in Transatlantic Dialogue* (New York: Palgrave Macmillan, 2006); James A. Noel, *Black Religion and the Imagination of Matter in the Atlantic World* (New York: Palgrave Macmillan, 2009). And on America's growth, see Samuel Eliot Morison and Henry Steele Commager, *The Growth of the American Republic: Volumes One & Two* (New York: Oxford Book Company, 1969).

3. See Robin D. G. Kelley and Earl Lewis, eds., *To Make Our World Anew: A History of African Americans* (New York: Oxford, 2000); Henry Hampton and Steve Fayer, *Voices of Freedom: An Oral History of the Civil Rights Movement from the 1950s through the 1980s* (New York: Bantam Books, 1990); Vincent Harding, *Hope and History: Why We Must Share the Story of the Movement* (Maryknoll, NY: Orbis, 1990).

4. See also Stokely Carmichael, *Ready for Revolution: The Life and Struggles of Stokely Carmichael {Kwame Ture}* (New York: Scribner, 2003).

5. See Dwight N. Hopkins and Edward P. Antonio, eds., *The Cambridge Companion to Black Theology* (Cambridge, UK: Cambridge University Press, 2012).

6. Gayraud S. Wilmore and James H. Cone, eds., *Black Theology: A Documentary History, 1966–1979* (Maryknoll, NY: Orbis, 1979).

7. James H. Cone, *Black Theology and Black Power* (Maryknoll, NY: Orbis, 1997), especially Chapter 2.

8. Clayborne Carson, *The Autobiography of Martin Luther King, Jr.* (New York: Grand Central Publishing, 1998), 350.

9. Joan Turner Beifuss, *At the River I Stand: Memphis, the 1968 Strike, and Martin Luther King* (Memphis, TN: B & W Books, 1985).

10. Malcolm X, *The Autobiography of Malcolm X* (New York: Grove, 1965).

11. Huey P. Newton, *To Die for the People: The Writings of Huey P. Newton* (New York: Random House, 1972).

12. Marvin Surkin and Dan Georgakas, *Detroit: I Do Mind Dying: A Study in Urban Revolution* (Chicago, IL: Haymarket, 2012); Jim Jacobs, *Our Thing Is DRUM: An Interview with Ken Cockrel and Mike Hamlin of the League for Revolutionary Black Workers* (Boston: New England Free Press, 1971).

13. See Abdul Hakimu Ibn Alkalimat, *Toward the Ideological Unity of the African Liberation Support Committee: A Response to Criticisms of the ALSC Statement of Principles Adopted at Frogmore, South Carolina, June–July, 1973* (city and publisher not known, 1974); Dawolu Gene Locke, *A Few Remarks in Response to Criticisms of ALSC* (city unknown: Lynn Eusan Institute, 1974); Edward O. Erhagbe, "The African-American Contribution to the Liberation Struggle in Southern Africa: The Case of the African Liberation Support Committee, 1972–1979," *The Journal of Pan African Studies* 4.5 (September 2011).

14. Scot Brown, *Fighting For US: Maulana Karenga, The US Organization, and Black Cultural Nationalism* (New York: New York University Press, 2005).

15. See Robert McDonald and Anna Paulson, "What Went Wrong at AIG," *Kellogg Insight* (August 3, 2015); Janice C. Eberly and Arvind Krishnamurthy, "Fixing the Next Mortgage Crisis," *Kellogg Insight* (December 1, 2004); Jeff Cockrell, "What Contributed Most to the Financial Crisis?," *Chicago Booth Review* (October 20, 2017); Atif Mian and Amir Sufi, *House of Debt: How They (and You) Caused the Great Recession, and How We Can Prevent It from Happening Again* (Chicago: University of Chicago, 2015); Union for Radical Political Economics, *Special Issue on the Financialization of Global Capitalism* (December 2009); John Quelch, "How Marketing the American Dream Caused Our Economic Crisis," *Harvard Business Review* (October 27, 2008); Colin McArthur and Sarah Edelman, "The 2008 Housing Crisis," *Center for American Progress* (April 13, 2017).

16. Martin Luther King Jr., "I Have a Dream," in *A Testament of Hope: The Essential Writings of Martin Luther King, Jr.*, ed. James M. Washington (San Francisco: Harper & Row, 1986), 217.

17. Ken Mondschein, "Introduction," in *The U.S. Constitution and Other Writings*, ed. Ken Mondschein (San Diego, CA: Canterbury Classics, 2017), ix.

18. Martin Luther King Jr, "MIA Mass Meeting at Holt Street Baptist Church. 5 December 1955. Montgomery, Ala," in *The Papers of Martin Luther King, Jr. Volume III: Birth of a New Age December 1955—December 1956*, ed. Clayborne Carson (Berkeley, CA: University of California Press, 1997), 72.

19. See Martin Luther King Jr., *Stride toward Freedom: A Leader of His People Tells the Montgomery Story* (New York: Harper & Row Publishers, 1958).

20. Cited in James M. Washington, *A Testament of Hope: The Essential Writings of Martin Luther King, Jr.* (San Francisco: Harper & Row, 1986), 232–233.

21. I have a copy of the speech in my possession.

22. On biblical interpretation, see Brian K. Blount, ed., *True to Our Native Land: An African American New Testament Commentary* (Minneapolis, MN: Fortress Press, 2007); Vincent L. Wimbush, ed., *African Americans and The Bible: Sacred Texts and Social Textures* (New York: Continuum, 2000); Tokunboh Adeyemo, ed., *Africa Bible Commentary: A One-Volume Commentary Written by 70 African Scholars* (Grand Rapids, MI: Zondervan, 2006).

23. Taken from the public poster issued prior to the DePaul Humanities Centers' sponsored event on "The Biblical Humanities: The Temptations of Christ" (January 16, 2017).

24. In a sense, one could intuit that Satan is tempting Jesus on another level. By representing fire, Satan can be seen as echoing what John the Baptist says in Luke 3:15 about Jesus, that the latter will come to baptize the masses with fire. Here fire signifies positive energy. Might the Satan figure try to confuse his negative energy fire with the life energy of John the Baptist type of fire?

25. See Davarian L. Baldwin, *Chicago's New Negroes: Modernity, the Great Migration, and Black Urban Life* (Chapel Hill, NC: University of North Carolina Press, 2007); Marcia Chatelain, *South Side Girls: Growing Up in the Great Migration* (Durham, NC: Duke University Press, 2015); Brian McCammack, *Landscapes of Hope: Nature and the Great Migration in Chicago* (Cambridge, MA: Harvard University Press, 2017); James R. Grossman, *Land of Hope: Chicago, Black Southerners, and the Great Migration* (Chicago: University of Chicago Press, 1991).

26. See Franklin Foer, *World without Mind: The Existential Threat of Big Tech* (New York: Penguin Press, 2017); Scott Galloway, *The Four: The Hidden DNA of Amazon, Apple, Facebook, and Google* (New York: Portfolio and Penguin, 2017); Tim Wu, *The Master Switch: The Rise and Fall of Information Empires* (New York: Vintage, 2011); David Maister, *Managing the Professional Service Firm* (New York: The Free Press, 2003), James Heskett, *Service Breakthroughs: Changing the Rules of the Game* (New York: The Free Press, 1990); James A. Fitzsimmons, *Service Management: Operations, Strategy, Information Technology* (New York: McGraw-Hill, 2010).

Chapter 10

In the Face of Empire

Postcolonial Theology from the Caribbean

Luis N. Rivera-Pagán

I originate from Puerto Rico, a Caribbean island that has been described by a foremost juridical scholar as "the oldest colony in the modern world."[1] Christopher Columbus claimed the island for the crown of Castile in 1493 and, after the defeat of a desperate native insurrection during the second decade of the sixteenth century, it remained part of the Spanish empire till 1898, when it was conquered by the United States.

The transfer of imperial sovereignty from Madrid to Washington was accomplished through the two classical ways of solving conflicts among powerful nations: war and diplomacy. War was perpetrated in the tropical Caribbean and the Philippines; diplomacy was negotiated later in elegant and cosmopolitan Paris.[2] No need to consult the natives. Washington, Madrid, and Paris were the sites of privileged historical agency. In early 1898 Puerto Rico was a Spanish colony; at the end of that fateful year, it had become a colony of the United States.

It was the end of the Spanish imperial saga and the initial stages of imperial *pax americana*.[3] It was part and parcel of the Age of Empire, so aptly named by the British historian Eric Hobsbawm.[4] From the Philippines, Guam, and Hawaii, in the Pacific, to Cuba and Puerto Rico, in the Caribbean, the American ideology of "manifest destiny,"[5] with its vigorous religious undertones, aggressive military perspectives, and strong commercial interests, was transgressing national boundaries. The military conquest of those Pacific and Caribbean nations, according to the president of the United States, William McKinley, took place "under the providence of God and in the name of human progress and civilization."[6]

We have learnt much from Edward Said, Homi Bhabha, Gayatry Spivak, and Walter Mignolo about *colonial discourse* and postcolonial critique.[7] Even before these four distinguished émigrés, there were the crucial analyses of colonial ideology and mentality drafted by Franz Fanon and Albert Memmi.[8] Also, the critical examination of the strategies of coloniality—military power, economic domination, racial hierarchy, cultural arrogance—by the Peruvian Aníbal Quijano.[9] The colonized subjects providing theoretical paradigms to their colonizers? Dislocated, "out of place"[10] Third World intellectuals giving lessons to the masters of the world and challenging their epistemic dominion? Quite a paradox of these postcolonial times!

Imperial power comprises at least three interrelated domains: political subordination, material appropriation, and ideological justification. Colonial discourse mystifies imperial dominion. It diffuses and affirms imperial ideological hegemony. It crafts by persuasion what the mechanisms of coercion are unable to achieve: the fine-tuned consent and admiration of the colonized subjects. "Rulers who aspire to hegemony . . . must make out an ideological case that they rule . . . on behalf of their subjects."[11] Its greatest creation is what V. S. Naipaul has called *mimic men.*[12]

In 1493 the Spaniards came to Puerto Rico with the proclaimed purpose of converting its idolatrous inhabitants to the one and only true religion, Christianity, to teach them how to live according to the European ethical norms of a civil and ordered society, and, as concurrent objective, to reap substantial material benefits for the imperial purveyors of those spiritual goods.[13] As Christopher Columbus wrote in his 1493 report of his transoceanic exploration: "All Christendom ought to feel joyful and make celebrations and give solemn thanks to the Holy Trinity with many solemn prayers for the turning of so many peoples to our holy faith . . . and afterwards for material benefits, since not only Spain but all Christians will hence have refreshment and profit."[14]

In 1898 the Americans came to impart upon us, poor tropical barbarians, the blessings of liberty, justice, humanity, and enlightened civilization. To crown its generosity, in 1917, without consulting "the Inhabitants of *Porto Rico*" (who cares about the views and feelings of colonized subjects?), Washington bestowed upon us the gift of American citizenship. That citizenship has allowed our people to participate in the military adventures of Washington to extend its "empire of freedom," from World War I trenches to the streets of Kabul and Baghdad. As an added bonus, we do not need to mess with any of the crucial decisions regarding our political condition and fate. We can rest assured that those decisions, usually important dimensions of democratic sovereignty, are well taken care by the wisdom and benevolence of the powers that be in Washington. How fortunately colonial we Puerto Ricans have been!

Maybe this is another occasion to reiterate Gayatri Spivak's famous query, "can the subaltern speak?"[15] A question that Edward Said dared to answer affirmatively: "Indeed, the subaltern *can* speak, as the history of liberation movements in the twentieth century eloquently attests."[16] The subaltern can also speak critically and prophetically, in dissension and with hope:

> The Bible . . . unlike the books of other ancient peoples, was . . . the literature of a minor, remote people—and not the literature of its rulers, but of its critics. . . . The prophets of Jerusalem refused to accept the world as it was. They invented the literature of political dissent and, with it, the literature of hope.[17]

COLONIALITY, MIGRATION, AND DIASPORA

To the ambivalence of a postcolonial colony, whose residents as citizens of the empire can claim in the courts the civil liberties of their citizenship but not its political rights, we should add the crucial fact that more than half of the Puerto Rican population resides in the mainland United States.[18] Legally, those Puerto Ricans are not migrants. Psychologically and culturally, they are. They belong to the history of modern diasporas. And diasporas are the source of the bewildering multiculturalism of the postmodern megacities.

Migration and diaspora are crucial dimensions of human history.[19] They constitute an experience shared by many former and present colonial peoples all over the world. Nowadays they have also become important themes of conversation in postcolonial cultural studies.[20] But, as Homi Bhabha has stressed, diaspora is an important object of critical analysis because it is the sociohistorical existential context of many displaced Third World peoples: "For the demography of the new internationalism is the history of postcolonial migration, the narratives of cultural and political diaspora . . . the poetics of exile."[21]

Diaspora entails dislocation, displacement but also a painful and complex process of forging new strategies to articulate cultural differences and identifications. In the Western *cosmopolis*, with its heterogeneous and frequently conflicting ethnocultural minorities that belie the mythical *e pluribus unum*, the émigré exists in ambivalent tension. More than half a century ago, Franz Fanon brilliantly described the peculiar gaze of so many white French people at the growing presence of black Africans and Caribbeans in their national midst.[22] Scorn and fear are entwined in that stare. The diasporic person frequently feels, alas, "like a man without a passport who is turned away from every harbour," the anguished dread that haunts the persecuted whisky priest of Graham Greene's novel, *The Power and the Glory*.[23] Frequently, nostalgia grips his/her soul, in the beautiful words of a painful biblical lamentation:

> By the rivers of Babylon –
> there we sat down and there we wept

when we remembered Zion.
. . .
How could we sing the Lord's song
in a foreign land? (Psalm 137:1,4; NRSV)

Often, however, and sometimes simultaneously, the displacement of migration creates a new space of liberation from the atavistic constraints and bondages of the native cultural community and opens new vistas, perspectives, and horizons. To repressed persons, exile in a metropolis like London, Paris, or New York could convey an expansion of individual autonomy, even if its hidden side might turn out to be despair or death.[24] Diasporic existence, as Bhabha has so forcefully reiterated, questions fixed and static notions of cultural and communal identity. In the diaspora, identity is not conceived as a pure essence to be nostalgically preserved but as an emancipatory project to be fashioned, in an alien territory, in a foreign language, as a polyphonic process of creative imagination. In many instances, yet, "the restoration of a collective sense of identity and historical agency in the home country may well be mediated through the diaspora."[25]

As Walter Mignolo has so provocatively asserted, diaspora, as a site of critical enunciation, compels the rethinking of the geopolitical distinction between center and periphery, and elicits a border thinking that changes not only the content but also the terms of intellectual global dialogue.[26] The émigré's cultural differences produce subaltern significations that resist the cultural cannibalism of the metropolitan melting pot. Diasporic communities are, to quote Bhabha once more, "wandering peoples who will not be contained within the *Heim* of the national culture and its unisonant discourse, but are themselves the marks of a shifting boundary that alienates the frontiers of the modern nation."[27]

Migration has become one of the main issues for theories of human rights and theological creativity done in solidarity with the pains and sorrows of displaced communities. Diasporic displacement has been an essential and historical consequence of imperial domination. "There are 65 million displaced persons around the globe. . . . And the mass drowning of migrants has become so routine that it scarcely qualifies as news."[28]

We have seen, during this last decade, extreme xenophobia in many Western and Northern nations. But it also conveys urgent challenges to the ethical sensitivity of religious people and persons of good will.[29] The first step we need to take is to perceive this issue from the perspective of the migrants, to pay cordial (i.e., deep from our hearts) attention to their stories of suffering, hope, courage, resistance, ingenuity, and as so frequently happens in the wildernesses of the American Southwest or deep in the Mediterranean waters, death.[30] Many of the unauthorized migrants have become *nobodies* (John

Bowe), *disposable people* (Kevin Bales), or *wasted lives* (Zygmunt Bauman).[31] They are the empire's new μέτοικοι, *douloi*, modern servants. Their dire existential situation cannot be grasped without taking into consideration the upsurge in global inequalities in these times of unregulated international financial hegemony.[32] For many human beings the excruciating alternative is between misery in their Third World homeland and marginalization in the rich West/North, both fateful destinies intimately linked.[33]

The existential dislocation of diaspora, its cultural hybridity, recreates the complex intertwined ethnic and racial sources of many migrant communities. Asked to whom does she owe allegiance, Clare, the Jamaican protagonist of Michelle Cliff's novel *No Telephone to Heaven*, replies, "I have African, English, Carib in me."[34] She is a mestiza moving between Kingston, New York, and London, searching for a place to call home, torn between the quest for solidarity in the forging of a common identity and the lure of solitude in a strange land. To be part of a pilgrim diaspora is a difficult and complex challenge, which, to avoid utopian illusions, must be faced having in mind the superb irony of that master of twentieth-century skepticism, himself a displaced wanderer, James Joyce: "We were always loyal to lost causes. . . . Success is for us the death of the intellect and of the imagination."[35]

From the margins of empires and metropolitan centers of powers, the crossroads of borders and frontiers, in the proximity of so many different and frequently conflictive cultural worlds, in the maelstroms of the global megacities and the virtual imagined communities of the internet arise constantly new challenges to the international structures of power and control.[36] There colonial discourses meet their nemesis: postcolonial defiance. In the ecumenicity of diaspora, to quote again Bhabha, "we must not change merely the narratives of our histories, but transform our sense of what it means to live, to be, in other times and different places, both human and historical."[37]

It is usually there, in the counter invasion of the "others," the colonized barbarians, deep into the realms of the lords of the world, that the silenced peoples find the sonority of their voices and reconfigure their historical sagas into meaningful human stories. The quasi-beastly shadows of Joseph Conrad's *Heart of Darkness* (1899) dare to disrupt the imperial monologue. They hybridize the language of the colonizers to reshape and narrate their own histories. As Chinua Achebe, engaged in a critical dialogue with the specter of Conrad, so eloquently has written in a text titled *Home and Exile*, "My hope for the twenty-first [century] is that it will see the first fruits . . . of the process of 're-storying' peoples who had been knocked silent by the trauma of all kinds of dispossession."[38]

For the early Christian communities, diaspora was a constant perspective in their way of living and understanding their faith, as expressed in a letter ("The Epistle to Diognetus") written by an anonymous Christian author in the second or third century: "They [Christians] take part in everything as citizens and put up with everything as foreigners. Every foreign land is their home, and every home a foreign land."[39] The Bible itself, as a canonic sacred text, is a literary creation of the diaspora,[40] for the Old Testament was born from the sufferings of the dispersed Hebrew nation and the New Testament was written in koine Greek, the lingua franca of many diasporic peoples of the Hellenistic age. The New Testament faith is, in many ways, a devout endless wandering, by a community of "aliens and exiles" (1 Peter 2:11), to the unreachable ends of the world and times, in search of God and solidarity.

The concept of diaspora could thus be a significant crossroad of encounter, a dialectical hinge, between postcolonial cultural studies and theological hermeneutics.[41] Compelled diaspora and exile, caused by violent imperial invasion, are essential elements in the biblical narratives. The desolation and destruction of the city of Jerusalem and its sacred temple, the dislocation and displacement suffered by its inhabitants, entailed a grave crisis of cultural and religious identity, the possibility of national dissolution, and the imposition of absolute hopelessness. Only the arousal of the strong prophetic voice advocating hope in the promises of Yahweh the Liberator was able to sustain courage in the midst of utter devastation.

Diaspora and exile are part and parcel of modern history and disturb deeply the identity of the displaced. For "identity—who we are, where we come from, what we are—is difficult to maintain in exile. . . . We are the 'other', an opposite, a flaw in the geometry of resettlement, an exodus."[42]

Pope Benedict XVI, in his 2009 social encyclical *Caritas in veritate*, rightly reminded the global community of the urgent necessity to develop international and ecumenical perspective of migration:

> [M]igration . . . is a striking phenomenon because of the sheer numbers of people involved, the social, economic, political, cultural and religious problems it raises . . . [We] are facing a social phenomenon of epoch-making proportions that requires bold, forward-looking policies of international cooperation. . . . We are all witnesses of the burden of suffering, the dislocation and the aspirations that accompany the flow of migrants . . . [T]hese laborers cannot be considered as a commodity or a mere workforce. They must not, therefore, be treated like any other factor of production. Every migrant is a human person who, as such, possesses fundamental, inalienable rights that must be respected by everyone and in every circumstance.[43]

Puerto Ricans constitute an important part of the U.S. Latino/Hispanic population, that sector of the American society whose growth, in the view of many, enriches multicultural diversity but has also led Samuel P. Huntington to warn that it constitutes a "major potential threat to the cultural and possibly political integrity of the United States."[44] How interesting that the former prophet of the "clash of civilizations," beyond the frontiers of the American colossus, became the apostle of the "clash of cultures," within its borders. According to this eminent Harvard professor, the main problem of Latino/ Hispanics is not the illegality in which many of them incur to reside in the United States but the threat they represent to the American national identity and its allegedly traditional "Anglo-Protestant" culture.

In that clash of cultures, we Puerto Ricans are distinguished warriors. We excel in the "double consciousness," the transculturation, and the border thinking that Walter Mignolo has so suggestively rescued from the African American W. E. B. Dubois, the Cuban Fernando Ortiz, and the Chicana Gloria Anzaldúa. In Puerto Rico, we take delight in our Spanish language, in the mainland we share the linguistic fate of the diaspora, we experience "the pain and perverse pleasure of writing in a second language," in the words of that exceptional Haitian scholar Michel-Rolph Trouillot.[45] The experience of *heteroglossia*, of thinking, speaking, and writing in a different language, opens unexpected spaces for a heterodox understanding of the hybridizing encounters of peoples and cultures. For, as Mikhail Bakhtin so adeptly has written, "the word lives, as it were, on the boundary between its own context and another, alien, context."[46]

The colonial situation, encompassing its political and juridical subjugation, its ensuing cultural symbiosis, and the persisting socioeconomic inequities, constitutes the historical matrix of many modern diasporas and, thus, a crucial source of the multicultural collisions in the imperial metropolitan centers. In the words of William Schweiker, University of Chicago professor of theological ethics,

> International cities are a "place" in which people's identities, sense of self, others, and the wider world, as well as values and desires, are locally situated but altered by global dynamics. . . . The compression of the world found in massive cities is thus a boon for the formation of new self-understandings, especially for dislocated peoples. . . . This is especially pointed when those "others" are implicated in histories of suffering. The compression of the world confronts us with the problem of how to live amid others, even enemies.[47]

The postmodern and postcolonial megacities compress times and spaces into borderlands of cultures, religiosities, traditions, and values. There it is impossible to evade the gaze of the others and the primordial biblical question—"am I my brother's keeper?"—acquires new connotations and urgency. A new sensitivity has to be forged to the rendering ambivalences, the sorrows and joys, of diasporic existence of the peoples who live day and night with the uncanny feeling of existing as Gentile aliens within the gates of holy Jerusalem.

In the borderlands, a new poetic of political resistance is developed, as the late Gloria Anzaldúa so hauntingly perceived. At the borderlands one is at once the battleground and the crossroads, the enemy and the kin of the enemies, the stranger who is at home and thus

> To survive in the Borderlands
> you must live *sin fronteras* [without borders][48]

THEOLOGY AND POSTCOLONIAL
STUDIES: A CRITICAL OBSERVATION

It is not surprising that biblical scholars—Fernando Segovia, R. S. Sugirth-arajah, Stephen D. Moore, Musa Dube, Roland Boer, Tat-Siong Benny Liew, Richard Horsley, and Leo G. Perdue, among others—have been foremost among the theological disciplines to pay close attention to postcolonial and decolonizing theories.[49] After all, it is impossible to evade the pervasive ubiquity of empires, imperial conquests, and anticolonial resistances in the Judeo-Christian sacred scriptures.

The geopolitical expansions or contractions of the Egyptian, Assyrian, Babylonian, Persian, Macedonian (Ptolemaic and Seleucid), and Roman empires constitute the main historical substratum of the entire biblical corpus. And let there be no doubt, imperial conquest constitutes a grave violation of human integrity. "There is no system of domination that does not produce its own routine harvest of insults and injury to human dignity."[50]

From the exodus saga to the anti-Roman apocalyptic visions of Revelation[51] only a fruitless strategy of hermeneutical evasion would be able to suppress the importance of imperial hegemony in the configuration of human existence and religious faith.[52] The dolorous cry of the conquered people was constant:

> Here we are, slaves to this day—slaves in the land that you gave to our ancestors
> to enjoy its fruit and its good gifts. Its rich yield goes to the kings [the Persian
> monarchy] whom you have set over us because of our sins; they have power
> also over our bodies and over our livestock at their pleasure, and we are in great
> distress. (Nehemiah 9:36–37)

Even a comprehensive study of gender and sex in the Bible has to take into consideration the different ways in which Esther and Judith use their female sexuality in critical historical instances in which the fate of the children of Abraham is at the stake of a powerful empire. How to forget that Jesus was executed by the Roman authorities as a political subversive? He was exposed to the horrendous rituals of moral denigration and physical assaults that traditionally constitute the tragic fate of colonized subjects who dare to defy imperial arrogance and dominion. Any theory of atonement that elides the intense political drama of the last days of Jesus transforms it in an abstract unhistorical dogma, or in a display of tasteless masochism à la Mel Gibson's *The Passion of the Christ* (2004).

Thus, it was to be expected that biblical scholars would be the first in the academic fields of religious studies to incorporate the emphases on geopolitical hegemony and resistance provided by postcolonial theories to the array of other contemporary hermeneutical perspectives. The observation by R. S. Sugirtharajah is poignant indeed:

> One of the weighty contributions of postcolonial criticism has been to put issues relating to colonialism and imperialism at the center of critical and intellectual inquiry. . . . What is striking about systematic theology is the reluctance of its practitioners to address the relation between European colonialism and the field. There has been a marked hesitancy to critically evaluate the impact of the empire among systematic theologians.[53]

To be fair, some theologians are beginning to wake from disciplinary slumber to take into consideration the crucial issues of geopolitical power. Creative theologians like Catherine Keller, Mark Lewis Taylor, Kwok Pui-lan, Wonhee Anne Joh, Mayra Rivera, and Joerg Rieger have begun to face with intellectual rigor and rhetorical elegance the challenges raised by postcolonial studies.[54] For those studies and dialogues, the Caribbean, where I live and work, might be a fine place to start.

Let me explain this last statement that many might find perplexing. Fernando Segovia has written a precise and concise exposition of the convergence between biblical scholarship and postcolonial studies.[55] Segovia raises several poignant critiques to the latter. Two of them are particularly relevant to the argument I want to develop: First, the lack of attention, by most postcolonial intellectuals, to the Latin American and Caribbean Iberian imperial formations as they developed between the end of the fifteenth century and the first decades of the seventeenth.[56] Second, the scarcity of analysis of religion as a crucial dimension of the imperial-colonial ideological frameworks. To quote Segovia on this second issue,

> It is almost as if religious texts and expressions did not form part of the cultural production and as if religious institutions and practices did not belong to the social matrix of imperial-colonial frameworks. I would argue . . . that religion is to be acknowledged and theorized as a constitutive component of such frameworks, and a most important one.[57]

The existential relevance of both issues for Segovia, a Cuban-born person who describes himself as "a student of religion in general and of the Christian faith in particular," seems obvious. I, as another Caribbean-born student of religion and theological ideas, share both concerns.

It is hard to deny that Segovia is *partially* right, for he is referring to post-colonial cultural studies as they emerged from the twilight of the European empires that developed in the wake of the Enlightenment. What has been named by some British historians as the classic age of empire is the basic matrix whence the critical texts of Said, Bhabha, and Spivak emerge. Even a useful introductory text in the field, *Post-Colonial Studies: The Key Concepts*,[58] proceeds as if the sixteenth-century Iberian empires never existed or as if religious discourses have never been used as motivation for conquest and colonization. The end result of those analytical occlusions is the homogenization of imperial experiences and, therefore, of colonial defiance.[59]

In many postcolonial texts we learn a lot about the multifarious resonances of the notorious 1835 Macaulay's Minute on Indian Education, but almost nothing about the intense theological controversies, juridical disputes and philosophical debates (Francisco de Vitoria, Bartolomé de las Casas, Juan Ginés de Sepúlveda, José de Acosta) during the sixteenth-century Spanish conquest of the Americas, despite the fact that they anticipate most of the latter colonial and anticolonial discourses.[60] The discussion by Vitoria about the justice of the wars against the Native Americans foreshadows all posterior arguments on the legitimacy of imperial wars.[61] The dispute between Las Casas and Sepúlveda about the rationality of the Native Americans and the adequacy of conversion by conquest inaugurates a long series of similar latter debates.[62] The lengthy treatise of Acosta on the Christianization and civilization of the American "barbarians" is paragon of subsequent analogous imperial justifications.[63]

Segovia is therefore right in his critique to the mainstream postcolonial studies. Yet, his critique reiterates that same mistake. He also excludes from the rather porous and vague boundaries of postcolonial studies authors that do in fact pay serious attention to both the Iberian sixteenth-century imperial formations and, as an unavoidable consequence, to the role of religious discourses in those geopolitical structures of control and dominion. The initial shaping of European global imperial expansion in Latin America and the Caribbean during the sixteenth century, in conjunction with the emergence of early modernity, capitalist accumulation, transatlantic slave trade, the proclamation of the Christian Gospel as imperial ideology, and the othering of non-European peoples, have been topics of rigorous academic research and publications by two Argentinean émigrés, Walter Mignolo and Enrique Dussel.[64] Lewis Hanke and Anthony Pagden have also dealt extensively with that complex configuration of themes, engaging frequently in a comparative critical analysis with more recent empires.[65] I myself have scholarly engaged the theological debates that accompanied the emergence of the transatlantic Iberian empire in the sixteenth century.[66]

GOD THE LIBERATOR

Liberation and decolonial theologies have stressed the priority, for its theoretical analysis, of the fate of the poor, the destitute, the "wretched of the earth" (Fanon) or "the least of these," in Jesus's poetic language.[67] The downtrodden people, to appropriate the words of T. S. Elliot, have survived torture and oppression, extortion and violence, destitution and disease, discomfort and hunger, unemployment and repression:

> We have seen the young man mutilated,
> The torn girl trembling by the mill-stream.[68]

Yet, even in these postmodernist and cybernetic times, people care about God. In the midst of present disturbances and conflicts, the "battle for God," as Karen Armstrong so aptly has named it, rages ferociously.[69] In the fascinating and perplexing kaleidoscope of human social existence, God is reimagined as the ultimate source of hope for the oppressed and downtrodden. When the social miseries that afflict so many communities become unbearable, beyond and besides the tiresome quarrels of religious fundamentalism and dogmatic secularism, the memory of God the Liberator erupts again and again: "When the Egyptians treated us harshly and afflicted us . . . we cried to the Lord, the God of our ancestors; the Lord heard our voice and saw our affliction, our toil, and our oppression. The Lord brought us out of Egypt with a mighty hand and an outstretched arm" (Deut 26:6–8). As the influential 1985 South African *Kairos* document categorically states:

> For most of their history from Exodus to Revelation, the people of the Bible suffered under one kind of oppression or another. . . . They were oppressed by the tyrannical, imperial nations around them. . . . The people of Israel were also for many centuries oppressed internally, with their own country, by the rich and the powerful and especially by the kings or rulers of Israel. . . .
> The Bible, of course, does not only describe oppression, tyranny, and suffering. . . . Throughout the Bible God appears as the liberator of the oppressed.[70]

These are the factors that counter and resist the ruling imperial project of controlling and policing the frontiers of human imagination. Deeply felt fears and hopes, as David Hume noted more than two centuries ago, are able to agitate hearts and spirits and to move minds to think the otherwise unthinkable.[71] Suddenly, at the end of the epoch so aptly named the "Age of Extremes" by Eric Hobsbawm,[72] two tendencies clash: the first announces with glib satisfaction "the end of history," the obliteration of transformative social utopias;[73] the second, from the entrails of the subordinated subjects,[74] proclaims a new insurrection of human hopes for "another possible world,"[75] in the words of Michel Foucault, "an *insurrection of subjugated knowledges.*"[76]

The essential imperative might be to remember and radicalize the prophetic words written by the imprisoned Dietrich Bonhoeffer, in a note surreptitiously preserved by his friend Eberhard Bethge: "We have for once learnt to see the great events of world history from below, from the perspective of the outcast, the suspects, the maltreated, the powerless, the oppressed, the reviled—in short, from the perspective of those who suffer."[77] This hermeneutical horizon, in constant critical and creative dialogue with contemporary liberation theologies and postcolonial theories, is strikingly analogous to Edward Said's representation of the intellectual as a person who unearths "the memory of forgotten voices . . . of the poor, the disadvantaged, the voiceless, the unrepresented, the powerless."[78] Its original source is an admonition on countless occasions reiterated by the Hebrew Bible itself:

> Speak out for those who cannot speak,
> for the rights of all the destitute . . .
> defend the rights of the poor and needy. (Prov 31:8–9)

For Oscar Romero, the ones who opt to speak out for and be on the side of vulnerable people must have courage:

> This is the commitment of being a Christian: to follow Christ in his incarnation. If Christ, the God of majesty, became a lowly human and lived with the poor and even died on a cross like a slave, our Christian faith should also be lived in the same way. . . . Christ invites us not to fear persecution.[79]

NOTES

1. José Trías Monge, *Puerto Rico: The Trials of the Oldest Colony in the World* (New Haven: Yale University Press, 1997), 4.

2. The war between the United States and Spain concluded with the Treaty of Paris, signed December 10, 1898. Spain, militarily defeated, was forced to relinquish its dominion over the Philippines, Cuba, Guam, and Puerto Rico to the new American colossus. See Alfonso García Martínez, ed., *Libro rojo/Tratado de París: Documentos presentados a las cortes en la legislatura de 1898 por el ministro de Estado* (Río Piedras, Puerto Rico: Editorial de la Universidad de Puerto Rico, 1988).

3. Stephen Kinzer, *The True Flag: Theodore Roosevelt, Mark Twain, and the Birth of American Empire* (New York, NY: Henry Holt, 2017).

4. Eric J. Hobsbawm, *The Age of Empire, 1875–1914* (New York: Pantheon Books, 1987).

5. See Albert K. Weinberg, *Manifest Destiny: A Study of Nationalist Expansionism in American History* (Baltimore: John Hopkins, 1935).

6. Cited in Kinzer, *The True Flag*, 132.

7. Edward W. Said, *Out of Place: A Memoir* (New York: Knopf. 1999); Homi Bhabha, *The Location of Culture* (London and New York: Routledge, 2001); Gayatri C. Spivak, *In Other Worlds: Essays in Cultural Politics* (New York and London: Routledge, 1998); Walter D. Mignolo, *The Darker Side of the Renaissance: Literacy, Territoriality, & Colonization* (Ann Arbor, MI: The University of Michigan Press, 1995).

8. Franz Fanon, *The Wretched of the Earth* (New York: Grove Press, 1968); Albert Memmi, *The Colonizer and the Colonized* (Boston: Beacon, 1965).

9. Aníbal Quijano, "Colonialidad del poder, cultura y conocimiento en América Latina," *Anuario Mariateguiano* 9.9 (1998): 113–121; Quijano, "The Colonial Nature of Power and Latin America's Cultural Experience," in *Sociology in Latin America (Social Knowledge: Heritage, Challenges, Perspectives)*, ed. R. Briceño H. R. Sonntag (Caracas, 1998), 27–38. Quijano, "Coloniality of Power, Eurocentrism, and Latin America," *Nepantla* 3 (2000): 533–580.

10. Said, Out of Place.

11. James C. Scott, *Domination and the Arts of Resistance: Hidden Transcripts* (New Haven, CT: Yale University Press, 1990), 18.

12. V. S. Naipaul, *The Mimic Men* (New York: Macmillan Naipaul, 1967).

13. Enrique Dussel, *1492: el encubrimiento del Otro* (Santafé de Bogotá: Ediciones Antropos, 1992).

14. Christopher Columbus, *A New and Fresh English Translation of the Letter of Columbus Announcing the Discovery of America* (Madrid: Gráficas Yagües, 1959), 15.

15. Gayatri C. Spivak, "Can the Subaltern Speak?" in *Marxism and the Interpretation of Culture*, ed. Cary Nelson and Lawrence Grossberg (Urbana and Chicago: University of Illinois Press, 1988), 271–313.

16. Edward W. Said, *Orientalism* (New York: Random House, 2003), 35.

17. Amos Elon, *Jerusalem: Battlegrounds of Memory* (New York: Kodansha International, 1995), 19.

18. Angelo Falcón, *Atlas of Stateside Puerto Ricans* (Washington, DC: Puerto Rico Federal Affairs Administration, 2004).

19. As Princeton University professor Arcadio Díaz-Quiñones has beautifully shown, Puerto Rican culture cannot be genuinely assessed if the creativity of its diaspora community is neglected or its significance diminished. See Arcadio Díaz-Quiñones, *El arte de bregar: ensayos* (San Juan: Ediciones Callejón, 2000).

20. Elazar Barkan and Marie-Denise Shelton, eds., *Borders, Exiles, Diasporas* (Stanford: Stanford University Press, 1998), 5.

21. Bhabha, *The Location of Culture*, 5.

22. Franz Fanon, *Peau Noir, Masques Blancs* (Paris: Éditions du Seuil, 1952).

23. Graham Greene, *The Power and the Glory* (London: Penguin, 1990).

24. This was the case for two creative Caribbean writers, marginalized and despised in their homelands, the Cuban Reinaldo Arenas and the Puerto Rican Manuel Ramos-Otero, who found in New York a wider horizon for their literary talents, a greater realm of personal freedom, and AIDS related death. See Rubén Ríos-Avila, "Caribbean Dislocations: Arenas and Ramos Otero in New York," in *Hispanisms and Homosexualities*, ed. Sylvia Molloy and Robert M. Irwin (Durham, NC: Duke University Press, 1998), 101–122.

25. Barkan and Shelton, *Borders, Exiles, Diasporas*, 5.

26. Walter D. Mignolo, *Local Histories/Global Designs: Coloniality, Subaltern Knowledges, and Border Thinking* (Princeton: Princeton University Press, 2000).

27. Bhabha, *The Location of Culture*, 164.

28. Jason DeParle, "The Sea Swallows People," *The New York Review of Books* 64.3 (February 23, 2017): 31.

29. Luis N. Rivera-Pagán, "Xenophilia or Xenophobia: Towards a Theology of Migration," *The Ecumenical Review* 64.4 (2012): 575–589.

30. See Jeremy Harding, "The Deaths Map," *London Review of Books* 33.20 (October 20, 2011): 7–13.

31. John Bowe, *Nobodies: Modern American Slave Labor and the Dark Side of the New Global Economy* (New York: Random House); Kevin Bales, *Disposable People: New Slavery in the Global Economy* (Berkeley, CA: University of California Press, 2004); Zygmunt Bauman, *Wasted Lives: Modernity and Its Outcasts* (Cambridge: Polity, 2004).

32. Slavoj Žižek, *Refugees, Terror and Other Troubles with the Neighbors* (Brooklyn, NY: Melville House, 2016).

33. Branko Milanovic, "Global Inequality and the Global Inequality Extraction Ratio: The Story of the Past Two Centuries," The World Bank, Development Research Group, Poverty and Inequality Group (September 2009).

34. Michelle Cliff, *No Telephone to Heaven* (New York: Plume Books, 1996), 189.

35. James Joyce, *Ulysses* (New York: Random House, 1946), 131–32.

36. Michael Hardt and Antonio Negri, *Multitude: War and Democracy in the Age of Empire* (New York: The Penguin Press, 2004).

37. Bhabha, *The Location of Culture*, 256.

38. Chinua Achebe, *Home and Exile* (New York: Anchor Books, 2000), 79.

39. Cited in Johannes Quasten and Joseph C. Plumpe, *Ancient Christian Writers: The Works of the Fathers in Translation* (Westminster, MD: The Newman Press, 1961), 139.

40. Daniel L. Smith-Christopher, *A Biblical Theology of Exile* (Minneapolis: Fortress Press, 2002).

41. René Krüger, *La diáspora: De experiencia traumática a paradigma eclesiológico* (Buenos Aires: ISEDET, 2008).

42. Edward W. Said, *After the Last Sky: Palestinian Lives* (New York: Pantheon Books, 1986), 16–17.

43. Pope Benedict, *Caritas in veritate*, 62.

44. Samuel P. Huntington, *Who Are We? The Challenges to America's National Identity* (New York: Simon & Schuster, 2004), 243.

45. Michel-Rolph Trouillot, *Silencing the Past: Power and the Production of History* (Boston: Beacon Press 1995), xv.

46. Mikhail Bakhtin, *The Dialogic Imagination: Four Essays* (Austin, TX: University of Texas Press, 2006), 284.

47. William Schweiker, *Theological Ethics and Global Dynamics in the Time of Many Worlds* (Malden, MA and Oxford: Blackwell, 2004), 6–7.

48. Gloria Anzaldúa, *Borderlands/La Frontera: The New Mestiza* (San Francisco: Aunt Lute, 1999), 216–217.

49. Stephen D. Moore and Fernando Segovia, *Postcolonial Biblical Criticism: Interdisciplinary Intersections* (London and New York: T & T Clark, 2005); R.S. Sugirtharajah (ed), *The Postcolonial Bible* (Sheffield, UK: Sheffield Academic Press, 1998); Sugirtharajah, *Postcolonial Criticism and Biblical Interpretation* (Oxford: Oxford University Press, 2002); Sugirtharajah, "Complacencies and Cul-de-sacs: Christian Theologies and Colonialism," in *Postcolonial Theologies: Divinity and Empire*, ed. Catherine Keller, Michael Nausner, and Mayra Rivera (St. Louis, MO: Chalice Press, 2004); Musa W. Dube, *Postcolonial Feminist Interpretation of the Bible* (St. Louis, MO: Chalice Press, 2000); Richard A. Horsley, *Paul and Empire: Religion and Power in Roman Imperial Society* (Harrisburg, PA: Trinity Press International, 1997); Horsley, *Jesus and Empire: The Kingdom of God and the New World Disorder* (Minneapolis: Fortress Press, 2003); Horsley, *Paul and the Roman Imperial Order* (Harrisburg, PA: Trinity Press International, 2004); Leo G. Perdue and Warren Carter, *Israel and Empire: A Postcolonial History of Israel and Early Judaism* (London: Bloomsbury, 2015).

50. Scott, *Domination and the Arts of Resistance*, 37.

51. João B. Libânio and Maria Clara L. Bingemer, *Escatologia Cristã: O Novo Céu e a Nova Terra* (Petrópolis, Brasil: Vozes, 1985); Pablo Richard, *Apocalipsis: reconstrucción de la esperanza* (San José: DEI, 1994); Brian K. Blount, *Can I Get a Witness? Reading Revelation Through African American Culture* (Louisville, KY: Westminster John Knox Press, 2005).

52. Giorgio Agamben, *The Kingdom and the Glory: For a Theological Genealogy of Economy and Government* (Stanford, CA: Stanford University Press, 2011).

53. Sugirtharajah, "Complacencies and Cul-de-sacs," 22.

54. Catherine Keller, *God and Power: Counter-Apocalyptic Journeys* (Minneapolis: Fortress, 2005); Mark Lewis Taylor, *Religion, Politics, and the Christian Right: Post-9/11 Powers and American Empire* (Minneapolis: Fortress Press, 2005); Pui-lan Kwok, *Postcolonial Imagination and Feminist Theology* (Louisville, KY: Westminster John Knox Press, 2005); Wonhee Anne Joh, *Heart of the Cross: A Postcolonial Christology* (Louisville, KY: Westminster John Knox Press, 2006); Joerg Rieger, *Christ & Empire: From Paul to Postcolonial Times* (Minneapolis: Fortress Press, 2007).

55. Fernando Segovia, "Mapping the Postcolonial Optic in Biblical Criticism: Meaning and Scope," in *Postcolonial Biblical Criticism: Interdisciplinary Intersections* (London and New York: T & T Clark, 2005), 23–78.

56. Ibid., 73.

57. Ibid., 74–75.

58. Bill Ashcroft, Gareth Griffiths, and Helen Tiffin, *Post-Colonial Studies: The Key Concepts* (London and New York: Routledge, 1998). Sometimes their disregard for the sixteenth century imperial formations leads them into egregious mistakes, like asserting that "in 1503, Bishop Las Casas . . . proposed . . . systematic importation of blacks" as "an alternative to indigenous labor" (1998, 212). In 1503 Bartolomé de Las Casas was not yet a bishop and he did not propose to bring black slaves to the new Spanish territories till the middle of the second decade of that century (cf. Rivera-Pagán 1992, 180–195; Rivera-Pagán 2003). Several of their statements regarding Latin America are not to be trusted ["the slave system . . . persisted in the Caribbean and some South American areas until the 1830s" [ibid., 214]—whereas slavery was not abolished in Puerto Rico until 1873, in Cuba until 1886 and in Brazil until 1888), which only shows the lack of attention to the colonial history of Latin America and the Spanish Caribbean.

59. Curiously, Chinua Achebe is mentioned once in Ashcroft *et al.*, *Post-Colonial Studies*, but his 1958 classic novel, *Things Fall Apart*, one of the foremost literary assessments of the convergence between European colonization of African and Christian missions, is not even alluded to.

60. Enrique Dussel, *Política de la liberación. Historia mundial y crítica* (Madrid: Editorial Trotta, 2007), 186–210.

61. Francisco de Vitoria, "On the American Indians" (*De indis*, I), *Political Writings*, trans. Jeremy Lawrance (Cambridge: Cambridge University Press, 1992), 231–292.

62. Bartolomé de las Casas, *In Defense of the Indians*, trans. Stafford Poole (DeKalb, IL: Northern Illinois University Press, 1992).

63. José de Acosta, *De procuranda indorum salute* (2 vols.), trans and ed G. Stewart McIntosh (Tayport and Scotland, UK: Mac Research, 1996).

64. Walter D. Mignolo, The Darker Side of the Renaissance: Literacy, Territoriality, & Colonization (Ann Arbor, MI: The University of Michigan Press, 1995); Enrique Dussel, Invention of the Americas: Eclipse of "the Other" & the Myth of Modernity (New York: Continuum, 1995).

65. Lewis U. Hanke, *The Spanish Struggle for Justice in the Conquest of America* (Philadelphia: University of Pennsylvania Press, 1949); Hanke, *Aristotle and the American Indians: A Study in Race Prejudice in the Modern World* (Chicago: Henry Regnery, 1959); Hanke, *All Mankind is One; A Study of the Disputation Between Bartolomé de Las Casas and Juan Ginés de Sepúlveda in 1550 on the Intellectual and Religious Capacity of the American Indians* (DeKalb, IL: Northern Illinois University Press, 1974); Anthony Pagden, *The Fall of Natural Man: The American Indian and the Origins of Comparative Ethnology* (Cambridge: Cambridge University Press, 1982); Pagden, *Spanish Imperialism and the Political Imagination* (New Haven and London: Yale University Press, 1990); Pagden, *Lords of all the World: Ideologies of Empire in Spain, Britain and France, c.1500—c.1800* (New Haven and London: Yale University Press, 1995).

66. Luis N. Rivera-Pagán, *A Violent Evangelism: The Political and Religious Conquest of the Americas* (Louisville, Kentucky: Westminster John Knox, 1992);

Rivera-Pagán, *Entre el oro y la fe: El dilema de América* (San Juan: Editorial de la Universidad de Puerto Rico, 1995). Among theologians, Joerg Rieger is a distinguished exception. He devotes a chapter of one of his books to the critical analysis of Bartolomé de las Casas's Christology in the context of the sixteenth century imperial expansion (Rieger 2007, *Christ & Empire*, 159–196).

67. Luis N. Rivera-Pagán, "God the Liberator: Theology, History, and Politics," in *Essays from the Margins*, ed. Luis N. Rivera-Pagán (Eugene, OR: Cascade, 2014), 63–83.

68. T. S. Eliot, "Murder in the Cathedral" (1935), in *The Complete Poems and Plays, 1909–1950* (New York: Harcourt, Brace and Company, 1952), 195.

69. Karen Armstrong, *The Battle for God* (New York: Knopf, 2000).

70. Willis H. Logan (ed), *The Kairos Covenant: Standing with the South African Christians* (New York, NY: Friendship Press, 1988), 27, 33.

71. David Hume, *The Natural History of Religion* (London: A. & C. Black, 1956).

72. Eric Hobsbawm, *Age of Extremes: The Short Twentieth Century, 1914–1991* (London: Michael Joseph, 1994).

73. Francis Fukuyama, *The End of History and the Last Man* (New York: Free Press, 1992).

74. Franz Hinkelammert, *El grito del sujeto: del teatro-mundo del evangelio de Juan al perro-mundo de la globalización* (San José, Costa Rica: DEI, 1998).

75. Jorge Pixley et al., *Por un mundo otro: alternativas al mercado global* (Quito, Ecuador: Consejo Latinoamericano de Iglesias, 2003).

76. Michel Foucault, *Power/Knowledge: Selected Interviews and Other Writings 1972–1977* (New York: Vintage Books, 1980), 81.

77. Dietrich Bonhoeffer, *Letters and Papers from Prison*, ed. Eberhard Bethge (London: Folio Society, 2000), 16.

78. Edward W. Said, *Representations of the Intellectuals* (New York: Vintage Books, 1996), 35, 113.

79. Oscar Arnulfo Romero, *The Violence of Love* (Farmington, PA: Plough, 1998), 191.

Chapter 11

Theological Shifts

From Multiculturalisms to Multinaturalisms

Cláudio Carvalhaes

The theological turn of the twentieth century has been, among other things, the movement from universal doctrines and beliefs about God to cultural, contextual ones. This move has helped us see that theologies have a cultural grid that defines not only the final result of the process of thinking but thinking itself. Thinking theology is a cultural creation, dependent on forms of knowledge that dominate that culture; then dominant cultures dominate the theological field and end up making universal claims.

Liberation theologies among other theologies have learned to be critical of knowledges located in centers of power and restore local "subjugated knowledges."[1] Also, a certain brand of Christian theology and liturgy started to think the necessity of multicultural theologies and liturgies as a way to produce justice-seeking congregations, hospitable worship services, and fair norms and forms of mutual conviviality and sharing of power. In all of these theological and liturgical efforts, including many liberation theologies, the multicultural efforts of inclusion focused solely on cultures and cultural battles forgetting and even denying the very condition of the organization of these theologies and liturgies: nature. My aim in this essay is to point to the ways in which multicultural theologies failed to engage the earth and the basic sustenance of our lives on earth. Introducing one aspect of the thought of Brazilian anthropologist Eduardo Viveiros de Castro, namely *Amerindian Perspectivism*, and offering some challenges for the theological thinking in our new twenty-first century, I hope to expand our possibility of thinking theology in more *natural* ways.

MULTICULTURALISM

When we talk about nature we are already engaging in separation. The rift between human beings and nature is the product of a cultural way of thinking prone to classification and/by separation. Human beings have always under-stood ourselves as being above nature. Our very identity as humans is a social construct crafted in contrast to the idea of "nature"; our very notion of what it is to be human entails a negative image of nature. For us, nature is subservi-ent, wild, uncontrollable, in need of being mastered, shaped, and organized. I was taught to think this way in Sunday School, as I listened to Bible studies and sermons based on Gen 1:28: "God blessed them, and God said to them, 'Be fruitful and multiply, and fill the earth and subdue it; and have dominion over the fish of the sea and over the birds of the air and over every living thing that moves upon the earth'" (NRSV).

The fundamental separation is between God and the earth! Ever since, inequality has prevailed. God versus us, nature versus us. We are taught to subdue "it"; nature has become a thing. Everything is now under our feet. "Dominion over": those magical words we love. Dominion over fish, birds, and anything that moves. What the writer of Genesis didn't know was that this form of relation would fit perfectly into a worldview of economic meth-ods, financial categories, forms of production within this developmental growth called capitalism, and its agribusiness force.

The advent of modernity radicalized this theological reading of the cre-ation story in rational, nonreligious ways. Immanuel Kant's desire for human autonomy shaped new forms of being human, providing us with new ways of engaging our minds and our many forms of reasoning. God, transformed now into abstract sublimity, was also able to be grasped by reason. Our task became mastering and controlling everything with the ability and power of our mind. Over and against the darkness of religion, Kantian reason enjoined us to move onward, even and fundamentally over nature. As Eduardo Viveiros de Castro and Déborah Danowski put it:

> Kant's misnamed "Copernican Revolution" is, as we know, the source of the official modern conception of Man (let us keep it masculine) as consistent power, the autonomic and sovereign lawgiver of nature, the only being capable of rising above the phenomenal order or causality of which his own understand-ing is a condition; "human exceptionalism" is a veritable ontological state of exception, grounded on the self-grounding separation between Nature and History.[2]

Gaining our humanity by placing ourselves over and against animal instincts, mastering the world through thinking, organizing our culture over and against an unruly nature, modernity asserted this theoretical division, imposing yet another disastrous hierarchical relationship between humans and the earth. With time, the rawness of the earth was lost to our new *oikos* in the form of a mechanized world, that rawness so deeply buried that many people are now clueless about what is entailed in processes such as water coming into our homes and out of the faucets; about who owns this resource or where it comes from. We not only eat without knowing where our food comes from or what happens to the animals and the earth that provide it; we also couldn't care less.

Theologian Vitor Westhelle writes about the ways in which Christian theology was caught in that web of time over against space. In his book *Eschatology and Space, the Lost Dimension in Theology Past and Present*, he shows how historically, the theological enterprise of the West was dependent on notions of time and how geographical spaces were never considered in theological formation of doctrines, faith, and general constructions. Following a theological construction of time that predates modernity and starts with Orosius and Augustine, Westhelle points to the ways in which modernity, following Hegel and his "the truth of space is time," continues this project of time against space in theologians and biblical scholars such as Paul Tillich, Karl Barth, Wolfart Pannenberg, Gerhard von Rad, and Juan Luis Segundo. Eschatology has only been viewed as it relates to time and not with space. Westhelle writes,

> The current crisis of eschatological thinking came through the backdoor of the historical project of the Western world with its colonial expansion and conquering enterprise. The face of the other and its truth came to the fore by a latitudinal advent. In the tradition of Hegel, the others of the Europeans were typically located either in the historical past (the Asians) or in the future (North Americans). But with the colonial backlash, thinking of the other could no longer be limited to a longitudinal and time-bound perspective. The others were "over-there." For many communities in the world, the movement of the Earth around the Sun—which registers time and is printed on the face of every analogical watch that we wear on our wrists or in clocks built into square towers—is not the dominant, or at least not the only frame to interpret reality and the experience of ultimacy. The other is definitely somewhere else and not *some-when* else.[3]

The "crisis of eschatological thinking" makes us think our present and our ends (*schata*) not in terms of geographical terms, thus geographically marked by power dynamics, race, politics and dominion, in an ecologically interdependent web but rather, as the fulcrum of our faith disassociate with pulsing markers of the conditions of our living. Since our theological knowledge is so bound to time, our sources are not to be taken from the earth, from the flowers, from the birds, from the rivers. Even many of our wise prophets know very little about the processes of the earth.

If we look at the liturgical calendar that many churches use, everything is organized between Chronos and Kairos times. Chronos is the sequential time that moves forward in linear ways toward an eschaton where God will disclose the fullness of the Kingdom of God. Kairos is the fulfillment of times, or time in fullness where a moment goes beyond its limits and is filled with the past, present, and future, like the coming of Jesus Christ on earth and the sacramental moments of history when we see God's inbreaking into human history. Very little of the *schata* of life is geographical, or taken from the living cycles of microorganisms, or animals or the air, water, earth or fire. There is no Christian liturgical calendar based on earthly events.

Our liturgies and theologies cannot stop us thinking that everything that exists, sentient and non-sentient beings, live either because of us or to fulfill our needs and desires. According to our timely knowledge and assumptions, the world is only possible if we, human beings, exist; without us the world would neither be, nor have meaning or purpose. Without our presence, the world, nature, and even some kinds of people cannot make sense, are often on the edge of living in bestial ways, and running the risk of destroying themselves. The prize of our rationality is to put proper order in the world—an order that subsumes earth to our hierarchical reasoning. We are on the side of socialization, but nature is in the side of anti-socialization; we have a culture to change things and the environment has a nature to be changed.

Moreover, modernity has made clear not only the distinction between time and space (history and nature) but also between the individual and society, nature and culture, tradition and originality, feeling and thinking, the sacred and the secular, the universal and the particular, objectivity and subjectivity, the physical and the moral, value and fact, immanence and transcendence, animal and human, body and spirit, and so on. Reasoning according to these absolute, mythological pairings runs contrary to the wisdom and ways of so many peoples across the world.

Christianity is a religion made of binaries. God is transcendent, we are immanent; history is where God plans God's salvation, culture is the place of God's incarnation, and nature seems to be at best a second-tier subject in the scheme of God's representation and at worse a totally unnecessary "thing" to understand God's love; the body is to be subsumed to the spiritual, animals are under the ruling of humans and the sacraments, while shaped by earthly elements, must be placed in an altar, above the earth. The sky has become too far from the earth. Theological nomos is marked by cultural autonomy rather than ecological relationality.

Faith is an inward gift to be lived as a testimony to the world. The way it happens is through culture, for faith is a cultural event and it happens in cultural locations. Faith in nature must be treated with caution because we could hit on animism. Nature carries a natural grace of God but it needs the redemptive, especial grace of God in Jesus. And Jesus is only understood through culture. As just one example, consider what many hold to be a classic of Christian theology, H. Richard Niebuhr's *Christ and Culture*.[4] The book describes Jesus Christ according to five different headings: *Christ against Culture, Christ of Culture, Christ above Culture, Christ and Culture in Paradox,* and *Christ the Transformer of Culture.* These five categories give Christians a sense of how to relate to, deny, oppose, or engage culture. This sort of Christ has nothing to do with nature at all.

Liberals and minority intellectuals quickly pick up on this Christological emphasis on culture and criticize the notion of dominant culture that controls the means of theological knowledge production. According to this criticism, minorities were relegated to the fringes of society, to subaltern places. Cultural differences are often asymmetric relations between them, and a new "multiculturalism" is necessary to even the plane of cultures. Grounded in politics of identity, cultures started to be a place of particular knowledge and power. In the United States, for instance, theological multiculturalism tried to engage with cultural differences by trying to create blended forms of worship, carving spaces for various cultures to participate in often white dominant services.[5]

As this scholarship helps to break the master cultural narrative, it is still grounded in the dominated culture/nature binary. Nature, ecology, environment, are all placed on the hidden spectrum of the multicultural enterprise sustaining the master and other narratives that structures life, religion, and ways of living. The theological axis is autonomous, self-referential, and revolves around culture. Ecology is, and has always been, the ground that sustains and supports its ways of thinking and its ways of keeping structures of domination.

The focus on culture is fundamental for liturgy. The *Nairobi Document of Worship and Culture* follows the same modern, humanistic assumptions we have been discussing but with a colonial hint of Christian traditions clearing up what is bad in culture.[6] In order to engage with worship and culture, we are admonished to think about worships as "transcultural," "contextual," "countercultural," and "cross-cultural." In each of these realms, we learn about the "nature" of each cultural assessment, its meaning, and uniqueness that separates one from the other. What we don't hear is the way in which nature itself is intertwined in everything, organizing life, providing the very possibility of any form of worship to exist. Contrary to what seems to be the case, Christian worship should not be understood as a form of colonialism that excludes or detaches us from the natural world. This exclusion, however, is nuanced since colonialism was deeply involved in the natural world of those it subjugated; it relied on natural resources to fuel empire, for example—the very business of colonialism was making use of human and nonhuman resources; even if it was an evil, dysfunctional relationship. The new forms of coloniality, the power structures of colonialism, continue to be dependent on the "natural" world while it works completely detached from it. In other words, the whole cultural diversity maintains the homogenous metanarrative of the master oppression. The proposed diversity of multicultural liberation continues to be the subjugation of the earth and thus leave the domination of the earth to be in the hands of those who control the forms of reproduction. The multicultural enterprise continues to be the subjugation of the earth.

MULTINATURALISM

The dualism culture/nature continues to be maintained under the reasoning and knowledge that continue to take place "outside" of nature. This "outside," beyond nature, is the ground from which multiculturalism and the politics of difference work in a somewhat unconscious level. In some ways, this relation can be described as an "ontological duality between nature, the domain of necessity, and culture, the domain of spontaneity, areas separated by metonymic discontinuity."[7]

The justice work intended under multiculturalism often forgets the complexities of the contexts of environmental relations. Environmental understandings are never engaged. What is at stake are the claims of various forms of culture, experience, and lately mostly around identity, with no connection to the larger productions of relations and the owning of natural resources. Moreover, the affirmation of identities, all kinds of identities, claim a place where often it entails a radical separation of identity of others, denying their interdependence with each other and with nature. While the professed value of multiculturalism and identity politics is centered on their goal of organizing society in a fair and just way, all the same, they reify the denial of the fact that these groups' very existence emerges from, takes place within, and depends upon nature.

Viveiros de Castro, a Brazilian anthropologist working with indigenous Latin Americans, developed the notion of *Amerindian perspectivism* and *multinaturalism* in order to offer a new way of thinking, feeling, and living life. It is worth the long quote:

In sum, animals are people, or see themselves as persons. Such a notion is virtually always associated with the idea that the manifest form of each species is a mere envelope (a "clothing") which conceals an internal human form, usually only visible to the eyes of the particular species or to certain trans-specific beings such as shamans. This internal form is the "soul" or "spirit" of the animal: an intentionality or subjectivity formally identical to human consciousness, materializable, let us say, in a human bodily schema concealed behind an animal mask. At first sight then, we would have a distinction between an anthropomorphic essence of a spiritual type, common to animate beings, and a variable bodily appearance, characteristic of each individual species but which rather than being a fixed attribute is instead a changeable and removable clothing. This notion of "clothing" is one of the privileged expressions of metamorphosis—spirits, the dead and shamans who assume animal form, beasts that turn into other beasts, humans that are inadvertently turned into animals—an omnipresent process in the "highly transformational world" (Riviere 1994, 256) proposed by Amazonian ontologies. Such an ethnographically-based reshuffling of our conceptual schemes leads me to suggest the expression, "multi-naturalism," to designate one of the contrastive features of Amerindian thought in relation to Western "multiculturalist" cosmologies. Where the latter are founded on the mutual implication of the unity of nature and the plurality of cultures . . . the Amerindian conception would suppose a spiritual unity and a corporeal diversity. Here, culture or the subject would be the form of the universal, whilst nature or the object would be the form of the particular.[8]

As opposed to the modern Western conception that sees one human nature within multiple cultures, meaning one human body contains one substance and the rest are animals without substance/soul, essentially different from humanity, indigenous thought asserts that there is instead one culture (the world) where we all live amidst multiple natures made of various forms of humanities where the human nature is one nature living among many other natures, such as animals and spirits.

"Perspectivism" describes the nature of Amerindian mythology, cosmology, and daily activities. Perspectivism is a unique way in which humans view themselves and other inhabitants of the universe, the same ways that animals and spirits see themselves as humans, even if some humans do not share that understanding. Perspectivism is a view from a point that is always changeable. It is in the body that we perceive and feel ourselves, others, objects, and the world. The human condition is everywhere, here and elsewhere. Each species is a center of conscience that varies in grade and situation. There is a relation between subjects and they dialogue about their differences. There is the unity of the spirit and diversity of bodies. While the Western modern conception of nature means one nature and multiple cultures, for the Amerindian perspective, culture is the universal and nature is the particular. Culture is what encompasses everything and within our realm, there are many naturalisms between human forms of humans and animals. "Perspectivism is not a relativism but a multinaturalism."[9]

Multinaturalism is perspectivism. Even while living within one culture, everyone has a different nature. These different natures—of human beings, animals, spirits and so on—display forms of relationality in which many ways of being human are possible. These natures have distinct ways of seeing each other. Viveiros de Castro adds:

In particular, individuals of the same species see each other (and each other only) as humans see themselves, that is, as beings endowed with human figure and habits, seeing their bodily and behavioral aspects in the form of human culture. What changes when passing from one species of subject to another is the "objective correlative," the referent of these concepts: what jaguars see as "manioc beer" (the proper drink of people, jaguar-type or otherwise), humans see as "blood." Where we see a muddy salt-lick on a river bank, tapirs see their big ceremonial house, and so on. Such difference of perspective—not a plurality of views of a single world, but a single view of different worlds—cannot derive from the soul, since the latter is the common original ground of being. Rather, such difference is located in the bodily differences between species, for the body and its affections . . . is the site and instrument of ontological differentiation and referential disjunction. Hence, where our modern, anthropological multicultur-alist ontology is founded on the mutual implication of the unity of nature and the plurality of cultures, the Amerindian conception would suppose a spiritual unity and a corporeal diversity—or, in other words, one "culture," multiple "natures." In this sense, perspectivism is not relativism as we know it—a subjective or cultural relativism—but an objective or natural relativism—a multinaturalism.[10]

In this way, to talk about human rights is to talk about the rights of many forms of humanities, many natures. This all encompassed, intertwined, inter-related reality of many natures lives mostly by the instincts of humanities rather than the control of its instincts as seen in institutions of human race. Our species need institutions such as the state and churches while for indig-enous thinking we rely and we wrestle in the instincts that organize our lives.

Multiculturalism works and relies on institutions that hope to tame the human Spirit through mediation, norms, and regulations. Multiculturalism relies on one nature, the human being nature, and in different cultures that try to compose the whole of cultures under the notion of one nature. This one nature has many spirits in competition with each other. In order to organize these spir-its, one has to organize the many cultures. This whole process often works with cultures as bodies subsumed from all its complexities and differences to flat notions of cultural representations. Multinaturalism works from a single spirit and a cultural background that shapes the I for each individual body and per-ceives culture differently. Multiculturalism is infused with a detachment from the earth and focus on representations of life, rather than means of production of life. The former shuffles us around according to the kindness of the prevalent culture and the latter calls into question the very structure of our living and who controls the natural sources that condition our living.

AGRI-CULTURE

In this way, eco-feminists are closer, while still in many ways caught in the binary culture/nature, to this view for they see the earth as indistinctively connected to the living-thinking of their theologies. The society means of production must engage animals, its biodiversity, and the multiverses (infinite number of parallel universes). From them we learn that the materiality of life, the flesh and bones and desires of our bodies, is deeply associated with soil and seeds, animals and biodiversities, and the needs of the earth. They say that these associations are related to the ownership of the earth and bodies, of sexualities and subjectivities, agribusiness, capitalistic exploitation, and they are all intertwined. Latin American Bible scholar Nancy Cardoso proposes:

> Economic reflection approached the field of amorous and erotic phenomena with the need to express an important perspective on property modes and forms of capital accumulation—two vital items for the understanding of the capitalist model, in a special way within capitalist agriculture—what we know as agribusiness.[11]

This immanent, intertwined notion of life, where everything is dependent on processes and movements, goes against the modern anthropocentrism that makes nature a subject of man's dominion and permanently subjugates the earth. This human prerogative is seen in the theological arrangement of creation, where God's preference for the human, the final product of creation, has been granted the ultimate blessing of dominion over everything—hence, the power to do anything required for the survival of the human species. The earth, a subject without rights, must indeed be under the control of human need and desire. Thus, the earth is to be conquered for our own survival, and to allow for the possibility of continuously changing social constructions.

This worldview ignores the question of agriculture, which many theologians do not think it applies to us because we are not farmers. But I want us to pause and think about the etymology of the term "agri-culture." The word "agri/acre" indicates a field, land, that which is sown. The word "culture" comes from the Latin *cultura*, meaning cultivation or culture, a term that itself derives from *cultus*,[12] the past participle of *colere* (to cultivate, worship), and is also related to *colonus* and *colonia*. This cultivation of what is active is a manufacturing of what is important to honor, worth working for and ascribing honor to it. Thus, agriculture points to a deep relation between land and people, to people living off and with the land in interdependence, cultivating each other's existence. Nonetheless, the *agri of culture*, the very land where we live and survive, has been invaded by the *culture of the agri* in our societies. We have been transformed from being people of the earth into people who own the earth. Detached by the rationalism of our humanitarian and now capitalistic ways of living-thinking, we have even let the earth be taken away from us. Since we have been detached for so long from the earth, we never understood that this process of exploitation of the earth would be akin to the exploitation of people everywhere.

The colonization and capitalist devouring of the world was and continues to be based upon worship of our culture, a *colos*, the bosom of empire in which society is cultivated. In this cultivation, colonizers, states, and bankers decided to get rid of our seeds and our spiritualities, our worship, and our ways of living with the earth. We ended up cultivating their own worship, their own ideas. Our ontologies became their epistemologies, our faith a mere feeling that sustains the market, our thinking a way of justifying our detachment from the earth.

It is thus our work to move away from a modernist humanist perspective that denies the very connectivity with the earth and the interdependency of environmental relations and eco-systems.

CONCLUSION

The theological cultural paradigm has contributed to cause the irreversible destruction of the earth. We must shift this paradigm to one that is grounded in multinaturalisms. This multinaturalism can be seen in the connection and equality found between people and animals, earth and the cosmos in the myths of the Aikewara in Brazil: "When the sky was still too close to Earth, there was nothing in the world except people and tortoises." But modernity widened the separation between the sky and the earth, between people and tortoises, by creating industries, artificial products, instrumental reasoning, notions of self, and new desires to be fulfilled. Now we are all separated and far from the sky; now the earth and the sky have been colonized. With our overpopulated world, the earth abused, and our cares directed away from creation, our gods have taken flight and left us. And we can no longer live with the tortoises.

Contrary to the discourse of autonomous beings, living in separated ways, we are all intertwined, interrelated, and interconnected. Christianity is a good example to show this denial of interdependency. The celebration of the ritual of the Eucharist elevates the sacramental elements above the ground. What is sacred is on the table, an altar, away from the floor, which is always dirty and detached from our holy things. If, God forbid, we drop the bread on the floor, it touches the ground (seen to be filthy) and runs a certain risk, even though we don't know exactly what this is. Is it the losing of power; lack of respect with the holy since we have desecrated the altar of God? Even though we disassociate the earth with ritual practices, the sacrament comes from the earth, the "dirt," and its elements—water, bread, and grapes—are sources of its life.

Multinaturalism calls for a reapproximation to what we are: several humanities living together in this cultural universe. It is only when we can live and protect the tortoises the same way we live and protect other human beings that we become fully connected with the Spirit of God and with the whole of our beings.

If we are to engage in multinaturalism and perspectivism, we must move away from our transcendental theologies and worship a God who lives in different natures and is felt, perceived and lived in different planes, forms, and structures. As the late Latin American theologian Jaci Maraschin said, "It is in the body that we are Spirit."[13] The culture of our times is the Spirit. The Spirit is what keeps our natures in relation. Leonardo Boff might help us think-feel, and feel-think the *ruach* of God, the Spirit that breathes in everything and in us. Using the Chinese tradition of Taoism, he expands this breath (*Tao*, spirit) as presence in many religious traditions:

> The *Tao* represents this integration, the integration of an indescribable reality and the person who seeks to unite itself with this reality. Tao means the path and the method, but it is also the mysterious and secret energy that produces all paths and projects all methods. It cannot be expressed in words, so when in front of it, silence is best. It is present in all things as the immanent principle that ascribes meaning. . . . To reach this union it is imperative to be in synchrony with the vital energy that weaves through the heavens and earth, *chi*. It is impossible to translate *chi*, but it is equivalent to the *ruach* of the Jewish people, to the *pneuma* of the Greeks, to the *spiritus* of the Latins, to the *axé* of the Yoruba/Nago; these are expressions that designate the universal breath, the supreme and cosmic energy. It is because of *chi* that everything changes and remains in a constant process of change.[14]

The Spirit is working within thinking, but it is also beyond thinking! It moves within and through history but also breaks into and causes history to move. The Spirit of God is our breathing sustenance but this breath does not only exist in our form of humanity. God's breathing Spirit is everywhere in every sentient and non-sentient beings. A godly animism if one needs a definition, even though God's Spirit is not confined to those beings only. God's Spirit goes beyond what we know and into the multi-universes. Thus, our breathing together must entail every other being we know and don't know. For instance, our theological thinking must gain an awareness that we can only actually breathe God's breath if we consider the oceans. Without the plants called phytoplankton, kelp, and algal plankton we simply cannot live the breath of God in us.[15]

It is this breathing together, in holy co-respiration with sentient and non-sentient beings that we can find the *schata*, the ends, and the beginnings, of our life! It is this breathing together, this holy co-respiration with other people, other humanities, other naturalisms that we can redeem not only our times but fundamentally our grounds and our spaces. The earth is the force of our times. The truth of time is space. It is this breathing together, in holy inspiration and transpiration, eco-supporting all of the endless complex systems of the earth, that we can level the plain of all sentient and non-sentient beings to actually be able to live together.

It is this eco-breathing together with God that makes the *ruach* become a force in the world. The *ruach* of God respiring in all things is what helps us see that we are not alone, that we are living together in the midst of many multinaturalisms. And we gain a new humanity, deeply connected with the earth, deeply humidified by the humus of our coexistence.

Can Christianity be a multinaturalist faith? Not in the way we know now. But since this knowledge was once invented, Christian knowledge can be reinvented under God's breath. If language is but means to receive God's Spirit, we can gain a new language to breath God's breath anew. Thus, it is our task and our challenge to expand the grammar of our faith. A grammar that will have a new alphabet, new languages, new wisdoms, new ontologies, new forms, new and old prayers, new and old songs, new paradigms, new rituals, and new Spirit. For the *ruach* of God is not one that is afraid. Rather, the *ruach* of God is the one who breaks into our lives with newness of a new world possible, with challenges that can only be faced with the grace of God.

From a Christian multinaturalism, we need liturgies that think-feel-believe in spirits incarnated in eagles and tortoises; liturgies that think-feel-believe in the long work of theory and praxis so that the Christian faith can become not only counterculture but also against culture when culture is detached from nature; liturgies that think-feel-hear the cries of the earth; liturgies that think-feel-believe-see what is happening to the destruction of our people and to the earth; liturgies that think-feel-listen to the birds, and learn the ways of the birds; liturgies that think-feel-believe-breath-co-inspire, respire a life lived in solidarity with sentient and non-sentient beings, striving for everyone's rights to live fully and well.

The breathing of the spirit is our multinatural possibility, the very possibility to live within and beyond natures, running against empire and for the sake of the wretched of the earth and the wretched earth.

NOTES

1. Michel Foucault, *Power/Knowledge. Select Interviews and Other Writings, 1972–1977* (New York: Pantheon Books, 1988), 81.

2. Eduardo Viveiros de Castro and Déborah Danowski, *The Ends of the World* (Cambridge: Polity Press, 2016), 28.

3. Vitor Westhelle, *Eschatology and Space: The Lost Dimension in Theology Past and Present* (New York: Palgrave Macmillan, 2012), xiv–xv.

4. H. Richard Niebuhr, *Christ and Culture* (New York: Harper & Row, 1975).

5. Sandra Maria Van Opstal, *The Next Worship: Glorifying God in a Diverse World* (Westmont: Intervarsity Press, 2016); Eunjoo Mary Kim, *Christian Preaching and Worship in Multicultural Contexts: A Practical Theological Approach* (Liturgical Press: Collegeville, 2017); Brian K. Blount and Leonara Tubbs Tisdale, *Making Room at the Table: An Invitation to Multicultural Worship* (Louisville: Westminster John Knox Press, 2000).

6. The Lutheran World Federation, "Nairobi Document of Worship and Culture" (http://www.smithseminary.org/wp-content/uploads/2016/02/Nairobi-Statement-and-Worshiping-Triune-God.pdf).

7. Eduardo Viveiros de Castro, "Cosmological Deixis and Amerindian Perspectivism," *The Journal of the Royal Anthropological Institute* 4.3 (1988): 473.

8. de Castro, "Cosmological Deixis and Amerindian Perspectivism," 470.

9. Eduardo Viveiros de Castro, n.d. "Perspectivismo e multinaturalismo na América indígena," in *O que nos faz pensar* No 18, setembro de 200, 239.

10. Eduardo Viveiros de Castro, "Perspectival Anthropology and the Method of Controlled Equivocation," *Tipití: Journal of the Society for the Anthropology of Lowland South America* 2.1 (2017): 6.

11. Nancy Cardoso Pereira, "Da agropornografia à agroecologia: uma aproximação queer contra as elites vegetais," in *História, saúde e direitos: sabores e saberes do IV Congresso Latino-Americano de Gênero e Religião*, ed. André Musskopf and Márcia Blasi (São Leopoldo, RS: CEBI, 2016), 35–41.

12. https://www.merriam-webster.com/dictionary/cult.

13. Jaci Maraschin, *The Transient Body: Sensibility and Spirituality*, paper presented at the event "Liturgy and Body," Union Theological Seminary, New York, October 20, 2003.

14. Leonardo Boff, *Essential Care. An Ethics of Human Nature*, trans. Alexandre Guilherme (Waco: Baylor University Press, 2008), 138–139.

15. See also Larry L. Rasmussen, *Earth-Honoring Faith: Religious Ethics in a New Key* (Oxford: Oxford University Press, 2015).

Chapter 12

Liturgy after the Abuse

Stephen Burns

In this chapter, I explore two foci within my own disciplines of liturgical and pastoral theology and try to think into some questions and possibilities that the legacy of church-based abuse might provoke for ministry practice and for Christian worship. My foci are only fragments, but I hope that they signal the depth of challenges yet to be faced within my fields.

I find my way into this by recalling the work of Ann Loades, among others, whose own writing on child sexual abuse was among the first theological engagements with the problem. Loades is important because she first wrote about the issue on the initial cusp of major publicity about abuse in church-based contexts. While there has in the meantime been some sensitive work on ministry with individuals affected by abuse,[1] very little reflection has stretched to the implications of growing public concern and mistrust of the church as a result of abuse by its representatives. So in what follows, I open up some thought on public symbols of ministry and practices of public worship which seem to me to now invite some new thinking.

SCOPE

As Ann Loades reminds, "ill-treatment [of children] rarely causes human beings sufficient disturbance to generate momentum for change," drawing this insight from what she herself describes as the "disturbing" work of Nigel Parton.[2] Her own disturbance, writing as she was at the turn of the millennium, places her near the beginning of Christian theologians' attempts to tackle this difficult topic. Her earlier papers, "A Climate of Oppression" and "Thinking about Child Sexual Abuse" of 1993 and 1994, respectively,[3] make her the first academic theologian in the UK to take on this agenda. In the United States, recognition of child sexual abuse (CSA) marked, though is not the focus of, some earlier theological work, such as Mary Pelleaur, Barbara Chester, and Jane Boyajian's *Sexual Assault and Abuse: A Handbook for Clergy and Religious Professionals* of 1987. Notably, the theologians named earlier—the first to be disturbed by child abuse, or at least to write about it—are all women, and indeed all firmly self-identify as feminist. One might hope that by now, late in the second decade of the new century, wider disturbance about abuse of children would have generated momentum for change in conditions that made church-based abuse possible. But theological disciplines have still *not* engaged deeply with the problem, and so this essay is one attempt to let my own disturbance stir some questions about change and cause some disruption in my own academic areas, as I think needs to happen right across the curriculum.

As it was, Loades's work accompanied then still fresh—and as yet unabated—revelations of sexual abuse in the context of the churches. In the United States, CSA in the Roman Catholic Church had begun to be publicized in 1985, with what was identified as a single instance in the diocese of Lafayette. Others followed in the 1990s in the like of Boston and Dallas.[4] Boston was again a focus in 2002, ironically from January 6, the Feast of the Epiphany, with the beginning of decisive revelations in the *Boston Globe*, the story of which are told in an understated way in the recent (2015) major movie *Spotlight*—itself just one instance of continuing public interest and concern about the issues it confronts. Once the Boston story was picked up by the *New York Times* "the firestorm from Boston swept across the country"[5] unearthing similar incidents. In the first decade of the new millennium multimillion-dollar lawsuits were being raised against dioceses across the United States that had sheltered dozens of abusers, exposing hundreds of victims.[6]

Neither the Roman Catholic Church nor the North American continent have been the only contexts for church-based abuse of children, with the (albeit Roman) church in Ireland providing a significant incidence of a wider phenomenon, provoking a public apology from the then-pope, Benedict XVI, in 2010. In fact, *Irish Times* had been investigating abuse in the church for as long as reporters at the *Boston Globe* on the other side of the Atlantic, and it transpired that abuse in Ireland stretched back at least until the 1980s when church-based abuse first began to be named in the United States. The movie *Spotlight* in fact ends with a (long) list of places in which church-based abuse has been uncovered.[7] In my own current setting in Australia, church-based abuse is a major current issue, with just the last months of 2017 involving two major scandals, one concerning the Roman Catholic diocese of Ballarat in northern Victoria, the other engulfing the Anglican diocese of Newcastle in New South Wales.

ELABORATIONS

The preceding information is important because understanding the scope of abuse—both geographical and numerical—can be one important way of beginning to become appropriately disturbed about it. And some important points should be made to clarify and elaborate those that I have made thus far. First, while I have given a brief account of revelation of abuse across the churches, it needs to be acknowledged that not all of the abuse just mentioned is of the same kind. While sexual abuse is clearly a feature in church-based contexts, physical abuse has also been a significant problem in some religious institutions. So it is important to recognize that "abuse" is not only a reference to sexual misdemeanor—indeed, it can refer quite widely, as in the National (British) Society for the Protection of Children's clarifying multiple definitions: domestic abuse, sexual abuse, neglect, online abuse, physical abuse, emotional abuse, child sexual exploitation, female genital mutilation, (cyber-) bullying, child trafficking, grooming, and harmful sexual behavior.[8] Questions can be asked about the lines between some of these and the authoritarian style that marks some churches in order to begin to explicate how churches could have become contexts in which abuse could occur.

Second, much of the abuse that has been and is reported in church-based contexts is "historic," that is referring to past episodes. The churches may now at least oftentimes have better processes in place both for screening candidates and reporting violations, but evidently there are dynamics in church life that have prohibited disclosure. These dynamics are wrapped up with at least how power operates, how secrecy has been fostered in certain practices of leadership, unexamined and uncontested gender prejudice in texts and doctrines, and stigmas around nonprescribed sexual behaviors. Abuse in the Anglican Church of Australia, for example, has taken, on average, 23.7 years to disclose, with a notably longer time lapse for male than female victims, perhaps because boys and men have received less family support on disclosure than women and girls, or because of the persistence of the idea that abused persons inevitably themselves become abusers, a lie that is quite likely to make disclosure more difficult.[9] In any case, many who come to speak of abuse are, in Jean Renvoise's term, "remembering abuse with concern"[10] and facing not only the abuse itself but its hidden legacy through years of nondisclosure. It also needs to be recognized that in at least some cases specific incidents of abuse were begun with "grooming," which the National Society for the Protection of Children rightly includes among categories of abuse. Abuse needs, then, to be seen across a long context that may encircle both before and after specific incidents.

Third, the aftermath of abuse is multifaceted and includes at least further trauma from bungled response to disclosure and, as has been widely noted as a matter of concern in a wide range of contexts, insufficient responses by church authorities. As one Roman Catholic priest from the United States put it, "While some did what they did, others looked away."[11] In the 1985 case in Lafayette, Louisiana, for example, church authorities did not report abuse to the police, a pattern which continued elsewhere. Joseph Bernardin, cardinal in Chicago, was the first bishop to appoint a board (significantly comprised mainly of laypeople) to investigate charges of church-based abuse, but this was in 1992, and it was then another ten years until the U.S. Conference of Catholic Bishops acted in concert to facilitate anything akin across the country, with their Charter for the Protection of Children and Young People and establishment of a National Review Board.[12] Even as they eventually did, the "zero tolerance" policy of the charter they authorized received much criticism, not least from priests who felt themselves to be wrongly exposed, with bishops "aggressive" toward them, "selling them out" in order to "cover" themselves.[13] That is to say that whatever measures to "safeguard" were put in place were also felt to undermine trust in dioceses, with lack of trust in church hierarchies remaining as an enduring feature of the situation in which the churches now find themselves. It must also be noted, however, that, in perhaps rare cases, it has been bishops who have promoted disclosure over-against aggressive cultures of secrecy among the clergy and other leaders. Greg Thompson, Anglican bishop of Newcastle (New South Wales, Australia), reported to the Royal Commission a culture of "life turned in on itself" within the diocese to which he came as bishop, and of encountering racket-like dynamics of collusion and silencing. In a most moving episode in the Royal Commission, the bishop—who himself confessed to being a survivor of church-based abuse—was addressed by the chair of the commission in the following, understated, way:

20 Q. Now, there is an expression, Bishop, "Cometh the hour,
21 cometh the man." Without wanting to embarrass you, it
22 would appear that as a consequence of your long-held
23 philosophical belief that the church should be a vehicle
24 for promoting social justice rather than pomp and ceremony,
25 your clear and unambiguous public support of those who have
26 been subjected to child sexual abuse, your continuing
27 support, in often stormy waters, of the commitment and work
28 of Mr Cleary and Bishop Peter as the Diocesan Executive and
29 Mr Elliott as the Professional Standards Director in this
30 area, and the courage and leadership which you have shown
31 in coming forward and making public your own abuse to
32 provide an example to others that they can do the same, you
33 seem to have given a voice to people who could not

34 previously speak, or perhaps in some cases could speak but
35 could not be heard. If I might be permitted an indulgence,
36 can I say that that fact, in combination with the pastoral
37 care and support that you have provided directly and in
38 good grace, whether on the streets of Newcastle or in the
39 corridors of this Royal Commission, to many survivors of
40 abuse and their families—I think it can be fairly said
41 that there are many people who would be very pleased that
42 you did come to this Diocese and at the hour in which you
43 did.
44 A. And I've drawn courage from them.[14]

Fourth, abuse revealed from the 1980s has some continuities with earlier phenomena, and not least social problems that those who might respectfully be labeled proto-feminists (and who were sometimes associated with the churches) made to counter such problems. Mary Wollstonecraft and Josephine Butler, for example, were, as Ann Loades again reminds, women who strived to change attitudes and legislation around marginalized women and children vulnerable in their own day, working, in their cases, to raise the age of consent, to establish the Sexual Diseases Act, and so on. It is significant, then, that feminist theology has so far been the main theological discipline to focus on abuse. But even then, it must be admitted, only sometimes, or by some. Some versions of feminist theology have not made much room for children—being, in Loades's judgment, "introspective," "narrowly self-referential," "narcissistic and self-absorbed"—while others have been key in advocacy, representing the kind of "enlarged feminism"[15] of which Loades finds germs in Wollstonecraft and Butler, and herself seeks to represent. Significantly, it is *religious* feminism that Loades finds able to promote a necessary "requirement to think beyond one's immediate concerns"[16] if abuse is to be tackled in the public realm—though the hope that this dynamic is always present with religious faith would not appear to be obviously borne out in all biblical study or systematic theology, at least with respect to this topic, which has gone largely ignored. But the contribution of feminist theology challenges not only what might sadly be expected to be patriarchally freighted modes of theology, but feminist theology's nearer neighbors like liberation and postcolonial theologies, which are each in their own way grounded in conviction about listening to the marginalized and subaltern but have not as yet used their resources as it might be imagined they could to consider and contest the abuse of children.

TESTIMONY

As and when theologians of whatever "school" start to listen to experience of abuse, there will be plenty of reasons to become appropriately disturbed. Hearing the testimony of those who find the courage to tell of their own experience can "humanize" statistics,[17] but conversely, at least potentially have a salacious aspect,[18] or else desensitize because it is so overwhelming. I have chosen just two fragments of testimony to give pause to my reflections, so that the speakers' words stand in clear relief. A victim's comment, recorded in Tracey Hansen's *Seven for a Secret That's Never Been Told*, is that "when I think of God the Father, I think of a man with a penis";[19] and then, from a statement made by Andrew Collins, an Australian victim traveling to Rome in 2016 to witness Cardinal George Pell's video-linked Royal Commission appearance, "we'll see all the crucifixes and collars and we'll be triggered."[20] Even these two brief comments confront core Christian symbols of God and the cross, and while another focus mentioned—clerical collars—can hardly be deemed central, because it is associated with some people's notions of supposedly "sacred persons," it cuts close to the heart of some views of divine mediation. In what follows, I want to engage these fragments in order to lever rethinking in my own fields of theology, to track some ways in which I at least have come to be disturbed by the lack of impact abuse has made on theological content in my own disciplines.

BROKEN SYMBOL

In the early 1990s, when Loades started writing about abuse, important books on church and ministry seemed undisturbed (or unaware) of the problem. Writings that could identify multiple "demands of the present" could make no reference to abuse.[21] This is harder to imagine in light of the interval of time since then. For example, Gautier et al.'s study of changes in the Roman Catholic ordained priesthood since Vatican II, a large amount of space is given to the impact of sexual abuse scandals in the church. Many priests in their study report their efforts to engage with the anger of persons both within the church and from the wider public. In parish life, "people were *really* pissed off,"[22] sometimes stopping their financial support if not stopping their attendance. In interactions with "strangers and the public" few met "naked hostility" but many felt "nervous" and "more wary" and some met "vitriol." This was especially so when wearing clerical collars, which variously evoked the sense of being an "invisible man," ignored, or else stared at with suspicion, either way uncomfortable, judged, and out of place. For example, clergy began to notice that others would not establish eye contact with them. Consequently, some clergy felt "ashamed" to wear representative dress in public spaces. Such sensibilities were by no means universal, and could indeed sometimes be quite minimal, especially in small-town communities where clergy were already well known so that "it doesn't matter what you wear" anyway.[23] In other places, however, especially where abuse was concentrated, the situation was very different. In Boston, for instance, priests reported not going out in their collar, as well as a sense of the church now "hunkered down into bunkers."[24]

These comments raise the interesting possibility that a symbol intended as a marker in public space (clerical collars are not liturgical vesture) had, at least sometimes, become a countersign. In Australia, among Roman Catholic priests at least, clerical attire had already become less used than elsewhere[25] such that Pope John Paul II had long ago written publicly in a so-called Statement of Conclusions of his concern about the loss of such attire as an example of what he perceived as needing greater differentiation between lay and ordained persons. Of course, not wearing collars did not and would not stop abuse, but after the abuse, the collar may have at least sometimes become a repellent, rather than, as in more favorable interpretations, an invitation to ministry. Some dogged wearers of the collar might now be unaware that it can hold pastoral engagement with others at arm's length—inhibiting it.

In this context, John Spong's reflection on what he calls the "haberdashery worn by the ordained"[26] may be apt. In his provocatively titled *Why Christianity Must Change or Die*, he is concerned about more central matters than such haberdashery but at one point reflects his assent to the idea of Richard Holloway, one-time primate of the Episcopal Church in Scotland, who enjoined his colleagues to ditch episcopal attire on account of its medieval and royal content. His particular target was, then, not the clerical collar but the like of the mitre, a hat that is a "thinly disguised crown." Likewise, he identified the cope, "an ecclesiastical version of the king's royal cape," and also ring, with its associations with a royal signet ring, and crozier, akin to royal staff, and chair, which is sometimes called a throne, at which in ritual others may kneel at the bishop's feet. Spong identifies this haberdashery among "dying church customs," means of bishops "fooling" themselves, for while these symbols may somehow have spoken more appropriately "in an era of ecclesiastical dominance," in the current time in which "the opinions of bishops on most subjects are widely ignored," they may not. Spong is forthright in his view that "our costumes seek to disguise the fact that we are engaged in a massively irrelevant charade of enormous pretension," and he assents to Holloway's suggestion: "Why not gather on the banks of the river Thames," at the Lambeth Conference, "and hurl our medieval mitres into its dark waters and be done with them forever?"[27] In his autobiography *Leaving Alexandria*, Richard Holloway reports that he did indeed throw his mitre into the river, this being his only "sweet memory" of the notorious 1998 Lambeth

Conference, which as he saw it had effectively proclaimed that "God hates fags."[28] Over time, Holloway "wanted nothing more to do with the men in pink dresses and their vehement opinions."[29]

One does not need to agree with either Holloway or Spong on these or other points they make to recognize that the symbols to which they refer are broken. But notably, even in the end matter of *Why Christianity Must Change or Die* John Spong is photographed in a clerical collar. Maybe the time has come to add that to the list of things to ditch?

At the same time, and more importantly, much more than attire needs to change. I am struck by how a local personality in my city has recently spoken of her "elation" and "relief" that a Roman Catholic Church building near my home was attacked and destroyed by an arsonist.[30] The church had been a center of abuse in which friends in the celebrity's circle had been victimized. She had herself attended the church as a child, witnessed the abuse of peers and friends, been caught up in the trauma caused to the community, moved away but somehow managed to retain a discipline of worship elsewhere, and could appreciate the destruction of this building. There may be little love lost, not only among strangers and the public but also those who retain some connection with Christian communities, for some so-called sacred symbols.

In *Becoming the Sign*, with its significant subtitle "Sacramental Living in a Post-conciliar Church," Kathleen Hughes narrates how Joseph Bernardin, the cardinal of Chicago (already mentioned), conducted himself on parish visits. We may see in the story something of the culture he tried to foster and in which the lay leadership that emerged, not least in investigating abuse allegations, was well fit. Before leading a rite of, or preaching on, reconciliation, Bernardin would ask forgiveness for his own sins and failings. He would also, as representative of the church, ask for forgiveness of damage done by the church: any harsh treatment, cause for scandal, withholding of love and unwelcoming behavior. *Only then* would he see himself as ready and able to lead a rite that invited the people to face their own sins.[31] Whatever clothes he wore for such occasions, his behavior represents a wise move away from the subtexts of medieval and regal plumage.

PITCHING THE SCRIPT

Apart from anything else, Hughes's story about Bernardin encourages some critical scrutiny of worship: how power-distance is maintained or collapsed, accountability is depicted, and values are affirmed in ritual inscriptions. The force of the comment made in Hansen's *Seven for a Secret* might be better felt by noting, as does Gail Ramshaw, that of all the "authorised rites of the Anglican Communion" in the twenty-first century the address to God as mother appears only once in Anglican churches anywhere around the world.[32] At the same time, it needs to be acknowledged that ditching metaphors of fatherhood and switching in maternal ones is unlikely in and of itself to help stifle and tackle abuse. While, clearly, an "omnipotent Father-God who is free to do what he likes" is a highly problematic model for fatherhood if it "licenses some fathers to interpret controlling and abusive power as an expression of love,"[33] the substantive challenge in changing this is *both* to construct "father" "in terms of intimacy, presence, protection where needed, willingness to listen, and availability,"[34] *and* to ensure that it is possible for mothers to have a developed sense of self in which they are not subject to patriarchal "lords."[35] In that respect, imaging God as mother may help but more than liturgical tinkering is needed.

The comment in Hansen's book about paternal imagery of God also raises questions not only about the "content" of prayers[36]—their metaphors and requests and so on—but the very forms in which prayers are voiced. In her remarkable book *Praying With Our Eyes Open*, Marjorie Procter-Smith considers among other things, "the need for heteroglossia" in resistance to "unison prayer," that being things said in common, scripted for the assembly.[37] Interestingly, even the most creative of examples of feminist liturgy in the like of Rosemary Redford Ruether's *Women-Church*—with its rites for crones or coming out as lesbian or other things for which official ecclesial resources do not provide—assume this "unison" mode of participation. But Procter-Smith points clearly to problems with it. Whatever its content, it runs the risk of becoming "patriarchal discourse," putting the "right" words into people's mouths. Unison texts, sometimes in bold-type—or most revealingly prefaced by "All":—assume "unified voice," "unitary discourse." Here is an example, and one I find particularly disturbing for being specially identified as suitable "when children are present":

> God our Shepherd, / we are lost in the darkness and danger of sin. / We are hungry and afraid, / and we cannot find our own way home. / We are sorry for our sins. / Search for us, / save us, / forgive us, / and bring us back to life, we pray, / through Jesus Christ our Lord. Amen.[38]

This is troubling not least because while replacing some patriarchal imagery (we have a "lord" but not a "father" and instead a "shepherd") it concentrates images of lostness, fear, and danger, juxtaposed to speech of "our sins," in a way that I can barely imagine being helpful to children, let alone abused ones, those who are certainly in need of being "saved" from distress because they are at the mercy of threatening and frightening others.

Procter-Smith links unison prayer to Nancy Jay's description of "A-Not A" thinking (which might also be associated with borderline personality traits) which thrives not only on dichotomy but exclusion, and Procter-Smith deftly makes the point that early attempts at unification of the church's public prayer coincided with repression of women's leadership as well as identification of women with heresy.[39] A unitary voice, she continues, can serve as "a defence against critics and attackers," confirming group identity, and operating as a means of setting boundaries. These dynamics conspire to suppress difference and dissent. But as Procter-Smith also points out in her own contribution to counter-hegemony, univocality can only be a *desire* because it is never actually achievable, "because of the diversity of participants."[40] As she attests, supposed pray-ers may be "defecting in place" as well they might need to when faced with such as the shepherd prayer mentioned, for example. Feminists, she avers and I agree, can teach ways of "praying between the lines," refusing to join in, uttering alternatives, and countering the dominance toward which unison text can tend. While one might be concerned about the place of unison prayer—and especially confession—for victims and survivors of abuse themselves, given reports of deeper "resistance" to church teachings in the light of the church's own clear moral failings in responding to revelations of abuse and the embrace of dysfunctional dynamics of silencing and denial about that abuse, unison prayer may do well to be reduced, if not pitched into the Mississippi, Tiber, Thames, or some other nearby watercourse along with the haberdashery. At the very least, I think unison prayer needs to revise the prefix "All": for something, albeit more cumbersome, more open-ended, seeking consent and not assuming agreement, like "Some/one/none/those so moved."

ENDING

My foci are only fragments, but even matters like clerical dress and unison prayer face challenges in the aftermath of church-based abuse, not only because they may "trigger" memory of traumatic events, or muddle appropriate navigation of sin, fault, blame, forgiveness, and a marsh of difficult concepts that cluster around confession by particular individuals. It is also now important to engage the depth of changed perceptions of the church and its representatives in the wider public and consider how symbols of ministry and invitations to unison prayer are perceived. Questions should be squared up against symbols of privilege associated with hierarchy and marking power-distance as well as scripted means of participation that smother and suppress what persons have to say for themselves. This is especially so if what people might have to say dissents from what are purported as moral truths by an organization that has damaged its own moral standing not only for including abusers in its ranks but also sometimes responding to abuse so ambiguously. So I have raised some of my questions for discernment.

NOTES

1. This includes attention to approaches to forgiveness as this is engaged in sacramental reconciliation and pastoral counselling. For some of my own attempts to think into this, see Stephen Burns, "Forgiveness in Challenging Circumstances," in *Forgiveness in Context: Theology and Psychology in Creative Dialogue*, ed. Fraser Watts and Elizabeth Gulliford (London: Continuum, 2004), 144–159.

2. Ann Loades, *Feminist Theology: Voices from the Past* (Oxford: Polity, 2001), 140.

3. "A Climate of Oppression: Is That All?" was the address at the inaugural gathering of Christian Survivors of Sexual Abuse. See Ann Loades, *Thinking about Child Sexual Abuse: The John Coffin Memorial Lecture (11 January 1994)* (London: University of London, 1994).

4. Jason Berry, *Lead Us Not Into Temptation: Catholic Priests and the Sexual Abuse of Children* (New York: Doubleday, 1992).

5. Mary L. Gautier, Paul M. Perl, and Stephen J. Fichter, *Same Call, Different Men: The Evolution of the Priesthood since Vatican II* (Collegeville, MN: Liturgical Press, 2012).

6. See https://www.ncronline.org/news/accountability/ncr-research-costs-sex-abuse-crisis-us-church-underestimated (accessed January 31, 2017).

7. See http://www.abc.net.au/news/2016-03-01/mcphillips-spotlight-on-the-church/7210404 (accessed January 31, 2017). The author of this informative piece is post-Christian feminist theologian Kathleen McPhillips.

8. https://www.nspcc.org.uk/preventing-abuse/child-abuse-and-neglect/ (accessed January 31, 2017).

9. Because "growing up in abusive family environments can teach children that the use of violence and aggression is a viable means for dealing with interpersonal conflict, which can increase the likelihood that the cycle of violence will continue when they reach adulthood," it is the case that some physically maltreated children are at greater risk of intergenerational abuse than those who were not maltreated in childhood, but it is clearly the case that the majority of maltreated children do not then maltreat children. For some pointers to current research, see https://aifs.gov.au/cfca/publications/effects-child-abuse-and-neglect-adult-survivors (accessed January 31, 2017).

10. Jean Renvoise, *Innocence Destroyed* (London: Routledge, 1993), 75.

11. Gautier et al., *Same Call, Different Men*, 114.

12. http://www.usccb.org/issues-and-action/child-and-youth-protection/charter.cfm (accessed January 31, 2017).

13. Gautier et al., *Same Call, Different Men*, 128–129.

14. https://www.childabuseroyalcommission.gov.au/downloadfile.ashx?guid=caf3421a-6ccc-451b-9628-ac318caeb354&type=transcriptdoc&filename=Transcript-(

Day-231)&fileextension=doc). The numbering on the left-hand column shows part of the transcript line reference. For another example, see https://www.irishtimes.co m/news/social-affairs/religion-and-beliefs/diarmuid-martin-remains-a-maverick-am ong-the-clergy-1.2746903 (accessed January 31, 2017).

15. Loades, *Feminist Theology*, 165, 3.

16. Ibid., 3.

17. I continue to much appreciate John Vincent's insistence that an "anatomy" of deprivation has "faces," and the importance of emphasising not abstract conditions but, for instance, segregated *people*, derelict *human* environment, and so on. See John Vincent, *Hope from the City* (Peterborough: Epworth Press, 2000), 15.

18. Close to what Lauren McGrow calls "tragedy porn." Lauren McGrow, "Doing It (Feminist Theology and Faith-Based Outreach) with Sex Workers—Beyond Christian Rescue and the Problem-Solving Approach," *Feminist Theology* 25 (2017): 150–169.

19. Tracey Hansen, *Seven for a Secret That's Never Been Told* (London: SPCK, 1991), 86.

20. http://www.abc.net.au/news/2016-02-28/child-abuse-survivors-arrive-in-rome-ahead-of-pell-testimony/7205696 (accessed January 31, 2017).

21. Note the influential text by Robin Greenwood especially its chapter "Demands of the Present," with an impressive range of concerns, but abuse never mentioned. See Robin Greenwood, *Transforming Priesthood: A New Theology of Mission and Ministry* (London: SPCK, 1994).

22. Gautier et al., *Same Call, Different Men*, 120.

23. Ibid., 133–135.

24. Ibid., 142. One priest relates seeing a monsignor in Rome, "in full regalia," being "hollered" at by passers-by who were making "all kinds of derogatory comments" (Gautier et al., *Same Call, Different Men*, 121–122).

25. And from personal experience, though from a different tradition, may not have had the intended effect of indicating public presence anyway. I found that younger people sometimes had no idea what it was. For reflection on the Statement of Conclusions, see Stephen Burns, "Formation for Ordained Ministry: Out of Touch?" in *Indigenous Australia and the Unfinished Business of Theology: Cross-Cultural Engagement*, ed. Jione Havea (New York, NY: Palgrave, 2013), 151–166.

26. John Spong, *Why Christianity Must Change or Die* (San Francisco, CA: HarperCollins, 1993), 181.

27. Ibid., 181–182.

28. Richard Holloway, *Leaving Alexandria: A Memoir of Faith and Doubt* (London: Canongate, 2013), 323, 320. Holloway linked his action to Thomas Merton's encouragement to undermine "comfortable and social Catholicism, this lining up of cassocks, this regimenting of birettas," and his (Merton's) own line, "I throw my biretta in the river" (Holloway, *Leaving Alexandria*, 326).

29. Holloway, *Leaving Alexandria*, 341.

30. Stephen Burns, *Pastoral Theology for Public Ministry* (New York, NY: Seabury Press, 2015), ix.

31. Kathleen Hughes, *Becoming the Sign: Sacramental Living in a Post-Conciliar Church* (Mahwah, NJ: Paulist Press, 2013), 5–6.

32. Gail Ramshaw, "A Look at New Anglican Eucharistic Prayers," *Worship* 86 (2012): 161–167.

33. Loades, *Feminist Theology*, 161.

34. Ibid., 162.

35. Ibid., 147.

36. It is striking that the Australian Anglican *A Prayer Book for Australia* (1995) includes a range of "prayers for various occasions," and notably two about "those suffering abuse," as well as one for "those who abuse" (209–210). This makes abuse, apart from ordained ministries, the major focus of this section of the book.

37. Marjorie Procter-Smith, *Praying with Our Eyes Open: Engendering Feminist Liturgical Prayer* (Nashville, TN: Abingdon Press, 1995), 17–40.

38. http://www.anglican.org.au/governance/commissions/documents/liturgy/ho ly%20communion%20for%20children%20shepherd%20theme.pdf (accessed January 31, 2017).

39. Procter-Smith, *Praying with Our Eyes Open*, 26.

40. Ibid.

Chapter 13

Embodied Epistemologies

Queering the Academic Empire

Sarojini Nadar and Sarasvathie Reddy

It is a Friday night at the end of April 2016, and the authors (Saras and Sarojini) are driving to fetch a friend to go watch a show. As they are driving, Sarojini receives a spine-chilling text on her phone—it is from a cherished relative to whom she had, until recently, been a guardian. He was tired of pretending to be a "he." She wanted the world to know who she was but the world did not like her—in fact this world was so violent toward her that on this Friday night she decided to exit it. This was a goodbye note that Sarojini received on her phone. She read the note out aloud to Saras in disbelief. Saras, being trained as an advanced life support paramedic, did not think twice—she swung the car around and headed straight to the little apartment on the rolling hills of KwaZulu-Natal, all the while giving Sarojini instructions about which emergency numbers to call.

They get to the apartment and the scene that unfolds before their eyes is like one from the movies. Saras scales the fence while the rest of the family, who have arrived by then, watch helplessly, and she emerges a few minutes later with a seemingly lifeless body in her arms, shouting instructions about how to get them to the car and to get to the nearest hospital. At the hospital, they try to pump out the liters of acetone and painkillers that were ingested, all the while reminding us that we did not have the necessary medical insurance to assure a stay at this private hospital—a ZAR 60,000 deposit (about US$5,000) could secure us a one night stay in ICU, excluding doctors' fees. Once stabilized, Saras calls a friend from the local emergency services to have her transferred to a public state hospital.

At the public state hospital, Sarojini almost faints at the sight of stabbed and wounded bodies sprawled throughout the emergency ward, nothing unusual on a Friday night in this gangster-ridden, apartheid-created township. Saras talks with the medical doctor on call (one of her ex-students from the medical school where she lectured), while he calmly stuffs his hand into the stab-wound on the neck of a victim to stop him from bleeding. Saras explains "the situation" to the intern doctor, who then explains that spending the weekend in that resource-constrained environment was not advisable for someone who's experiencing this kind of "gender dysphoria," as he described it, and wants to know whether to admit Z (pseudonym) to the male or female ward. Notwithstanding that this is not the ideal environment to leave Z in, we give in to the financial dictates.

A week later, we pick Z up from the hospital and she has to face the world again. The struggle with her bodily dissonance continues, as is evident from an excerpt of a poem she posts on social media not too long after (quoted here with Z's permission):

Lost through visions in a life of paradise
Keeping up an image is never an easy vice
Each time the look lessens, the effort grows
Becoming him when she's all he knows

Drifting, floating, soaring in his life
Hiding, down-sizing, minimizing her life
Finding a balance between he and she
Justice, equality or the life of a wannabe

A step-ford fit in, another face in the crowd
Changing of settings and to lifestyles of the proud
Lost in this hierarchy so traditional, so old
To the rich and surviving in the drought of winters cold

Torn between two worlds, two souls,
two people, two individuals,
two images, two personalities,
two identities, too much, too soon, too needed, too good, too
    bad, too nice, too kind, too much lies, too much,
not enough, too dire, to end, to start, Lets go from John doe, to Jane doe,
    to John once again, to be, for whom, too just, or sudden doom,
too him, too her, to them, to us,
to the sky, to the moon, to the sun, to be gone, to be gone too soon?
To a memory, of a guy, of girl, of a woman, of a man, for technicality, to a baby,
    to a gay, to a Trans, to a queer, to a hidden, to a loss and all for what cost.
I am not who I am because who I am is what I'm not,
forgive me, forget me, remember me, maybe not, to be a him,
who's a her, who's a him or a them,
to go there like they do, when it's not really you,
to be living, to be happy, to love and say it's true, is it
    for him or for her or to me that you refer to.

SEXUAL AND REPRODUCTIVE HEALTH

As we reflected on the events of that April evening, we contemplated the irony of just finishing, on that very same Friday afternoon, the last of the seminars we co-facilitated in the master's program in gender, religion, and health (GRH) at the University of KwaZulu-Natal, South Africa, a program which focused on the intersections of religion with sexual and reproductive health rights. This program was the academic component of a tripartite collaboration between faith leaders and community health outreach, and was funded by the Church of Sweden in three African countries (Ethiopia, Tanzania, and South Africa). The Church of Sweden, the actor from the North (ostensibly and contestably an imperial context), in 2012 identified that the lack of access to sexual and reproductive health rights, which the United Nations articulated in its Millennium Development Goals three, four, and five, was a result of religious and cultural beliefs, and faith leaders' authorities in this area. The concept note circulated to the partners included the following:

> The religious and cultural understanding in a larger number of churches in Africa on issues related to sexual and reproductive health rights (SRHR) and sexual orientation and gender identity (SOGI) has often helped to reduce the ability of men and women to live equally, to decide over their own bodies and sexuality and has limited their reproductive choices. Through the church and church leaders' authority in the African context access to SRHR is not promoted.

The authority of church leaders to control the choices of people to decide over their own bodies and sexuality is exactly the reason why Sarojini had guardianship over Z—a few years earlier she escaped a pastor who tried via her parents to "cast out the demon of femininity from her body." Sarojini's lived experience with Z and the lived experiences Saras and Sarojini shared in the classroom resonate in this collection of essays on body, person, and empire because to truly discern our role as educators in a higher education context is to radically engage and break down bodily binaries—the real and enfleshed bodies of our sexual and gendered selves, and those whom we love, as well as the bodies of knowledge we help to cocreate with our students. Each of these bodies—the physical and the epistemic, the experiential and the intellectual—must, we argue, constantly and radically engage and hold each other accountable if we are to overcome the violence that is done to bodies that are constantly resisting the imperial binaries on their personhood and sense of self.

In that final seminar on that Friday, we focused on the bodies of knowledge that the students were required to engage in for their research which straddled the intersections of three disciplines—gender, religion, and SRHR. The title of this section of the core module we co-facilitated together with a third colleague was called "Intersectionality, Trans-disciplinarity and Intentionality"—the objective was to teach students to work among the disciplines while maintaining integrity of the bodies of knowledge within the disciplines. The students were being taught how to be transdisciplinary with the bodies of knowledge they were learning. The ways in which the GRH curriculum enabled students to demonstrate transdisciplinarity by crossing epistemological, ontological and religious boundaries has been published elsewhere,[1] drawing on Sue McGregor's definition of transdisciplinarity which she frames as,

> an integrated combination of disciplinary work, scholarship between and among disciplines (interdisciplinarity) and knowledge generation beyond academic disciplines and across sectors external to the university (at the interface between the academy and civil society).[2]

Navigating and negotiating between intersectional bodies of knowledge was what we were calling our students' attention to earlier in the day, then we embodied that in this almost lifeless body inscribed with the wounds of empires: a sexuality empire which dictates coherence between our gender and sexual identity; an economic empire which controlled the kind of medical treatment this queer body receives; a religious empire that tells this body she is not a full person created in the image of God. We were trying to make sense of these empires within an academic empire that tells us that our knowledge must be neatly disciplined into packages—what are you really studying? Is it systematic theology? Biblical studies? Surely this belongs in practical theology, and nowhere else? Does such a study even belong in the university? And how do we put this round peg of gender into the square hole of the study of religion and theology? How do we do this while holding this real, seemingly lifeless body in our arms? How do we reconcile "real bodies" (queer and lifeless bodies) with epistemological bodies that we deal with in the classroom?

Drawing from various scholars, Jessica Richard, a master's graduate whom Sarojini supervised in 2010 within the gender and religion program, puts it perfectly:

> Our bodies are not mere coverings of our "real" personhood, but are integral to our personhood. The body is not a vessel but the being itself. The mind and spirit are not higher forms of the body, but methods of the body's workings. Our bodies are basic to our knowing and our understanding of salvation.[3]

As a feminist academic working in the discipline of higher education, Saras is interested in *what* bodies of knowledge are produced and *how* such knowledge is produced within the academy—students often joke that she is the intellectual police officer of the gender and religion program—ensuring that academic standards required at a master's level are met. As a feminist scholar working at the intersections of disciplines, Sarojini is interested in the politics of that knowledge production—who produces the knowledge and for whose benefit is as important as the content of what is produced. Having both worked in the program from 2013 until 2016, where each year, ten new master's students were enrolled in the program, we thought that our task was clear—as feminist teachers in a higher education context, we were developing bodies of knowledge around the embodied realities regarding the lack of access to SRHR. Our understanding did not correlate with the funding body from the North—ostensibly the funding empire. In a review of the "outcomes" of the program, one of the questions we were asked was, "how many lives of mothers and children, do you estimate, have been saved through this intervention program?" Our colleague from Stellenbosch University often answers, firmly tongue in cheek, in response to this overwhelmingly quantitative question, "FIVE." After all, how does one measure the intellectual project in which we are involved?

BACKGROUND TO THE INTELLECTUAL PROJECT: TEACHERS IN THE GRH PROGRAM

How does one measure a shaping of the mind that is informed by lived experiences of the real bodies we encounter in and outside of the classroom? For the purpose of background information and our context as teachers in the GRH program, we will briefly describe what has already been published elsewhere regarding the pedagogical underpinnings of the GRH program and our positioning as teachers. In a roundtable response article entitled "From Instrumentalization to Intellectualisation: Response to Silent Scripts and Contested Spaces,"[4] we reflected on our experiences as black South African women educators involved in teaching and supervising students in the GRH program. The response article focused on our positioning as black women who were working in a "massified" neoliberal global higher education context located in a paradigm that sought to "instrumentalize" knowledge production feeding into the "funding empire." In that piece we reflected on our experiences of teaching in a Global South program that was funded by the partner from the Global North. Harris, Medine, and Rhee who were the authors of the lead-in piece at the roundtable, pointed out that it seemed as if women of color struggled to "establish and maintain" authority.[5] We engaged with this claim by bringing into dialogue two areas of "progress and pedagogy" together with the notion of authority as it related to the GRH program. The first point on progress we were making was that there seems to be a disconnect between how Africa is positioned when it receives aid and how we as African feminist teachers were repositioning ourselves based on the work in which we were engaging with students. We were . . . through an insistence on critical intellectual development *as* development, claiming an authoritative space in the wider context of globalized development for gender and social transformation.[6]

The second point on progress was:

By teaching our students transformative feminist theories that respond to religion, we were, as women of colour, bringing up for scrutiny previously held notions of development and 'progress' shifting these ideas from "instrumentalisation" to "intellectualisation"; to more critical transformative work that undergirds the kind of intellectual development we were interested in enabling our students to acquire.[7]

The postcolonial gaze that we imposed on the development discourse as conceptualized by our partners from the North enabled us to *deconstruct Development and expose the mechanisms and tropes of power which Development as a discourse has in common with colonial discourse and modernity as a project.* It was in the preceding pedagogical ways that we challenged the Northern conceptions of development.

The other focus of the response article was on pedagogy, and our reflections on the pedagogical underpinnings of the GRH program in that article also provides a context for this chapter. It is useful to begin with the overall module outcomes which are taken from the GRH Module Template:[8]

At the end of this module, students will be equipped with knowledge, skills and attitudes to critically assess the intersections of gender, religion and sexual and reproductive health rights. Students will have:

- Knowledge of critical debates at the intersections of gender, religion and sexual and reproductive
- Skills for critical analysis of issues of gender, religion, and sexual and reproductive health rights
- An understanding of and ability to negotiate critical debates in gender, religion and sexual and reproductive health rights.

In the Harris, Medine, and Rhee (2016) lead-in piece that we were responding to, they raised the point that women teachers of color are often questioned about the subject matter that they teach because of the interdisciplinary approaches that are adopted and their challenging of "epistemologies, theories and methods." We shared our own experiences of being questioned about our methods of teaching in the GRH program: "Our methods of teaching disrupt the notion of the 'authoritative' teacher through the cohort model of supervision that we practice in this programme."[9] The teaching approach that is used here represented a paradigm shift from the traditional "master-apprentice" model that the predominantly Western male academy adopted as the norm for research training for many years. What we were replacing this traditional model with was a democratic space embraced by feminist principles of mentoring and collaboration. We created in our classroom a community of learning with no single individual being given any power or authority over another. This paradigm of community learning is aligned with the bodies of knowledge we were invoking within the program: African feminist, queer, and decolonized bodies of knowledge.

BODIES OF KNOWLEDGE OF AFRICAN FEMINISTS AND AFRICAN FEMINISM

In the GRH program we drew from rich and strong, resilient African feminist roots born out of enormous pain and suffering and nurtured by our foremothers. This body of knowledge was birthed long before the funding empire decided that sexual and gender norms are regulated and policed by religious and cultural beliefs. We are fortunate that these roots were anchored for us already in the Circle of Concerned African Women Theologians by scholars such as Mercy Oduyoye, Musimbi Kanyoro, Nyambura Njoroge, Isabel Phiri, and Denise Ackermann, to name a few. These scholars worked tirelessly at the intersections of faith and feminism, concepts which they tirelessly interrogated with all the analytical tools they could muster, in the service of life. And so when we taught in a program such as the GRH, we named and claimed our African feminist roots. Gender is but an analytical tool within feminist discourse, a tool that helps us interrogate power, privilege, and politics. Josephine Ahikre reflects on the recent depoliticization of the feminist project. She says:

> In order to be effective in the global development arena, great effort was put into making feminist change agendas intelligible to bureaucrats and development actors. . . . On the ideological front there is increasing de-politicisation arising out of the false popularity of the term gender. As a result, what Tamale refers to as the "F-word" being increasingly demonised. It is not uncommon to encounter such statements as:
>
> *I am a gender expert but I am not a feminist*
> *I am a gender activist but I do not like feminism*
> *Feminism is a luxury for the west and not for African women*
> *We need a gender consultant who is practical and not abstract.*[10]

We argue that these kinds of statements and this kind of rhetoric is mischief making. We recognize African feminism as a body of knowledge which we have the responsibility of shaping and developing for ourselves and our students. This intersectional feminism birthed knowledge that enhanced and enabled innovative theoretical and methodological paradigms within our students' research. Nowhere is this innovative theoretical and methodological shift clearer than in the research produced by two of our students, who went through the gender and religion program. The two students whose work we choose to present contribute to the body of knowledge that exists on queer bodies in Africa—in particular on gay men in Zambia and South Africa respectively. It is to this body of knowledge that we now turn.

BODIES OF QUEER KNOWLEDGE

We write this section with deep sadness, noting that one of the students whose work we are drawing from in this chapter, Lilly Phiri, died in February 2017 at the age of thirty-three, having just submitted for examination her PhD thesis entitled "'Construction Sites': Exploring Queer Identity and Sexuality at the Intersections of Religion and Culture in Zambia."[11] She graduated posthumously on April 11, 2017. As we explore the body of knowledge Lilly produced, we are painfully aware that while Lilly's body is no more, the body of knowledge she has left behind remains as her legacy.

"'Born This Way': A Gendered Perspective on the Intersectionality between Same-Sex Orientation and the Imago Dei: A Case Study of Men Who Love Other Men in Lusaka-Zambia" was the title of Lilly Phiri's 2013 master's dissertation that identified the issue of "men who have sex with other men" as the public health issue. She looked at this phenomenon through the lenses of postcolonial queer theory and identified that "a plethora of literature about same-sex orientation and the imago Dei reveals that heterosexism is generally regarded as the authentic image of God while same-sex orientation continues to be regarded as an affront to the image of God."[12] She subsequently identified the need to merge the two terms "same-sex orientation" and "imago Dei" in order to deconstruct and reconstruct how sexuality and God are understood within prevailing theologies, using emerging theologies from Zambian Christian "Men who Love other Men."[13] What is noticeable was how she engaged with the public health term "men who have sex with other men" and reinterpreted and converted it to how the men themselves express their orientation as "men who love other men." Hence the significant contribution of this dissertation was to move the public health discourse from "men who have sex with other men" to "men who love other men" by discursively subverting the dominant discourse and replacing it with how the men theologically understood their sexuality. Theologically, the student shifted the paradigm from a "hermeneutic of sexuality" to a "hermeneutic of love."

The purpose of Lilly's PhD study was to examine how gay Christians construct their identities and sexualities within the social contexts of religion and culture in Zambia. Drawing on the African feminist roots of the program, Lilly sought to understand the construction of gay identity in the Zambian context through the lenses of masculinity studies. While masculinity and femininity are explained as hierarchical concepts within feminist theorizing, Lilly increasingly found that masculinity was an unhelpful tool in understanding how her participants understood their identity. In fact, one of her findings was that the gender binary was unhelpful. Her research showed the importance of engaging gender outside of the sex difference binaries which feminism has helped demystify but which queer theorizing is taking to a new level. Thembani Chamane, a master's student in the GRH program who was supervised by Sarojini and Saras, provided a theoretical explanation for the performance of gender. Chamane builds upon Butler's understanding of gender and identity as fluid:[14]

> Regulating gender and sexuality into a social and gender order creates what Butler calls "gender performativity" in line with, and in contrast to heteronormativity and cultural expectations of men and women in the society. . . . Flowing from this arises . . . "Queer Theory" (Butler 1993)[15] [. . . insists] that all sexual behaviors, sexual identities and all categories of normative and defiant sexualities are social constructs. . . . Butler (1993) argues that categories of normative and defiant of sexual behavior are not biological but rather socially constructed. . . . Butler further points out that discrimination against gays is not a function of their sexuality but rather point to a failure to perform according to heterosexual gender norms.[16]

BODIES OF DECOLONIZING KNOWLEDGE

A significant body of work which exists on gay men in Africa portrays gay men largely as victims of homophobia. Thembani's dissertation focused on the coming-out experiences of Zulu, Christian gay men. His research confirmed the literature in the field regarding the struggles and complexities of the coming-out process faced by gay men but challenged the colonial narrative that seeks to valorize the black victim. In fact, his study showed the remarkable agency demonstrated by this group of men in taking ownership and creating a conducive and supportive environment for each other. This study showed the power of such resilience and agency in the face of religious and cultural discrimination. Despite the challenges faced by Zulu gay men, participants from the research affirm that negotiating the boundaries of their

Christian and cultural identity and their sexuality is possible by reconceptualizing their sexuality within a religious and cultural context that emphasizes the concepts of love and compassion as characteristics associated with God. In line with Adriaan van Klinken's work which emphasizes African gay agency,[17] Zulu gay men are reclaiming space and visibility by not divorcing their Christian faith and their cultural beliefs but rather continuing to find their own meaningful contribution by reconciling both their religious and cultural beliefs with their sexual identity.

In his dissertation Thembani argues that LGBTI people are deeply religious; however, their religious beliefs may be viewed by religious authoritative bodies as sinful. He further states,

> Togarassei and Chitando [2011][18] point out that the Bible plays a major role in influencing attitudes towards same-sex relationship in Africa in general. . . . It continues without saying that, how the Bible is read, understood and acted upon will continue to be a major reference in debates on same-sex relationships and on people of different sexual orientation. West et al [2016][19] points out that there is an important role for critical Biblical scholarship to expose the problems with using the Bible against same-sex relationship. It is the popular Bible readings of Leviticus and some of Paul's statements that continue to be used to condemn homosexuality. Critical engagement in the discourse of sexuality remain crucial in the context of contextual reading and interpretation of scriptures.[20]

The bodies of queer and decolonial knowledge produced by these two students show their intellectual sophistication in talking back to an empire that dictates not just what knowledge is produced but how such knowledge is produced. Their works show the importance of recognizing intellectual development as development!

CONCLUSION

In asking us "how many bodies were saved" a funding empire that seeks to quantify salvation not only misses the importance of bodies of knowledge we birthed in the program but entrenches the image of the white male university professor—at worst distanced from his students and society in a hierarchical relationship of master-apprentice, and at best the paternalistic savior offering solutions akin to Gayatri Spivak's "white men saving brown women from brown men."[21] As black feminist teachers we were trying to model something different not just through our embodied identities and presence in the classroom but through the bodies of knowledge we were cocreating. Bodies of knowledge produced on the authority and power of faith traditions in both maintaining and critiquing normative social and cultural ideals of gender and sexuality cannot be determined from the outside—by a funder. The sexual revolution will be African feminist, embodied, queer, and decolonial.

NOTES

1. Sarojini Nadar and Sarasvathie Reddy, "Undoing 'Protective Scientism' in a Gender, Religion and Health Masters Curriculum," in *Disrupting Higher Education Curriculum*, ed. Michael A. Samuel et al. (Rotterdam/Boston/Taipei: Sense Publishers, 2016), 229–245.

2. Sue McGregor, "Transdisciplinary Methodology," *International Journal of Home Economics* 4.2 (2011): 105.

3. Jessica Richard, "Resisting Bodies as a Hermeneutical Tool for a Critical Feminist Christology of Liberation and Transformation" (Masters diss., University of KwaZulu-Natal, 2010), 10.

4. Nadar and Reddy, "Undoing 'Protective Scientism,'" 229–245.

5. Harris, Medine and Rhee (2016, 105).

6. Nadar and Reddy, "Undoing 'Protective Scientism,'" 138–139.

7. Ibid.

8. Gender, Religion and Health Masters Module Template, University of Kwa-Zulu-Natal (2015).

9. Nadar and Reddy, "Undoing 'Protective Scientism,'" 140.

10. Josephine Ahikire, "African Feminism in Context: Reflections on the Legitimation Battles, Victories and Reversals," *Feminist Africa* 19 (2014): 7–23.

11. Lilly Phiri, "Exploring Queer Identity and Sexuality at the Intersections of Religion and Culture in Zambia" (PhD diss., University of KwaZulu-Natal, 2017).

12. Lilly Phiri, "Born This Way—A Gendered Perspective on the Intersectionality Between Same-Sex Orientation and the Imago Dei: A Case Study of Men Who Love Other Men in Lusaka-Zambia" (Masters diss., University of KwaZulu-Natal, 2013), viii.

13. Ibid., viii.

14. Judith Butler, *Gender Trouble: Feminism and Subversion of Identity* (New York: Routledge, 2011).

15. Judith Butler, "Critically Queer," *GLQ: A Journal of Lesbian and Gay Studies* 1.1 (1993): 17–32.

16. Thembani Bright Chamane, "An Exploration of How Zulu Gay Men Negotiate Their Christian and Cultural Beliefs in the Process of Coming Out" (Master's Diss., 2017), 21.

17. Adriaan Van Klinken, "Queer Love in a 'Christian nation': Zambian Gay Men Negotiating Sexual and Religious Identities," *Journal of the American Academy of Religion* 83.4 (2015): 947–964.

18. Lovemore Togarasei and Ezra Chitando, "Beyond the Bible: Critical Reflections on the Contributions of Cultural and Postcolonial Studies on Same-Sex Relationships in Africa," *Journal of Gender and Religion in Africa* 17.2 (2011): 109–125.

19. Gerald West, Charlene Van der Walt, and Kapya John Kaoma, "When Faith Does Violence: Reimagining Engagement between Churches and LGBTI Groups on Homophobia in Africa," *HTS Theological Studies* 72.1 (2016): 1–8.

20. Chamane, *An Exploration of How Zulu Gay Men Negotiate Their Christian and Cultural Beliefs*, 43.

21. Gayatri Chakravorty Spivak, "Can the Subaltern Speak?" in *Can the Subaltern Speak? Reflections on the History of an Idea* (New York: Columbia University Press, 2010): 21–78.

Chapter 14

Esse Quam Videri . . . to
Be and Not to Seem

Jenny Te Paa Daniel

In early 2017, as many in the United States and around the world were expressing unbounded angst about what the U.S. presidential election had unleashed on that nation and the world, there was just one short commentary in the veritable torrent of public media critique that especially touched my theological educator's heart.

The occasion was soon after the inauguration. Trump invited a select and primarily deeply conservative group of religious leaders to the White House. In they poured like grateful puppies eager simply to sniff around inside the grand kennel of power. William Barber II, in his always trenchant but powerfully theologically reasoned way, not only echoed my disgust at the spectacle but more so expressed the deeper obscenity of seeing so many senior faith leaders so obviously utterly seduced by their experience of proximity to secular power. Virtually without exception apart from their cringe-worthy photo op with Trump, they presented themselves as submissive, acquiescent, lacking in courage:

> [T]he awkward silence of so-called faith leaders as they listened
>   to a braggart drone on about himself was revelatory.
> The emperor had no clothes, but there wasn't a prophet in the house who
>   was prepared, like the boy in the story, to point out the obvious.[1]

Indeed, there was not on that occasion nor since from any one of the leaders gathered as much as a prophetic word related to any one of the myriad issues affecting those most vulnerable in U.S. society, there have since been no voices of outrage raised, no overturned tables, nothing, just shameless fawning and faking at the feet of the emperor.

For a long time now, I have been crying out in what often feels like the theological education wilderness at the way in which our very own intellectual enterprise is proving to be complicit in producing such leaders. Leaders that are ill-equipped for the pressing demands of Christlike ministry, in particular, are utterly ill-equipped for the offering of ministry with and for those who are the least among us.

For nearly twenty-five years I worked first as a teacher and then as dean of an Anglican seminary in Aotearoa, New Zealand. During my tenure I struggled relentlessly as a pioneering lay indigenous woman theological educator, as a faith-filled activist Anglican, to persuade my colleagues, my board, my church, that the traditional unapologetically Eurocentric means of devising, delivering, and validating theological education was systemically outdated, outmoded, unjust.

I insisted ad nauseum that their collective failure to recognize the monumental insufficiencies within their epistemological assumptions, institutional structures, and skewed geographical frames of reference rendered us all complicit with the insidious oppressions of ongoing colonial imperialism.

I insisted ad nauseum that as self-respecting twenty-first-century postcolonial Christians and theological educators we ought to be capable of articulating with Gospel confidence our understanding of how all elaborations of knowledge including theological knowledge always reflect dominant power interests. Following on from this we ought also to have been the first to adopt scholarly practices committed to equitable and mutually beneficial forms of collaboration with subaltern individuals and communities. How else would the long-standing Eurocentric hegemonies so deeply entrenched in theological curricula, pedagogy, assessment, and accrediting ever be disrupted, exposed, and transformed?

For good measure I suggested ever so politely that I thought the primary focus of theological education ought not be abstract theorizing about the meaning of God, the history of the church, the personhood of Christ, or the complexity of biblical studies but should also and predominantly be about a search for justice, liberation, and human transformation in the face of brutally dehumanizing forms of oppression and increased human suffering in the world.

It seemed self-evident to me that surely of all the academic disciplines, with its unassailable literary franchise on all the good words such as justice, freedom, liberation, equality, compassion, mercy, truth, and so on, that theology in the hands of faith-filled theologians ought to be opened to the postcolonial task of reexamining its hegemonic, North Atlantic-dominated intellectual tradition, one so uncritically perpetuated as the theological educational systems of both the old and new empires. Surely (I figured) seminaries would be concerned to critically address the colonial biases of their entire institutional base to become more appropriately polyvocal, receptive to and empowering of global cultures and epistemologies.

I was wrong. After thirty years of valiant struggle, I can confidently report that still too many theological seminaries across the denominational spectrum are to the largest extent not open to the kind of radical critique, let alone transformation, I have long been suggesting.[2] The extent therefore to which empire even in supposedly postcolonial institutions of higher learning continues to render traditional seminary-based theological education so bereft of context, validity, creativity, relevance, transformative power.

It is still extremely rare to find leaders prepared to radically disrupt the received intellectual and theological "traditions" of their seminaries especially since most who do dare end up as I did. They find themselves constantly on the receiving end of relentless clerical bullying, collegial undermining, and ecclesial outrage for "daring" to suggest there is just possibly a problem in the seminary household with racism, sexism, clericalism, and homophobia![3]

And yes, politically, this reluctance to be disruptive is to do with empire and hegemony, domination and oppression, patriarchy and imperialism, and so, inevitably, all of these structural injustices are also increasingly finding expression in the personal. In today's completely skewed moral universe, even the personal within seminaries has so ironically resulted in professional relationships becoming devoid of decency, kindness, courage, intellectual solidarity, empathy, and indeed, often, of Christian love. Is it really any wonder that women, especially indigenous women and women of color, are utterly underrepresented in seminary leadership?

The "pain" of recognizing my "wrongness," far from deterring me, has only increased my determination to figure a way of redeeming my beloved academic field, my beloved academic profession, and my beloved academic institutions. Just like Atticus Finch in Harper Lee's enduring novel *To Kill a Mocking Bird*, I figured that although "I maybe licked before I begin, I am going to begin anyway and see it through no matter what."[4]

DARING THEOLOGICAL EDUCATION

More recently it was in contemplating the words *Esse Quam Videri*—to Be and Not to Seem—that I was inspired to think anew about how best to confront what I see as an acute level of hypocrisy and professional malaise in much of the leadership of traditional seminary-based theological education. By this I mean the entire structure of leadership, not simply individual leaders.

If only theological education would *dare* to be what it ought to be. If only theological education would no longer be content with its largely colonially derived monolingual and monocultural façades—façades which so cleverly mask the deeply embedded injustices of racism, sexism, classism, homophobia. If only theological education would *dare to be* and not simply to *seem to be* the authoritative intellectual enterprise responsible for explaining and enabling the radically compassionate activist nature of God and of God's sacred relation to the world.

Justo Gonzalez's enduring quote from his book *Mañana* encapsulates something of my exasperation with those responsible for providing theological education relevant to and effective for God's most urgent mission tasks in the twenty-first century:

> North American male theology is taken to be basic, normative, universal theology, to which then women, other minorities, and people from the younger churches may add their footnotes. What is said in Manila is relevant for the Philippines. What is said in Tübingen, Oxford or Yale is relevant for the entire church. White theologians do general theology, black theologians do black theology. Male theologians do general theology; female theologians do theology determined by their sex. Such a notion of "universality" based on the present unjust distribution of power is unacceptable to the new theology. If the nature of truth is . . . both in its historical concreteness and in its connection with orthopraxis, it follows that every valid theology must acknowledge its particularity and its connection with the struggles and vested interest in which it is involved. A theology that refuses to do this and that leaps to facile claims of universal validity will have no place in the post reformation church of the twenty first century.[5]

It is not, however, only North American male theology that is problematic. It is, beyond that, the entire North Atlantic intellectual tradition, an intellectual tradition so deeply grounded in empire, where the root of the problem lies. For it is within this largely uncontested "tradition" that, regrettably, much global seminary-based theological education still intellectually ingratiates itself, from it still derives its intellectual validity, and still uses it determinedly to deny and/or obstruct epistemologies outside of its own. It is in this way that those seminaries most privileged by empire have been enabled over the years to establish and maintain such safe and erstwhile impenetrable intellectual havens where their institutional interests alone are so very well protected.

That is, until the advent of postcolonial theology, which because of its focus on redemptive justice and on radical inclusivity, readily made its way into the hearts and minds of the underside faithful, particularly indigenous people. It has therefore been this intellectual tour de force, combined with the unstoppable political projects of reclaiming indigenous and cultural rights by faith-filled minorities all over the world, that has provoked a determination among postcolonial indigenous people to look again at the theological academy and to wonder very critically about its as-yet under-realized potential.

What needs to be understood is that without fail, in spite of the multiple devastations inflicted upon indigenous peoples and in spite of much of the secularized rhetoric around indigenous spirituality, it remains that virtually all postcolonial indigenous elders have maintained an unyielding faith in God, combined with an irrepressible yearning for access to quality education. Both have always been seen by traditional indigenous leaders as crucial to the liberation of indigenous peoples and to the liberation of those who have so determinedly sought to oppress, suppress, or even to eliminate indigenous humanity.

Although small and still somewhat incoherent, there is an informal group of indigenous theologians whose scholarly postcolonial critiques of seminary-based theological education are now beginning to emerge.[6] Following on from and in the spirit of early liberation theologians, but with an eye to gender equality, indigenous educators are offering with generosity and confidence something of the vision, ideals, aspirations, insights, and intellectual gifts unique to indigenous epistemology, unique to indigenous spirituality, unique to indigenous wisdom.

As always, there is among those both *with the least* and *who are the least*, an unending faith-filled spirit of generosity, a willingness to contribute into the project of educating for future liberation and not simply to benefit from it.

What follows therefore is a substantial rewrite of one such contribution. It is one originally prepared for a gathering of leaders of Anglican Colleges and Universities in Seoul, Korea, in 2013 and then revised for presentation to a group of ecumenical church leaders in Cuba in 2015. It was the negative reaction of a number of seminary leaders at the Cuba gathering that further encouraged me to persist with challenging what I saw as blatant protectionism of their substantial, institutionally endowed privileges.

Mine is in essence both a moral challenge and an intellectual proposition to those faith-based leaders entrusted with the sacred work of leadership in seminary-based theological education. My particular project is to increase the numbers of indigenous peoples and of minority peoples across all levels of theological education, especially going into positions of leadership within denominational seminaries.

Notwithstanding the always negatively politicized semantics around definitions of just who is indigenous, it remains that there are unacceptably few postcolonial indigenous men or women holding positions of significant leadership in denominational seminaries anywhere in the world. My challenge therefore has always been leveled at nonindigenous leaders, especially at those who so readily proclaim their own solidarity with the indigenous struggle but who in fact are often demonstrably unwilling to genuinely share anything of the power and privileges they so enjoy.

We live now in times of massive social upheaval, of unprecedented political instability, of increasing risk not only to personal security but to the future security of our entire ecosystem—that complex interconnected global community where too many of those glorious gifts of God's creation given so freely into our care are now constantly under threat on so many fronts.

Is it not time, therefore, for faith-based educational leaders of all our seminaries to be more than just professionally aloof symbols of institutional power but to be hands-on deliverers and receivers of hope for and with the powerless, the disenfranchised, the oppressed, and the excluded? Is it not time for faith-based leaders to be radically activist exemplars of faith rather than simply professional purveyors of it?

If nonindigenous leaders are indeed to be capable of and trusted to reach out to those traditionally excluded, marginalized, and structurally deterred from institutional sites of teaching and learning, then they need first to be capable of engaging in mutually respectful collaboration and not well-meaning condescension. They need to be critically aware of the often-tempestuous politics that swirl throughout underside, indigenous, and other marginalized communities, for these politics are always profoundly complex and at times utterly unpredictable.

It is not acceptable for nonindigenous allies to enthusiastically and uncritically romanticize what they superficially perceive as indigenous reality while simultaneously demonizing their own. It is so often this ultimately ill-judged patronage that is in effect the greatest deterrent to building enduring relationships of deep mutuality.

What is needed, therefore, is a shared spirit of generosity, of humility, of vulnerability, and of willingness to struggle together in the project of envisioning afresh ways of teaching and learning, of seeing education as the pathway to acquiring a critical capacity enabling radical intervention in any unjust reality.

Prerequisite is seeing education itself as perhaps the most radical of interventions and in doing so to being accord with Freire, in knowing there is never to be anything neutral about it:

> All education has an intention, a goal which can only be political. Either it mystifies reality by rendering it impenetrable and obscure—which leads people to a blind march through incomprehensible labyrinths or it unmasks the economic and social structures which are determining the relationships of exploitation and oppression among persons, knocking down those labyrinths and allowing people to walk their own road. So we find ourselves confronted with a clear option: to educate for liberation or to educate for domination.[7]

Two years ago, I spoke to graduating students at the Church Divinity School of the Pacific, the Episcopal seminary in Berkeley, California. Here in part is what I said to them:

> I implore you not to be conformed to the prevailing ideologies of this world, to the mere rhetoric of freedom and of justice being articulated so hypocritically by

the powerful. Rather as with Paul, I implore you to go on being transformed by the continuous renewing of your minds and not simply for the sake of acquiring new knowledge but in order that everything about your future ministry is indeed based always on your unerring discernment of the will of God, to do only that which is good and acceptable and perfect, in other words to endeavor always to do only that which is courageous, compassionate and costly.

I do not presuppose for a moment the road ahead will be easy, for we each undertake our works of ministry in nations which sit inside a global community wherein so many places the scale of human suffering threatens daily to overwhelm and where genuinely selfless humanitarian responses to that suffering are increasingly difficult to identify.

As graduates you step out not into a brave new world but into an increasingly cowardly old world where greed trumps egalitarianism, where charity is contingent upon its tax advantages, where violence, public and private, is endemic, where morality, let alone human decency, appears now as untranslatable into the discourses and behaviors of the public square, where the milk of human kindness is daily soured by the unbidden human additives of prejudice and bigotry, of race and or religious hatred.[8]

I spoke this way because I do not think it is fair or helpful for theological educational leaders and teachers to minimize or obscure the sociopolitical realities for which students both deserve and openly yearn to be adequately and intentionally prepared.

This increasingly "cowardly old world" to which I referred is our contemporary reality. This is the twenty-first-century mission field which seminaries are responsible for preparing future leaders to step out into. This is the world to which the people of God are responsible for attending, for it is here that the least among us struggle daily for the mere necessities of life. It is here, too, that the scale of human injustice is more than matched by the unconscionable scale of human indifference on the part of those whose lives are characterized by more than sufficiency. It is here, therefore, in the brokenness and injustice of human existence that seminaries must discern and teach of theologically informed solutions for pressing political problems.

DARE TO QUESTION

My question remains—are denominational seminaries doing what they ought?

Are those responsible in our church communities for seminary governance and leadership, those called, commissioned, anointed, and blessed into ministries of leadership and teaching as theological educators, even cursorily acquainted with the underside communities in their respective societies? And by this, I mean to ask if they are acquainted as seasoned radical activist agents for change, as insiders within underside communities, or are they merely occasional well-meaning outsider cross-bearing visitor voyeurs?

Are those responsible in our church communities who are called, commissioned, anointed, and blessed into ministries of teaching as theological educators, professionally capable of teaching and learning alongside those from underside communities? And by this I mean are they capable as theological educators of radically disrupting and of relocating traditional classrooms, traditional practices of "education," traditional understandings of what counts as knowledge, or are they trained instead to uncritically uphold the tradition of highly prized subjectivist idealism, that which so neatly serves to preserve the institutional status quo and thus to preserve the interests of empire?

It is for the same reasons that I always react instinctively when I hear seminary-based theologians as educators speaking of "our common world" as if there is indeed a shared sociopolitical reality. But what is it that most seminary leaders really share in common with the "too many poor," with those who suffer the terror of armed conflict, the horror of political and or religious oppression, the debasement of being trafficked for sex, the ignominy of being exploited or enslaved as cheap human labor, the outrage of being unlawfully detained, the inexpressible grief of being so cruelly politically divided from those one loves?

Have they genuinely the intellectual will, the personal experience, the moral courage and empathy necessary to identify the deep and insidious causes of the global threats to human rights and thus to human freedom? And more than this, have they genuinely the intellectual will and skill, the personal experience, the moral courage, and the impassioned outrage to speak and teach of these things and simultaneously to be taught by those whose lives are daily demarcated by deep injustice?

Have they the determination and the critical insight needed to create such conditions that preclude educational injustice and inequity in denominational seminaries from ever again occurring? Have they the faith-filled passion for God's justice that seminary students rightly expect us as leaders to have? Have they the faith-filled passion for God's justice that those like my historically disenfranchised indigenous relatives so desperately and determinedly saw as their only real hope? How many are (as invited in the DARE 2017 call for papers) "daring to rethink ways of engaging more radically, more creatively, more justly in the pursuit of fullness in Christ for all Creation"? Or are they essentially ivory tower leaders and educators who know only too well how to objectify the distressing experiences of others but have never really thought, for example, about drawing those from the mission fields of suffering into the ivory tower theological academy, where, as valued partners and collaborators, the politically, economically, and socially marginalized could well assist in subjectifying their lived reality, in their own words and in their own languages, into the existential reality of the seminary classroom?

Do twenty-first-century seminary leaders have the critical capacity and the spirit of daring to struggle within the traditional ivory towers of seminary teaching and learning, those institutional bastions of empire, of male, clerical, and colonial privilege, and to radically transform these unjust structures?

Esse Quam Videri—To Be and Not to Seem! Do we want seminary-based theological education to be truly what it ought, or are we content for it to continue just to *seem* to be what it ought? Empire as the perfect breeding ground for elitist complacency is what has readily enabled seminary leaders to become impervious to the fact that too many graduates are now becoming church leaders such as those who recently gathered around Emperor Trump. These are the kind of leaders whose passivity and complicity with the interests of empire so inevitably impedes the liberation of those most vulnerable. I lay the blame for this firmly upon those responsible for teaching, forming, and preparing servant leaders for the work of God's mission.

Surely, unless all those with seminary leadership responsibility are able to answer in the affirmative to most of the earlier questions, I want respectfully and confidently to suggest that their professional credibility is justifiably called into question.

TRANSFORMATIVE THEOLOGICAL EDUCATION

So what might comprehensively inclusive, culturally expansive, contextually embedded, justice-seeking, seminary-based theological education for the twenty-first century require of us, apart from doing justice, loving mercy, and walking humbly with God? Many years of teaching, researching, speaking, and writing on the subject of transforming theological education have enabled me to identify four key attributes essential to enabling transformative theological educational work to proceed, let alone to flourish. These four are readily evident among staff, students, and governors alike in those seminary communities where there is deep and abiding commitment to radically realigning theological education toward meeting the urgent and unprecedented demands of the twenty-first-century mission fields. The following attributes are by no means exhaustive but rather the fundamental requirements to be taken into account, when we begin the unenviable task of transforming what is to what it ought to be:

First, *transcendent imagination*, or having both the capacity and the will to transcend the way things are. Far from being impotent, faith-filled human beings possessing immeasurable God-given agency have both freedom and obligation to act and think in new ways. They also have both the responsibility and the Gospel mandate to transform what is currently inequitable and thus unjust. Much seminary-based theological education globally is currently inequitable and unjust in terms of its lack of representation, outreach, or life-giving effect in the lives and upon the life chances of those traditionally marginalized, those who are the least in any given society.

Transcendent imagination inculcates a critical determination to refuse to see history as what took place but rather to see it as what all people, irrespective of their particular context, are now in the process of making. It enables an instinctive ability to stop trying to normalize the present and to stop seeing the future as a *fait accompli*. Both views negate the extraordinary political agency of real people and both therefore lack any real sense of hope. Surely Christian leaders and educators would want now to redress all extant inequities to ensure that justice prevails within the academic household of God.

Second, *transcendent praxis*. As Freire insisted, societal transformation cannot occur from a position of educational stasis, rather, "education itself must be an instrument of transforming action, a political praxis at the service of permanent human liberation. This does not happen only in the consciousness of people but it presupposes a radical change of structures, in which process consciousness itself will be transformed."[9]

In the new educational paradigm, the role of expert must be repositioned; teachers and students together become inquisitive learners empowering one another by their ability to produce knowledge and to challenge the knowledge that the old paradigm produced and presumed to be utterly sufficient. All existential realities have validity and are to be valued. It is in this way that curriculum deficit can be readily ameliorated in a mutually respectful and collaborative way.

Christian leaders and educators need have no fear but only gratitude, because the form of authority the new paradigm promotes draws on a variety of theological traditions in its unequivocal assertions that the greatest among us must become servant of all.

Third, *declericalizing and demystifying theological education*. Encouraging and enabling theological education of laypeople is not simply by way of a counterpoint to clericalism but rather is considered as a pragmatic solution to enabling desperately needed wisdom, insight, and critique from maybe up to 90 percent of the church to enter into academic discourse, and thus to properly disrupt so-called theological truths over which global elites have for too long maintained total control. Imagine what a radically different intellectual harmony empowered and liberated lay voices might contribute into the theological academy!

Fourth, *contextualization*. Reinforced by the advent of globalization and thus increased demand for inclusion and diversity, contextualization quickly became a fundamental characteristic of contemporary secular education. Secular education has thus led the way by underscoring the essential redemptive justice requirement of enabling and validating multivalent voices, epistemologies, and imaginings. Theological education has been a reluctant latecomer to the contextualization celebration and might otherwise have remained so had it not been for the vigilance and prophetic outrage of liberation theologians and more recently that of indigenous theologians.

Globally, the contemporary theoretical deployment of contextualization within seminaries is significantly uneven. I agree with Whiteman in his assertion that the problem is often ethnocentrism and ecclesiastical hegemony.[10] These two human constructs can, however, and must be intentionally deconstructed to avert the alternative phenomenon of contextual desolation. It is this insidious, ideologically rooted phenomenon of desolation that readily translates itself into attitudes of intolerance and mistrust, of increasing ecclesiological conservatism and confusion, of increased academic elitism, of neoliberal flight from public responsibility.

There are countless other attributes unique to seminary-based theological education that could and should be attended to—there is curriculum, assessment, environment, and accreditation, and within each of these discrete portfolios are many more layers, all of crucial importance. However, at this time, it seems so much more important to deal with the spiritual obligations at stake rather than dwell on matters of instrumentality.

After bearing firsthand witness to so many of the desperately poignant ongoing struggles for dignified self-determination across God's world, I cannot understand why there are still church leaders and seminary leaders who choose to remain aloof from the unavoidably serious educational challenges which are implicit in every cry for justice, every yearning for freedom.

I do not understand how any church leaders can for a moment remain unaffected by the starkness, the horror, the sheer outrage of what are so rightly described as the global obscenities of our times—the too many poor, a massively eco-damaged planet, monumental levels of political corruption, wanton warmongering, human trafficking, preventable disease, religious bigotry.

It is for all of these reasons that I remain utterly convinced that the ecclesiastically hegemonic and ethnocentric status quo of ecumenical- and indeed of any denominational-based theological education ought not remain as it is. I am in agreement with Freire in insisting that a radical change of consciousness is imperative "through the existential experience of dying to the current reality and being resurrected on the side of the oppressed or by being born again with the beings who are not allowed to be."[11]

Any radically new theological educational paradigm will of necessity undermine existing hierarchies of institutionally legitimated expertise. And so it must, because while the majority of any educational discussion focuses of necessity on students and their learning needs, I remain adamant that teachers and governors must never be exempt from responding to any of the extant challenges that are now being so eloquently and urgently laid out by those traditionally denied access to the theological academy.

Over the many years now of my academic leadership, I have found that the greatest deterrent to radicalizing minds and thus behaviors in favor of the least among us is the steadfast refusal of church leaders, of elite academics, of people with power over others, to forsake any of the considerable privileges of their offices, whatever they may be. It would seem necessary, therefore, that perhaps the hands, the feet, the hearts, and the minds of those with leadership responsibility are in need of being reconsecrated for the uncommon underside work of making all things here on earth to be as they are in heaven.

Remaking all seminaries as places "where faith and scholarship meet to reimagine the work of justice"[12] would be a very fine Gospel response to that work. Education requires relentless passion, a humanitarian vision, and a critical posture. It ought to stir the soul; expand the imagination; impart critical skills; energize the body; and secure justice, compassion, empathy, and ecological sustainability. Critical educators do more than simply study and transmit subject matter; they examine and critique social structures, they are intimately acquainted with community issues, and they are powerfully committed to helping others, especially those on the underside, to live meaningful lives.[13]

For those who, like me, either have been or still are in positions of seminary-based leadership, the critical questions remain—have we the passion, the vision, and the posture to do this work? Have we the requisite attitude of daring to imagine a completely radical new way of being the theology we speak of and teach, have we the courage to act boldly in spite of the costliness, have we the depth and breadth of loving empathy needed to be fully, credibly present to any and all "others" especially those on the underside, and have we the humility, the compassion, the kindness *to be* and not ever again to simply *seem to be* Christlike—*Esse Quam Videri*?

NOTES

1. William J. Barber II, "OpEd: Prophetic Moral Challenge after the National Prayer Breakfast," *NBC News* (February 3, 2017), (https://www.nbcnews.com/news/nbcblk/oped-moral-outrage-after-national-prayer-breakfast-n716261).

2. I can confidently attest to this being a reality throughout the Anglican Communion. Only once during my tenure was there a global meeting of seminary deans. Very few attended and many of those who did reported similar frustrations. Seven years of serving as Chair of the Ecumenical Theological Education Commission for the World Council of Churches further served to support my claim. Seriously problematic is the unacceptable gender imbalance among seminary leaders.

3. I acknowledge that globally, there are a very small number of standout denominational seminary exceptions to this claim.

4. Harper Lee, *To Kill a Mockingbird: 50th Anniversary Edition* (San Francisco: Harper Collins, 2010), 10.

5. Justo Gonzalez, *Mahana: Christian Theology from a Hispanic Perspective* (Nashville: Abingdon, 1990), 52.

6. We are especially indebted to Miguel A. de la Torre for his scathing yet powerful public critiques of racism in theological schools. His work has resonance with all theologians of color and with indigenous theologians.

7. Freire cited in bell hooks, *Talking Back: Thinking Feminist, Thinking Black* (New York: Routledge, 2015), 101.

8. Jenny Te Paa Daniel, Notes from Commencement Address at Church Divinity School of the Pacific, Berkeley, CA (May 2015).

9. Paulo Freire, *The Politics of Education: Culture, Power and Liberation* (Westport, CT: Bergin & Garvey, 1985), 140.

10. Darrell Whiteman, "Contextualization: The Theory, the Gap, the Challenge" (spu.edu/temp/denuol/context.htm).

11. Freire cited in James D. Kirylo and Drick Boyd, eds., *Paulo Freire: His Faith, Spirituality and Theology* (Rotterdam: Sense, 2017), 15.

12. This quote is taken from the website of Union Theological Seminary, https://utsnyc.edu.

13. See Joe L. Kincheloe et al., eds., *Contextualizing Teaching: Introduction to Education and Educational Foundations* (London: Longman, 2000).

Bibliography

Achebe, Chinua. 2000. *Home and Exile*. New York: Anchor Books.

Ackermann, Denise M. 2006. "From Mere Existence to Tenacious Endurance: Stigma, HIV/AIDS and a Feminist Theology of Praxis." In *African Women, Religion, and Health: Essays in Honor of Mercy Amba Ewudziwa Oduyoye*, ed. Isabel A. Phiri and Sarojini Nadar, 221–242. Maryknoll, NY: Orbis Books.

Acosta, Alberto. 2016. *O Bem Viver. Uma Oportunidade para Imaginar Outros Mundos*. São Paulo: Editora Elefant.

Adeyemo, Tokunboh, ed. 2006. *Africa Bible Commentary: A One-Volume Commentary Written by 70 African Scholars*. Grand Rapids, MI: Zondervan.

Agamben, Giorgio. 2011. The Kingdom and the Glory: For a Theological Genealogy of Economy and Government. Stanford, CA: Stanford University Press.

Ahikire, Josephine. "African Feminism in Context: Reflections on the Legitimation Battles, Victories and Reversals." *Feminist Africa* 19 (2014): 7–23.

Aichele, George, Fred W. Burnett, Robert M. Fowler, David Jobling, Tina Pippin and Wilhelm Wuellner, eds. *The Postmodern Bible: The Bible and Culture Collective*. New Haven: Yale University, 1995.

Althaus-Reid, Marcella. 2000. *Indecent Theology: Theological Perversions in Sex, Gender and Politics*. London and New York: Routledge.

———. 2003. *The Queer God*. London and New York: Routledge.

Anglican Church of Australia. 1995. *A Prayer Book for Australia*. Alexandria, NSW: Broughton Books.

Anglican Church of Australia, Liturgical Commission. "The Holy Communion, Also Called the Lord's Supper or the Eucharist for Situations When Children are Present." http://www.anglican.org.au/governance/commissions/documents/liturgy/holy%20communion%20for%20children%20shepherd%20theme.pdf (accessed 31 January 2017).

Antonio, Edward P. 2010. "'Eros', AIDS, and African Bodies: A Theological Commentary on Deadly Desires." In *The Embrace of Eros: Bodies, Desires and Sexuality in Christianity*, ed. Margaret D. Kamitsuka, 181–196. Minneapolis: Fortress Press.

Anzaldúa, Gloria. 1999. *Borderlands/La Frontera: The New Mestiza.* San Francisco: Aunt Lute.

Armstrong, Karen. 2000. *The Battle for God.* New York: Knopf.

Ashcroft, Bill, Gareth Griffiths, and Helen Tiffin. 1998. *Post-Colonial Studies: The Key Concepts.* London and New York: Routledge.

Australian Broadcasting Company. 2016. "Child Abuse Survivors Arrive in Rome ahead of George Pell's Royal Commission Appearance." http://www.abc.net.au/news/2016-02-28/child-abuse-survivors-arrive-in-rome-ahead-of-pell-testimony/7205696 (accessed January 31, 2017).

———. 2016. "Spotlight on the Church: An Uncomfortable Story That Must Be Told." http://www.abc.net.au/news/2016-03-01/mcphillips-spotlight-on-the-church/7210404 (accessed January 31, 2017).

Australian Institute of Family Studies. "Effects of Child Abuse and Neglect for Adult Survivors." https://aifs.gov.au/cfca/publications/effects-child-abuse-and-neglect-adult-survivors (accessed January 31, 2017).

Bakhos, Carol. "Genesis, the Qur'ān and Islamic Interpretation." In *The Book of Genesis: Composition, Reception, and Interpretation,* ed. Craig A. Evans, Joel N. Lohr and David L. Petersen, 607–634. Leiden and Boston: Brill, 2012.

Bakhtin, Mikhail. 2006. *The Dialogic Imagination: Four Essays.* Austin, TX: University of Texas Press.

Baldwin, Davarian L. 2007. *Chicago's New Negroes: Modernity, the Great Migration, and Black Urban Life.* Chapel Hill, NC: University of North Carolina Press.

Bales, Kevin. 2004. *Disposable People: New Slavery in the Global Economy.* Berkeley, CA: University of California Press.

Bar, Shaul. 2016. *A Nation is Born: The Jacob Story.* Eugene, OR: WIPF and Stock.

Barkan, Elazar, and Marie-Denise Shelton, eds. 1998. *Borders, Exiles, Diasporas.* Stanford: Stanford University Press.

Bauman, Zygmunt. 2004. *Wasted Lives: Modernity and Its Outcasts.* Cambridge: Polity.

Beifuss, Joan Turner. 1985. *At The River I Stand: Memphis, the 1968 Strike, and Martin Luther King.* Memphis, TN: B & W Books.

Berry, Jason. 1992. *Lead Us Not into Temptation: Catholic Priests and the Sexual Abuse of Children.* New York: Doubleday.

Bhabha, Homi. 2001. *The Location of Culture.* London and New York: Routledge.

Bhabha, Homi K. 2010. *The Location of Culture.* London and New York: Routledge.

Blount, Brian K. 2005. *Can I Get a Witness?: Reading Revelation Through African American Culture.* Louisville, KY: Westminster John Knox Press.

———, ed. 2007. *True to Our Native Land: An African American New Testament Commentary.* Minneapolis, MN: Fortress Press.

Blount, Brian K., and Leonara Tubbs Tisdale. 2000. *Making Room at the Table: An Invitation to Multicultural Worship.* Louisville: Westminster John Knox Press.

Blythe, Carolyne. 2008. *Terrible Silence, Eternal Silence: A Consideration of Dinah's Voicelessness in the Text and Interpretive Traditions of Genesis 34.* PhD Diss., University of Edinburgh. http://www.era.lib.ed.ac.uk/handle/1842/2593.

Bock, Darrel L. 1994. *Luke: 1:1–9:50*. Baker Exegetical Commentary on the New Testament. Grand Rapids, MI: Baker Books.

———. 1996. *Luke 9:51–24:53*. Baker Exegetical Commentary on the New Testament. Grand Rapids, MI: Baker Books.

Boesak, Allan Aubrey. 2015. *Kairos, Crisis, and Global Apartheid: The Challenge of Prophetic Resistance*. New York: Palgrave Macmillan.

Boff, Leonardo. 2008. *Essential Care. An Ethics of Human Nature*. Trans and notes Alexandre Guilherme. Waco: Baylor University Press.

Bonhoeffer, Dietrich. 2000. *Letters and Papers from Prison*, ed. Eberhard Bethge. London: Folio Society.

Bottomley, Frank. 1979. *Attitudes to the Body in Western Christendom*. London: Lepus Books.

Bottrel, Fred and Larissa Kümpel. 2017. *Agora o Rio corre calado*. https://www.em.com.br/app/noticia/gerais/2017/11/05/interna_gerais,914115/agora-o-rio-corre-cal ado-barragem-de-mariana-destruiu-a-fe-do-povo.shtml (accessed November 5, 2017).

Bowe, John. 2007. *Nobodies: Modern American Slave Labor and the Dark Side of the New Global Economy*. New York: Random House.

Boyarin, Daniel. 1995. "Are There Any Jews in 'The History of Sexuality'?" *Journal of the History of Sexuality* 5: 333–355.

Brett, Mark. 2000. *Genesis: Procreation and the Politics of Identity*. London and New York: Routledge.

———. 2014. "The Priestly Dissemination of Abraham." *Hebrew Bible and Ancient Israel* 3: 87–107.

Brown, Scot. 2005. *Fighting For US: Maulana Karenga, The US Organization, And Black Cultural Nationalism*. New York: New York University Press.

Brueggemann, Walter. 1982. *Genesis*. Interpretation. Atlanta: John Knox Press.

Budden, Chris. 2009. *Following Jesus in Invaded Space: Doing Theology on Aboriginal Land*. Princeton Theological Monograph Series 116; Eugene, OR: Pickwick Publications.

Burke, Cormac. 2006. "Saint Augustine and Conjugal Sexuality." *Church History Information Centre*. http://www.churchinhistory.org/pages/booklets/augustine.pdf (accessed May 15, 2017).

Burns, Stephen. 2004. "Forgiveness in Challenging Circumstances." In *Forgiveness in Context: Theology and Psychology in Creative Dialogue*, ed. Fraser Watts and Elizabeth Gulliford, 144–159. London: Continuum.

Burns, Stephen. 2013. "Formation for Ordained Ministry: Out of Touch?" In *Indigenous Australia and the Unfinished Business of Theology: Cross-Cultural Engagement*, ed. Jione Havea, 151–166. New York: Palgrave.

Burns, Stephen. 2015. *Pastoral Theology for Public Ministry*. New York, NY: Seabury Press.

Butler, Judith. 1993. "Critically Queer." *GLQ: A Journal of Lesbian and Gay Studies* 1.1:17–32.

———. 2009. *Frames of War. When Is Life Grievable?* London: Verso.

———. 2004. *Precarious Life: The Power of Mourning and Violence*. New York: Verso Books.

————. 2011. *Gender Trouble: Feminism and Subversion of Identity.* New York: Routledge.

————. 2015. *Gender Trouble: Feminism and the Subversion of Identity.* New York: Routledge.

Camp, Claudia V. 2000. *Wise, Strange and Holy: The Strange Woman and the Making of the Bible.* JSOTS 320. Sheffield: Academic Press.

Cardoso Pereira, Nancy. 2016. "Da Agropornografia à Agroecologia: Uma Aproximação Queer Contra as Elites Vegetais... Em Comunicação com o Solo." In *História, Saúde e Direitos. Sabores e Saberes do IV Congresso Latino-Americano de Gênero e Religião,* ed. André S. Musskopf and Marcia Blasi, 35–41. São Leopoldo: CEBI.

Cardozo, Ivaneide Bandeira, and Israel Correa Vale Júnior, eds. 2012. *Diagnóstico etnoambiental participativo, etnozoneamento e plano de gestão Terra Indígena Igarapé Lourdes.* Porto Velho, RO: Kanindé.

Carmichael, Stokely. 2003. *Ready for Revolution: The Life and Struggles of Stokely Carmichael {Kwame Ture}.* New York: Scribner.

Carmichael, Stokely, and Charles V. Hamilton. 1967. *Black Power: The Politics of Liberation in America.* New York: Vintage Book.

Carson, Clayborne, ed. 1998. *The Autobiography of Martin Luther King, Jr.* New York: Grand Central Publishing.

Chamane, Thembani. 2017. "An Exploration Of How Zulu Gay Men Negotiate Their Christian and Cultural Beliefs in the Process of Coming Out." Masters diss., University of KwaZulu-Natal.

Chapman, Cynthia R. 2004. *The Gendered Language of Warfare in the Israelite-Assyrian Encounter.* University Park, PA: Eisenbrauns.

Chatelain, Marcia. 2015. *South Side Girls: Growing Up in the Great Migration.* Durham, NC: Duke University Press.

Choquehancua, David. N.d. "Viver bem: Chanceler explica experiência da Bolívia." http://www.cut.org.br/imprimir/news/2b718747c195879070e9c28f90336587/ (accessed April 18, 2017).

Clark, J. Michael. 1993. *Beyond Our Ghettos. Gay Theology in Ecological Perspective.* Cleveland: Pilgrim.

Cliff, Michelle. 1996. *No Telephone to Heaven.* New York: Plume Books.

Clines, David. 1998. "Ecce Vir or, Gendering the Son of Man." In *Biblical Studies/ Cultural Studies: The Third Sheffield Colloquium,* ed. J. Cheryl Exum and Stephen D. Moore, 352–375. JSOTS 266. Sheffield: Sheffield Academic Press.

Cockburn, Harry. 2016. "Having Sex Increases Spirituality and 'makes people likely to believe in God.'" *Independent.* September 26. http://www.independent.co.uk/life-style/health-and-families/health-news/having-sex-believe-in-god-research-rel igion-duke-university-patty-van-cappallen-a7330076.html (accessed January 15, 2017).

Cockrell, Jeff. 2017. "What Contributed Most to the Financial Crisis?," *Chicago Booth Review* (October 20, 2017).

Cohen, Cathy J. 2017. "Punks, Bulldaggers, and Welfare Queens: The Radical Potential of Queer Politics?" In *Feminist Theory Reader: Local and Global Perspectives,* ed. Carole R. McCann and Seung-Kyung Kim, 419–435. New York/London: Routledge.

Columbus, Christopher. 1959. *A New and Fresh English Translation of the Letter of Columbus Announcing the Discovery of America*, trans. and ed. Samuel Eliot Morison. Madrid: Gráficas Yagües.

Cone, James H. 1997. *Black Theology and Black Power*. Maryknoll, NY: Orbis.

Connell, Raewyn W. 1987. *Gender and Power: Society, the Person and Sexual Politics*. Sydney: Allen & Unwin.

Connell, Raewyn W., and James W. Messerschmidt. 2005. "Hegemonic Masculinity Rethinking the Concept." *Gender & Society* 19.6: 829–859.

Connell, Robert. 2003. *Masculinidades*. Mexico: UNAM/PUEG.

Conway, Colleen M. 2008. *Behold the Man: Jesus and Greco-Roman Masculinity*. Oxford: Oxford University Press.

Copeland, M. Shawn. 2010. *Enfleshing Freedom: Body, Race and Being*. Minneapolis: Fortress Press.

Corley, Kathleen E. 1993. *Private Women, Public Meals: Social Conflict in the Synoptic Tradition*. Peabody, MA: Hendrickson.

Crossan, John Dominic. 1991. *The Historical Jesus: The Life of a Mediterranean Jewish Peasant*. San Francisco: HarperCollins.

CWM (Council for World Mission). 2017. *Discernment and Radical Engagement (DARE), Concept Note*. Singapore: Council of World Mission.

Davis, Patricia H. 2001. *Beyond Nice: The Spiritual Wisdom of Adolescent Girls*. Minneapolis: Fortress Press.

Day, Keri. 2016. *Religious Resistance to Neoliberalism: Womanist And Black Feminist Perspectives*. New York: Palgrave Macmillan.

de Acosta, José. 1996. *De procuranda indorum salute* (2 vols.), trans. and ed. G. Stewart McIntosh. Tayport and Scotland, UK: Mac Research.

de Castro, Eduardo Viveiros. 1998. "Cosmological Deixis and Amerindian Perspectivism." *The Journal of the Royal Anthropological Institute* 4.3: 469–488. http://www.jstor.org/stable/3034157 (accessed November 6, 2017).

de Castro, Eduardo Viveiros. "Perspectival Anthropology and the Method of Controlled Equivocation." *Tipití: Journal of the Society for the Anthropology of Lowland South America* 2.1:6. http://digitalcommons.trinity.edu/cgi/viewcontent.cgi?article=1010&context=tipiti (accessed November 6, 2017).

———. n.d. "Perspectivismo e multinaturalismo na América indígena," In *O que nos faz pensar* No 18, setembro de 200, page 239, http://oquenosfazpensar.fil.puc-rio.br/import/pdf_articles/OQNFP_18_13_eduardo_viveiros_de_castro.pdf (accessed November 6, 2017).

de Castro, Eduardo Viveiros, and Déborah Danowski. 2016. *The Ends of the World*. Cambridge: Polity Press, 2016.

de Certeau, Michael. 1984. *The Practice of Everyday Life*. Trans. Steven F. Rendall. Berkeley: University of California Press.

de Jong, Wietske. 2010. "How Do You Solve a Problem Like Maria?" In *Onder de Regenboog. De Bijbel Queer Gelezen*, ed. Adriaan van Klinken and Nienke Pruiksma, 71–80. Vught: Skandalon.

de las Casas, Bartolomé. 1992. *In Defense of the Indians*, trans. Stafford Poole. DeKalb, IL: Northern Illinois University Press.

de Vitoria, Francisco. 1992. "On the American Indians" (*De indis*, I). In *Political Writings*, trans. Jeremy Lawrance, 231–292. Cambridge: Cambridge University Press.

DeConick, April D. 2003. "The Great Mystery of Marriage: Sex and Conception in Ancient Valentinian Traditions." *Vigiliae Christianae* 57.3: 307–342.

Deifelt, Wanda. 2001. "Beyond Compulsory Motherhood." In *Good Sex: Feminist Perspectives from the World's Religions*, eds. Patricia Jung, Mary Hunt & Radhika Balakrishnan, 96–112. New Brunswick: Rutgers University Press.

———. 2016. "Teologia Feminista: Uma História Construída em Mutirão." In *História, Saúde e Direitos. Sabores e Saberes do IV Congresso Latino-Americano de Gênero e Religião*, ed. André S. Musskopf and Marcia Blasi, 17–26. São Leopoldo: CEBI.

———. 2017. "And G*d Saw That it Was Good – *Imago Dei* and Its Challenge to Climate Justice." In *Planetary Solidarity: Global Women's Voices on Christian Doctrine and Climate Justice*, eds. Grace Ji-Sun Kim and Hilda P. Koster, 119–132. Minneapolis: Fortress Press.

Denham, Greg. 2015. "Adam Goodes Booing Controversy: 'Can't blame him if he quits.'" *The Australian*. July 29. http://www.theaustralian.com.au/sport/afl/adam-goodes-booing-controversy-cant-blame-him-if-he-quits/news-story/162cd69f17eceb9f149c728df46df728.

DeParle, Jason. 2017. "The Sea Swallows People." *The New York Review of Books* 64.3 (February 23): 31.

Diamant, Anita. 2002. *The Red Tent*. London: Pan McMillan.

Díaz-Quiñones, Arcadio. 2000. *El arte de bregar: ensayos*. San Juan: Ediciones Callejón.

Dorham, Elliot T. 2015. "A Brief Consideration of Human Sexuality through the Lens of the Theology of the Body." *NDGS-Spring* 1–15.

dos Santos, Francisco Rokán. 2013. "Viver com a natureza." In *O Bem Viver na Criação*, ed. Cledes Markus and Renate Gierus, 69–70. São Leopoldo: Oikos.

Douglas, Mary. 1971. "Deciphering a Meal." In *Myth, Symbol and Culture*, ed. C. Geertz, 61–81. New York: W. W. Norton and Co.

Dube, Musa. 2017. "Dinah (Genesis 34) at the Contact Zone: Shall Our Sister Become a Whore?" In *Feminist Frameworks and the Bible: Power Ambiguity and Intersectionality*, eds. Juliana Classens and Carolyn Sharp, 39–49. London: Bloomsbury T & T Clark.

Dube, Musa W. 2000. *A Postcolonial Feminist Hermeneutics of the Bible*. St. Louis: Chalice.

———. 2000. *Postcolonial Feminist Interpretation of the Bible*. St. Louis, MO: Chalice Press.

———. 2007. *A Theology of Compassion in the HIV and AIDS Era. Module 7 of the HIV and AIDS Curriculum for TEE Programmes and Institutions in Africa*. Geneva: WCC Publications.

———. 2009. "HIV and AIDS Research and Writing in the Circle of African Concerned African Women Theologians 2002–2006." In *Compassionate Circles: African Women Theologians Facing HIV*, ed. Ezra Chitando and Nontando Hadebe, 173–196. Geneva: WCC Publications.

Dupont, Florence. 1989. *Daily Life in Ancient Rome*. Oxford, UK and Cambridge, US: Blackwell.

Dussel, Enrique. 1992. *1492: el encubrimiento del Otro*. Santafé de Bogotá: Ediciones Antropos.

———. 1995. *Invention of the Americas: Eclipse of "the Other" & the Myth of Modernity*. New York: Continuum.

———. 2007. *Política de la liberación. Historia mundial y crítica*. Madrid: Editorial Trotta.

Eberly, Janice C., and Arvind Krishnamurthy. 2004. "Fixing the Next Mortgage Crisis," *Kellogg Insight* (December 1) a Publication of the Kellogg School of Management at Northwestern University.

Efi, Tui Atua Tupua Tamasese. "More on Nuance, Meaning and Metaphor." Keynote Speech at the Pacific Fono: Moving Ahead Together, Pataka Museum. Porirua NZ: Capital Coast District Health Board, 2002.

———. "Whispers and Vanities in Samoan Indigenous Religious Culture." In *Whispers and Vanities: Samoan Indigenous Knowledge and Religion*, ed. Tamasailau M. Suaalii-Sauni, Maualaiva Albert Wendt, Vitolia Mo'a, Naomi Fuamatu, Upolu Luma Va'ai, Reina Whaitiri, and Stephen L. Filipo, 37–76. Wellington NZ: Huia Publishers, 2014.

Eldredge, John. 2001. *Wild at Heart: Discovering the Secret of a Man's Soul*. Nashville: Thomas Nelson.

Eliot, T. S. 1952. "Murder in the Cathedral" (1935). In *The Complete Poems and Plays, 1909–1950*. New York: Harcourt, Brace and Company.

Ellens, J. Harold. *Sex in the Bible: A New Consideration*. London: Praeger, 2006.

Elon, Amos. 1995. *Jerusalem: Battlegrounds of Memory*. New York: Kodansha International.

Erhagbe, Edward O. 2011. "The African-American Contribution to the Liberation Struggle in Southern Africa: The Case of the African Liberation Support Committee, 1972–1979." *The Journal of Pan African Studies* 4.5 (September 2011).

Falcón, Angelo. 2004. *Atlas of Stateside Puerto Ricans*. Washington, DC: Puerto Rico Federal Affairs Administration.

Faludi, Susan. 2011. *Stiffed: Betrayal of the Modern Man*. London: Random House.

Fanon, Franz. 1952. *Peau Noir, Masques Blancs*. Paris: Éditions du Seuil.

———. 1968. *The Wretched of the Earth*. New York: Grove Press.

Felzke, Lediane Fani. 2017. *Dança e imortalidade. Igreja, festa e xamanismo entre os Ikólóéhj Gavião de Rondônia*. http://repositorio.unb.br/handle/10482/22959 (accessed April 16, 2017).

Fewell, Danna N., and David Gunn. 1991. "Tipping the Balance: Steinberg's Reader and the Rape of Dinah," *JBL* 110: 193–211.

Fitzmyer, Joseph A. 1985. *The Gospel According to Luke X–XXV*. AB 28a; Garden City: Doubleday.

Fitzsimmons, James A. 2010. *Service Management: Operations, Strategy, Information Technology*. New York: McGraw-Hill.

Foer, Franklin. 2017. *World Without Mind: The Existential Threat of Big Tech*. New York: Penguin Press.

Foucault, Michel. 1980. *Power/Knowledge: Selected Interviews and Other Writings 1972–1977*. New York: Vintage Books.

———. 1988. *Power/Knowledge. Select Interviews and Other Writings*, 1972–1977, Colin Gordon, ed. New York: Pantheon Books.

Freire, Paulo. 1985. *The Politics of Education. Culture, Power and Liberation*. Westport, CT: Bergin & Garvey.

———. 1996. *Pedagogy of the Oppressed*. San Francisco: Penguin.

Freitas, Donna. 2008. *Sex and the Soul: America's College Students Speak out about Hookups, Romance, and Religion on Campus*. New York: Oxford.

Frilingos, Christopher A. 2003. "Sexing the lamb." In *New Testament Masculinities*, ed. Janice Capel Anderson and Stephen D. Moore, 297–317. Atlanta: Society of Biblical Literature.

Frye, Marilyn. 1983. "On Being White: Thinking toward a Feminist Understanding of Race and Race Supremacy." In *The Politics of Reality: Essays in Feminist Theory*, 110–127. Berkeley: Crossing Press.

Fukuyama, Francis. 1992. *The End of History and the Last Man*. New York: Free Press.

Galloway, Scott. 2017. *The Four: The Hidden DNA of Amazon, Apple, Facebook, and Google*. New York: Portfolio and Penguin.

García Martínez, Alfonso.ed. 1988. *Libro rojo/Tratado de París: Documentos presentados a las cortes en la legislatura de 1898 por el ministro de Estado*. Río Piedras, Puerto Rico: Editorial de la Universidad de Puerto Rico.

Garner, Stephen, ed. 2011. *Theology and the body: reflections on being flesh and blood*. Hindmarsh: ATF Theology.

Gautier, Mary L., Paul M. Perl, and Stephen J. Fichter. 2012. *Same Call, Different Men: The Evolution of the Priesthood since Vatican II*. Collegeville, MN: Liturgical Press.

Globo. 2014. "Em vídeo, deputado diz que índios, gays e quilombolas 'não prestam'." http://g1.globo.com/rs/rio-grande-do-sul/noticia/2014/02/em-video-deputado-diz-que-indios-gays-e-quilombos-nao-prestam.html (accessed March 16, 2017).

Gnanadason, Aruna. 1988. "Women's Oppression: A Sinful Situation." In *With Passion and Compassion: Third World Women Doing Theology*, ed. Virginia Fabella and Mercy Amba Oduyoye, 69–76. Maryknoll: Orbis.

Goh, Joseph N. 2017. "From Polluted to Prophetic Bodies: Theo-Pastoral Lessons from the Lived Experiences of Gay, HIV-Positive Christian Men in Singapore." *Practical Theology* 10.2: 133–146.

Gonzalez, Justo. 1990. *Mañana: Christian Theology from an Hispanic Perspective*. Nashville: Abingdon.

Goodman, Martin. 2008. *Rome and Jerusalem: The Clash of Ancient Civilizations*. London: Penguin.

Goss, Robert E., and Mona West, eds. 2000. *Take Back the Word. A Queer Reading of the Bible*. Cleveland: Pilgrim.

Greene, Graham. 1990. *The Power and the Glory*. London: Penguin (orig. 1940).

Greenwood, Robin. 1994. *Transforming Priesthood: A New Theology of Mission and Ministry*. London: SPCK.

Grossman, James R. 1991. *Land of Hope: Chicago, Black Southerners, and the Great Migration.* Chicago: University of Chicago Press.

Guest, Deryn. 2005. *When Deborah Met Jael. Lesbian Biblical Hermeneutics.* London: SCM.

Gunkel, Hermann. 1997. *Genesis.* Trans. *Mark E. Biddle* (3rd ed.). Macon, GA: Mercer University Press.

Haddox, Susan E. 2016. "Is there a Biblical Masculinity?: Masculinities in the Hebrew Bible." *Word & World* 36.1 (Winter): 5–14.

Halperin, David M. 1990. *One Hundred Years of Homosexuality: And Other Essays on Greek Love.* London and New York: Routledge.

Hampton, Henry, and Steve Fayer. 1990. *Voices of Freedom: An Oral History of the Civil Rights Movement from the 1950s Through the 1980s.* New York: Bantam Books.

Hanke, Lewis U. 1949. *The Spanish Struggle for Justice in the Conquest of America.* Philadelphia: University of Pennsylvania Press.

———. 1959. *Aristotle and the American Indians: A Study in Race Prejudice in the Modern World.* Chicago: Henry Regnery.

———. 1974. *All Mankind is One; A Study of the Disputation Between Bartolomé de Las Casas and Juan Ginés de Sepúlveda in 1550 on the Intellectual and Religious Capacity of the American Indians.* DeKalb, IL: Northern Illinois University Press.

Hankore, Danile. 2013. *The Abduction of Dinah: Genesis 28:10–35:15 as a Votive Narrative.* Cambridge: James Clarke & Co.

Hansen, Tracey. 1991. *Seven for a Secret That's Never Been Told.* London: SPCK.

Harding, Jeremy. 2011. "The Deaths Map." *London Review of Books* 33.20 (October 20): 7–13.

Harding, Vincent. 1990. *Hope and History: Why We Must Share the Story of the Movement.* Maryknoll, NY: Orbis.

Hardt, Michael, and Antonio Negri. 2004. *Multitude: War and Democracy in the Age of Empire.* New York: The Penguin Press.

Harris, Melanie et al. 2016. "Silent Scripts and Contested Spaces." *Journal of Feminist Studies in Religion* 32.1: 101–114.

Harvey, Brian K. 2016. *Daily Life in Ancient Rome: A Sourcebook.* Indianapolis, IN: Hackett Publishing.

Hau'ofa, Epeli. *We are the Ocean: Selected Works.* Honolulu: University of Hawaii Press, 2008.

Havea, Jione. "Bare Feet Welcome: Redeemer Xs Moses @ Enaim." In *Bible, Borders, Belonging(s): Engaging Readings from Oceania,* ed. Jione Havea, David J. Neville, and Elaine M. Wainwright, 209–222. Atlanta: SBL, 2014.

Hawkes, Gail. 2007. "The Problem of Pleasure and the making of Sexual Sin in early Christianity." Presentation made at *The Society for the Scientific Study of Sexuality, in cooperation with The Kinsey Institute 50th Anniversary: Honoring our Past and Envisioning our Future* (November 7–11 at Hyatt Regency, Indianapolis, IN).

Hernandez Castillo, R. Aída. 2017. "Confrontando la Utopía Desarrollista: El *Buen Vivir y la Comunalidad* en las luchas de Mijeres Indígenas." In *Feminismo y Buen*

Vivir. Utopias Decoloniales, eds. Soledad Varea and Sofía Zaragocin, 26–43. Cuenca: Pydlos Ediciones.

Heskett, James. 1990. *Service Breakthroughs: Changing the Rules of the Game*. New York: The Free Press.

Hinga, Teresia M. 2008. "AIDS, Religion and Women in Africa: Theo-Ethical Challenges and Imperatives." In *Women, Religion and HIV/AIDS in Africa: Responding to Ethical and Theological Challenges*, ed. Teresia M. Hinga, Anne N. Kubai, Philomena Mwaura, and Hazel Ayanga, 76–104. Pietermaritzburg: Cluster Publications.

Hinkelammert, Franz. 1998. *El grito del sujeto: del teatro-mundo del evangelio de Juan al perro-mundo de la globalización*. San José, Costa Rica: DEI.

Hobsbawm, Eric. 1994. *Age of Extremes: The Short Twentieth Century, 1914–1991*. London: Michael Joseph.

Hobsbawm, Eric J. 1987. *The Age of Empire, 1875–1914*. New York: Pantheon Books.

Holloway, Richard. 2013. *Leaving Alexandria: A Memoir of Faith and Doubt*. London: Canongate.

Holt, Simon Carey. 2013. *Eating Heaven: Spirituality at the Table*. Melbourne, Australia: Acorn Press Ltd.

hooks, bell. 2015. *Talking Back: Thinking Feminist, Thinking Black*. New York: Routledge.

Hopkins, Dwight N. 2017. *Black Theology – Essays on Gender Perspectives*. Eugene, OR: Cascade Books.

Hopkins, Dwight N., and Edward P. Antonio, eds. 2012. *The Cambridge Companion to Black Theology*. Cambridge, UK: Cambridge University Press.

Horsley, Richard A. 1995. *Galilee: History, Politics, People*. Valley Forge: Trinity Press International.

———. 1997. *Paul and Empire: Religion and Power in Roman Imperial Society*. Harrisburg, PA: Trinity Press International.

———. 2003. *Jesus and Empire: The Kingdom of God and the New World Disorder*. Minneapolis: Fortress Press.

———. 2004. *Paul and the Roman Imperial Order*. Harrisburg, PA: Trinity Press International.

Hughes, Kathleen. 2013. *Becoming the Sign: Sacramental Living in a Post-Conciliar Church*. Mahwah, N.J.: Paulist Press.

Hume, David. 1956. *The Natural History of Religion*. London: A. & C. Black.

Hunt, Hannah. 2012. *Clothed in the Body: Asceticism, the Body and the Spiritual in the Late Antique Era*. Burlington, VT: Farnham.

Huntington, Samuel P. 2004. *Who Are We? The Challenges to America's National Identity*. New York: Simon & Schuster.

Hyatt, J. P. 1962. "Circumcision." In *The Interpreters Dictionary of the Bible*, Vol 1, ed. Keith R. Crim and George A. Buttrick. Nashville: Abingdon.

Ibn Alkalimat, Abdul Hakimu. 1974. *Toward the Ideological Unity of the African Liberation Support Committee: A Response to Criticisms of the ALSC Statement of Principles Adopted at Frogmore, South Carolina, June–July, 1973* (city and publisher not known).

Ingram, Airileke. 2016. *Sorong Samarai.* https://www.youtube.com/watch?v=faJ fu-FJVt0 (accessed December 01, 2018).

Introvigne, Massimo. 2009. "Of Cultists and Martyrs: The Study of New Religious Movements and Suicide Terrorism in Conversation." In *Dying for Faith: Religiously Motivated Violence in the Contemporary World*, ed. Madawi al Rasheed and Marat Shterin, 43–48. London: I. B. Tauris.

Isherwood, Lisa. 2000a. "Erotic Celibacy: Claiming Empowered Space." In *The Good News of the Body. Sexual Theology and Feminism*, ed. Lisa Isherwood, 149–163. New York: New York University Press.

———. 2000b. "Sex and Body Politics: Issues for Feminist Theology." In *The Good News of the Body. Sexual Theology and Feminism*, ed. Lisa Isherwood, 20–34. New York University Press.

Isherwood, Lisa, and E. Stuart. 1998. *Introducing Body Theology.* Sheffield: Sheffield Academic Press.

———. 1998. *Introducing Body Theology.* Cleveland: Pilgrim Press.

Jacobs, Jim. 1971. *Our Thing is DRUM: An Interview with Ken Cockrel and Mike Hamlin of the League for Revolutionary Black Workers.* Boston: New England Free Press.

Jenkins, Philip. 2011. *Laying Down the Sword: Why We Can't Ignore the Bible's Violent Verses.* New York: HarperOne.

Jerome. 1893. "Letter XXII to Eustochium." In *The Principal Works of St. Jerome*, Trans. W.H. Fremantle. New York: Parker.

Joh, Wonhee Anne. 2006. *Heart of the Cross: A Postcolonial Christology.* Louisville, KY: Westminster John Knox Press.

Johnson, Cedric C. 2016. *Race, Religion, and Resilience in the Neoliberal Age.* New York: Palgrave Macmillan.

Johnson, Luke Timothy. 1991. *The Gospel of Luke.* Sacra Pagina 3. Collegeville, MN: Liturgical Press.

Joyce, James. 1946. *Ulysses.* New York: Random House.

Kahne, Joseph, and Ellen Middaugh. 2006. "Is Patriotism Good for Democracy? A Study of High School Seniors' Patriotic Commitments." *Phi Delta Kappan* 87.8: 600–607.

Keller, Catherine. 2005. *God and Power: Counter-Apocalyptic Journeys.* Minneapolis: Fortress.

Kelley, Robin D.G., and Earl Lewis, eds. 2000. *To Make Our World Anew: A History of African Americans.* New York: Oxford.

Kim, Eunjoo Mary. 2017. *Christian Preaching and Worship in Multicultural Contexts: A Practical Theological Approach.* Liturgical Press: Collegeville.

Kimmel, Michael. 2013. *Angry White Men: American Masculinity at the End of an Era.* New York: Nation Books.

Kimmel, Michael S. 1994. "Masculinity as Homophobia: Fear, Shame and Silence in the Construction of Gender Identity." In *Theorizing Masculinities*, ed. Harry Brod and Michael Kauffman, 119–141. London: Sage Publishing Press.

Kincheloe, Joe L. et al., eds. 2000. *Contextualizing Teaching: Introduction to Education and Educational Foundations.* London: Longman.

King, Jr., Martin Luther. 1958. *Stride Toward Freedom: A Leader of His People Tells The Montgomery Story*. New York: Harper & Row Publishers.

———. 1986. "I Have a Dream." In *A Testament of Hope: The Essential Writings of Martin Luther King, Jr.*, ed. James M. Washington, 217. San Francisco: Harper & Row.

———. 1997. "MIA Mass Meeting at Holt Street Baptist Church. December 5, 1955. Montgomery, Ala." In *The Papers of Martin Luther King, Jr. Volume III: Birth of a New Age December 1955 – December 1956*, ed. Clayborne Carson. Berkeley, CA: University of California Press.

Kinzer, Stephen. 2017. *The True Flag: Theodore Roosevelt, Mark Twain, and the Birth of American Empire*. New York, NY: Henry Holt.

Kirylo, James D., and Drick Boyd, eds. 2017. *Paulo Friere: His Faith, Spirituality and Theology*. Rotterdam: Sense.

Kolone-Collins, Sueala. "Fagogo: "Ua Molimea Manusina": A Qualitative Study of the Pedagogical Significance of Fagogo-Samoan Stories at Night-for the Education of Samoan Children." MThesis, Auckland University of Technology, 2010.

Krüger, René. 2008. *La diáspora: De experiencia traumática a paradigma eclesiológico*. Buenos Aires: ISEDET.

Kwok, Pui-lan. 2005. *Postcolonial Imagination and Feminist Theology*. Louisville, KY: Westminster John Knox Press.

Lee, Harper. 2010. *To Kill a Mockingbird: 50th Anniversary Edition*. San Francisco: Harper Collins.

Levine, Amy-Jill. 2002. "Introduction." In *A Feminist Companion to Luke*, ed. Amy-Jill Levine, London: Sheffield Academic.

Libânio, João B., and Maria Clara L. Bingemer. 1985. *Escatologia Cristã: O Novo Céu e a Nova Terra*. Petrópolis, Brasil: Vozes.

Loades, Ann. 1994. *Thinking About Child Sexual Abuse: The John Coffin Memorial Lecture (11 January 1994)*. London: University of London.

———. 2001. *Feminist Theology: Voices from the Past*. Oxford: Polity.

Locke, Dawolu Gene. 1974. *A Few Remarks in Response to Criticisms of ALSC* (city unknown: Lynn Eusan Institute).

Logan, Willis H. ed. 1988. *The Kairos Covenant: Standing with the South African Christians*. New York, NY: Friendship Press.

Lorde, Audre. 1984. "The Power of the Erotic." In *Sister Outsider: Essays and Speeches*. New York: Crossing Press.

Luther, Martin. 1956."The Magnificat." In *Luther's Works*. Vol. 21, ed. Jaroslav Pelikan. Saint Louis: Concordia Publishing House.

———. 1961. "Sermons on the Gospel of St. John: Chapters 14–16." In *Luther's Works*. Vol. 24, ed. Jaroslav Pelikan and Daniel E. Poellot. Saint Louis: Concordia Publishing House.

———. 1962. "The Freedom of a Christian." In *Martin Luther: Selections from His Writings*, ed. John Dillenberger. New York: Anchor.

———. 1964. "Lectures on Genesis: Chapters 21–25." In *Luther's Works*. Vol. 4, ed. Jaroslav Pelikan. Saint Louis: Concordia Publishing House.

———. 1970. "Lectures on Genesis: Chapters 31–37." In *Luther's Works*. Vol. 6, ed. Jaroslav Pelikan and Helmut T. Lehmann. Saint Louis: Concordia.

Lutheran World Federation. 2016. "Nairobi Document of Worship and Culture." http://www.smithseminary.org/wp-content/uploads/2016/02/Nairobi-Statement-a nd-Worshiping-Triune-God.pdf.

———. "Churches Say NO to Violence Against Women." Available at https://ww w.lutheranworld.org/content/resource-churches-say-no-violence-against-women -action-plan-churches.

MacLeod, Jason. 2015. *Merdeka and the Morning Star: Civil Resistance in West Papua.* Peace and Conflict Series. St. Lucia: University of Queensland Press.

Maister, David. 2003. *Managing the Professional Service Firm.* New York: The Free Press.

Malcolm X, 1965. *The Autobiography of Malcolm X.* New York: Grove.

Malina, Bruce J. 1981. *The New Testament World: Insights from Cultural Anthropology.* Atlanta: SCM Press.

Maluleke, Tinyiko S. 2001. "The Challenge of HIV/AIDS for Theological Education in Africa. Towards an HIV/AIDS Sensitive Curriculum." *Missionalia* 29.2: 125–143.

Maraschin, Jaci. 2003. *The Transient Body: Sensibility and Spirituality.* Paper presented at the event "Liturgy and Body;" Union Theological Seminary, New York, October 20.

Mark, Joshua. 2011."Enuma Elish – The Babylonian Epic of Creation." *Ancient History Encyclopedia.* http://www.ancient.eu/article/225/ (accessed May 15, 2017).

Martinez, Julia, and Claire Lowrie. 2009. "Colonial Constructions of Masculinity: Transforming Aboriginal Australian Men into 'Houseboys.'" *Gender & History* 21.2: 305–323.

Mbembe, Achille. 2001. *On the Postcolony.* Berkeley: University of California Press.

McArthur, Colin and Sarah Edelman. 2017. "The 2008 Housing Crisis." *Center for American Progress* (April 13).

McCammack, Brian. 2017. *Landscapes of Hope: Nature and the Great Migration in Chicago.* Cambridge, MA: Harvard University Press.

McDonald, Robert, and Anna Paulson. 2015. "What Went Wrong at AIG." *Kellogg Insight* (August 3), a publication of the Kellogg School of Management at Northwestern University.

McGregor, Sue. 2011. "Transdisciplinary Methodology." *International Journal of Home Economics* 4.2: 105–123.

McGrow, Lauren. 2017. "Doing It (Feminist Theology and Faith-Based Outreach) with Sex Workers – Beyond Christian Rescue and the Problem-Solving Approach." *Feminist Theology* 25: 150–169.

Memmi, Albert. 1965. *The Colonizer and the Colonized.* Boston: Beacon.

Mendelsohn, Isaac. 1898. *Slavery in the Ancient Near East.* West Port, CT: Greenwood Press.

Mendoza, Breny. 2015. "La epistemologia del sur, la colonialidad del género y el feminism latinoamericano." https://simposioestudosfeministasct.files.wordpres s.com/2015/03/mendoza_la_epistemologia_del_sur.pdf (accessed April 26, 2017).

Mettinger, Tryggve, N. D. *The Eden Narrative: A Literary and Religio-Historical Study of Genesis 2–3.* Winona Lake: Eisenbrauns, 2007.

Mian, Atif, and Amir Sufi. 2015. *House of Debt: How They (and You) Caused the Great Recession, and How We Can Prevent It from Happening Again.* Chicago: University of Chicago.

Mignolo, Walter D. 1995. *The Darker Side of the Renaissance: Literacy, Territoriality, & Colonization.* Ann Arbor, MI: The University of Michigan Press.

———. 2000. *Local Histories/Global Designs: Coloniality, Subaltern Knowledges, and Border Thinking.* Princeton: Princeton University Press.

Milanovic, Branko. 2009. "Global Inequality and the Global Inequality Extraction Ratio: The Story of the Past Two Centuries." The World Bank, Development Research Group, Poverty and Inequality Group (September 2009).

Min, Anselm Kyongsuk. 2004. *The Solidarity of Others in a Divided World: A Postmodern Theology after Postmodernism.* New York: T&T Clark.

Mondschein, Ken. 2017. "Introduction." In *The U.S. Constitution and Other Writings*, ed. Ken Mondschein. San Diego, CA: Canterbury Classics.

Moore, Stephen D. 2003. "'O Man Who Art Thou?': Masculinity Studies and New Testament Studies." In *New Testament Masculinities*, ed. Janice Capel Anderson and Stephen D. Moore, 297–317. Atlanta: Society of Biblical Literature.

Moore, Stephen D., and Fernando Segovia. 2005. *Postcolonial Biblical Criticism: Interdisciplinary Intersections.* London and New York: T & T Clark.

Morgensen, Scott Lauria. 2012. "Theorising Gender, Sexuality and Settler Colonialism: An Introduction." *Settler Colonial Studies* 2.2: 2–22. http://www.tandfonli ne.com/doi/abs/10.1080/2201473X.2012.10648839#.VbHiAniZbww.

Morison, Samuel Eliot, and Henry Steele Commager. 1969. *The Growth of the American Republic: Volumes One & Two.* New York: Oxford Book Company.

Moyo, Fulata L. 2002. "'Singing and Dancing Women's Liberation': My Story of Faith." In *Her-Stories: Hidden Histories of Women of Faith in Africa*, ed. Isabel A. Phiri, Devaraksham Betty Govinden, and Sarojini Nadar, 389–408. Pietermaritzburg: Cluster.

Moyo, Fulata L. 2006. "Navigating Experiences of Healing: A Narrative Theology of Eschatological Hope as Healing." In *African Women, Religion and Health: Essays in Honor of Mercy Amba Ewudziwa Oduyoye*, ed. Isabel A. Phiri and Sarojini Nadar, 243–257. Maryknoll, NY: Orbis Books.

Muhammad, Elijah. no date. *Message to the Black Man in America.* Philadelphia, PA: Hakim's.

Nadar, Sarojini, and Sarasvathie Reddy. 2016a. "From Instrumentalization to Intellectualisation: Response to Silent Scripts and Contested Spaces." *Journal of Feminist Studies in Religion* 32.1: 136–141.

———. 2016b. "Undoing 'Protective Scientism' in a Gender, Religion and Health Masters Curriculum." In *Disrupting Higher Education Curriculum*, ed. Michael A. Samuel et al, 229–245. Rotterdam/Boston/Taipei: Sense Publishers.

Nadar, Sarojini. 2009. "Her-Stories and Her-Theologies: Charting Feminist Theologies in Africa." *Studia Historiae Ecclesiasticae* 35: 135–150.

Naipaul, V. S. 1967. *The Mimic Men.* New York: Macmillan.

National Catholic Reporter. "NCR Research: Costs of Sex Abuse Crisis to US Church Underestimated." https://www.ncronline.org/news/accountability/ncr-research-c osts-sex-abuse-crisis-us-church-underestimated (accessed January 31, 2017).

National Society for the Prevention of Cruelty to Children. https://www.nspcc.org.uk/ preventing-abuse/child-abuse-and-neglect/ (accessed January 31, 2017).

Newton, Huey P. 1972. *To Die For The People: The Writings of Huey P. Newton.* New York: Random House.

Nicolacopoulos, Toula, and George Vassilacopoulos. 2014. *Indigenous Sovereignty and the Being of the Occupier: Manifesto for a White Australian Philosophy of Origins.* Melbourne: re.press. http://re-press.org/books/indigenous-sovereignty-and-the-being-of-the-occupier-manifesto-for-a-white-australian-philosophy-of-origins/

Niebuhr, H. Richard. 1975. *Christ and Culture.* New York: Harper & Row.

Nissinen, Marti. 1998. *Homoeroticism in the Biblical World: A Historical Perspective.* Minneapolis, MN: Augsburg Fortress.

Noel, James A. 2009. *Black Religion and the Imagination of Matter in the Atlantic World.* New York: Palgrave Macmillan.

Oduyoye, Mercy Amba. 2001. *Introducing African Women's Theology.* Cleveland: The Pilgrim Press.

Pagden, Anthony. 1982. *The Fall of Natural Man: The American Indian and the Origins of Comparative Ethnology.* Cambridge: Cambridge University Press.

———. 1990. *Spanish Imperialism and the Political Imagination.* New Haven and London: Yale University Press.

———. 1995. *Lords of all the World: Ideologies of Empire in Spain, Britain and France, c.1500 – c.1800.* New Haven and London: Yale University Press.

Pelleaur, Mary, Barbara Chester, and Jane Boyajian, eds. 1987. *Sexual Assault and Abuse: A Handbook for Clergy and Religious Professionals.* San Francisco, CA: HarperCollins.

Perdue, Leo G., and Warren Carter. 2015. *Israel and Empire: A Postcolonial History of Israel and Early Judaism.* London: Bloomsbury.

Philo. 1854. "Commentary on Genesis" In *The Works of Philo Judaeus.* Vol. 1. Trans. C.D. Younge. London: Henry G. Bohn.

Phiri, Isabel A., Beverley Haddad, and Madipoane Masenya, eds. 2003. *African Women, HIV/AIDS and Faith Communities.* Pietermaritzburg: Cluster Publications.

Phiri, Lilly. 2013. "Born this way- A Gendered Perspective on the Intersectionality Between Same-Sex Orientation and the Imago Dei: A Case Study of Men Who Love Other Men in Lusaka-Zambia." Masters diss., University of KwaZulu-Natal.

———. 2017. "Exploring Queer Identity and Sexuality at the Intersections of Religion and Culture in Zambia." PhD diss., University of KwaZulu-Natal.

Picq, Manuela Levinas, and Josi Tikuna. 2015. "Sexual Modernity in Amazonia." http://www.e-ir.info/2015/07/02/sexual-modernity-in-amazonia/ (accessed March 30, 2017).

Pieter, Van Niekerk. 2012. "Towards a theology of the body. A spirituality of imperfection." *Towards a Theology of the Body* 53.3&4: 369–375.

Piper, John, and Wayne Grudem. 2006. "An Overview of Central Concerns: Questions and Answers." In *Recovering Biblical Manhood and Womanhood: A Response to Evangelical Feminism*, ed. John Piper and Wayne Grudem. Wheaton, IL: Crossway.

Pixley, Jorge et al. 2003. *Por un mundo otro: alternativas al mercado global.* Quito, Ecuador: Consejo Latinoamericano de Iglesias.

Povos Indígenas no Brasil. n.d. "Quadro Geral dos Povos." https://pib.socioambienta
l.org/pt/c/quadro-geral (accessed April 25, 2017).

Pratt, Mary Louis. 1991. Arts of the Contact Zone." *Profession* 91.

Procter-Smith, Marjorie. 1995. *Praying With Our Eyes Open: Engendering Feminist Liturgical Prayer.* Nashville, TN: Abingdon Press.

Quasten, Johannes, and Joseph C. Plumpe, eds. 1961. *Ancient Christian Writers: The Works of the Fathers in Translation.* Vol. 6. Westminster, MD: The Newman Press.

Quelch, John. 2008. "How Marketing The American Dream Caused Our Economic Crisis." *Harvard Business Review* (October 27).

Quijano, Aníbal. 1998a. "Colonialidad del poder, cultura y conocimiento en América Latina." *Anuario Mariateguiano* 9.9: 113–121.

———. 1998b. "The Colonial Nature of Power and Latin America's Cultural Experience." In S*ociology in Latin America* (*Social Knowledge: Heritage, Challenges, Perspectives*), Proceedings of the Regional Conference of the International Association of Sociology, ed. R. Briceño and H. R. Sonntag, 27–38. Caracas: IAS.

———. 2000. "Coloniality of Power, Eurocentrism, and Latin America." *Nepantla* 3: 533–580.

Rajan, Rajeshwari Sunder. 1999. *Real and Imagined Woman: Gender, Culture and Postcolonialism.* London, NY: Routledge.

Ramshaw, Gail. 2012. "A Look at New Anglican Eucharistic Prayers." *Worship* 86: 161–67.

Rasmussen, Larry L. 2015. *Earth-honoring Faith: Religious Ethics in a New Key.* Oxford: Oxford University Press.

Reddie, Anthony G. 2006. *Black Theology in Transatlantic Dialogue.* New York: Palgrave Macmillan.

Renvoise, Jean. 1993. *Innocence Destroyed.* London: Routledge.

Richard, Jessica. 2010. "Resisting Bodies as a Hermeneutical Tool for a Critical Feminist Christology of Liberation and Transformation." Masters diss., University of KwaZulu-Natal.

Richard, Pablo. 1994. *Apocalipsis: reconstrucción de la esperanza.* San José: DEI.

Rieger, Joerg. 2007. *Christ & Empire: From Paul to Postcolonial Times.* Minneapolis: Fortress Press.

Ríos-Avila, Rubén. 1998. "Caribbean Dislocations: Arenas and Ramos Otero in New York." In *Hispanisms and Homosexualities*, ed. Sylvia Molloy and Robert M. Irwin, 101–122. Durham, NC: Duke University Press.

Rivera-Pagán, Luis N. 1992. *A Violent Evangelism: The Political and Religious Conquest of the Americas.* Louisville, Kentucky: Westminster John Knox.

———. 1995. *Entre el oro y la fe: El dilema de América.* San Juan: Editorial de la Universidad de Puerto Rico.

———. 2003. "Freedom and Servitude: indigenous Slavery in the Spanish Conquest of the Caribbean." In *General History of the Caribbean. Volume I: Autochthonous Societies*, ed. Jalil Sued-Badillo. London: UNESCO Publishing and Macmillan Publishers.

———. 2012. "Xenophilia or Xenophobia: Towards a Theology of Migration." *The Ecumenical Review* 64.4: 575–589.

———. 2014. "God the Liberator: Theology, History, and Politics." In *Essays from the Margins*, 63–83. Eugene, OR: Cascade.

Romero, Oscar Arnulfo. 1998. *The Violence of Love*. Compiled and translated by James R. Brockman. Farmington, PA: Plough.

Rosner, Brian. 1998. "Temple Prostitution in 1 Corinthians 6:12–20." *Novum Testamentum* 40: 336–351.

Royal Commission into Institutional Responses to Child Sexual Abuse. 2016. "Case Study 42: August and September 2016, Newcastle and Sydney, Transcript (Day 231), November 24." https://www.childabuseroyalcommission.gov.au/downloadfile.ashx?guid=caf3421a-6ccc-451b-9628-ac318caeb354&type=transcriptdoc&filename=Transcript-(Day-231)&fileextension=doc) (accessed January 31, 2017).

Ruether, Rosemary Radford. 1983. *Sexism and God-Talk: Toward a Feminist Theology*. Boston: Beacon Press.

———. 1998. *Women and Redemption: A Theological History*. Minneapolis: Fortress Press.

Safi, Michael. 2015. "AFL Great Adam Goodes Is Being Booed Across Australia. How Did It Come to This?" *The Guardian* (July 29, 2015). http://www.theguardian.com/sport/blog/2015/jul/29/afl-great-adam-goodes-is-being-booed-across-australia-how-did-it-come-to-this?CMP=soc_567.

Said, Edward W. 1986. *After the Last Sky: Palestinian Lives*. New York: Pantheon Books.

———. 1993. *Culture and Imperialism*. New York: Knopf.

———. 1994. *Culture and Imperialism*. New York: Vintage Books.

———. 1996. *Representations of the Intellectuals*. New York: Vintage Books.

———. 1999. *Out of Place: A Memoir*. New York: Knopf.

———. 2003. *Orientalism* (25th anniversary edition). New York: Random House.

Sandbach, F. H. 1989. *The Stoics* (2nd ed.). London: Gerald Duckworth.

Scholz, Suzanne. 2010. *Sacred Witness: Rape in the Hebrew Bible*. Minneapolis: Fortress.

Schweiker, William. 2004. *Theological Ethics and Global Dynamics in the Time of Many Worlds*. Malden, MA and Oxford: Blackwell.

Scott, James C. 1990. *Domination and the Arts of Resistance: Hidden Transcripts*. New Haven, CT: Yale University Press.

Segovia, Fernando. 2005. "Mapping the Postcolonial Optic in Biblical Criticism: Meaning and Scope." In *Postcolonial Biblical Criticism: Interdisciplinary Intersections*, 23–78. London and New York: T & T Clark.

Shire, Warshan. 2011. "In Love and in War." In *Teaching My Mother How to Give Birth*. London: Flipped eye publishing. https://www.goodreads.com/work/quotes/18606097-teaching-my-mother-how-to-give-birth.

Smith, Linda Tuhiwai. *Decolonizing Methodologies: Research and Indigenous Peoples*, 2nd ed. London and New York: Zed Books, 2012.

Smith-Christopher, Daniel L. 2002. *A Biblical Theology of Exile*. Minneapolis: Fortress Press.

Sölle, Dorothee, and Shirley A. Cloyes. 1984. *To work and To love: A Theology of Creation*. Philadelphia: Fortress.

Spivak, Gayatri C. 1988a. "Can the subaltern speak?," In *Marxism and the Interpretation of Culture*, eds. Cary Nelson and Lawrence Grossberg, 271–313. Urbana and Chicago: University of Illinois Press.

———. 1998b. *In Other Worlds: Essays in Cultural Politics*. New York and London: Routledge.

———. 2010. "Can the Subaltern Speak?" In *Can the Subaltern Speak? Reflections on the History of an Idea*, ed. Rosalind C. Morris, 21–78. New York: Columbia University Press.

Spong, John. 1993. *Why Christianity Must Change or Die*. San Francisco, CA: HarperCollins.

Squires, John T. 2000. *At Table with Luke*. Sydney: UTC Publications.

Stacey, Jim. 2015. *Liberating Jesus from Christianity: Healing from the Fear and Shame of Religious Dogma*. New York: Page Publishing.

Stalker, Peter. 2000. *Workers Without Frontiers: The Impact of Globalization on International Migration*. Geneva: International Labor Organization.

Sugirtharajah, R. S. 2002. *Postcolonial Criticism and Biblical Interpretation*. Oxford: Oxford University Press.

———. 2004. "Complacencies and Cul-de-sacs: Christian Theologies and Colonialism." In *Postcolonial Theologies: Divinity and Empire*, ed. Catherine Keller, Michael Nausner, and Mayra Rivera. St. Louis, MO: Chalice Press.

Sugirtharajah, R. S, ed. 1998. *The Postcolonial Bible*. Sheffield, UK: Sheffield Academic Press.

———, ed. 2006. *The Postcolonial Biblical Reader*. Malden, MA and Oxford: Blackwell.

Surkin, Marvin, and Dan Georgakas. 2012. *Detroit: I Do Mind Dying: A Study in Urban Revolution*. Chicago, IL: Haymarket.

Taylor, Adam. 2017. "There Are Now 3 Rivers That Legally Have the Same Rights as Humans." https://www.washingtonpost.com/news/worldviews/wp/2017/03/21/there-are-now-3-rivers-that-legally-have-the-same-rights-as-humans/?utm_term=.c4b660838ebd (accessed April 28, 2017).

Taylor, Mark Lewis. 2005. *Religion, Politics, and the Christian Right: Post–9/11 Powers and American Empire*. Minneapolis: Fortress Press.

Te Paa Daniel, Jenny. 2015. Notes from Commencement Address at Church Divinity School of the Pacific, Berkeley, CA. May 2015.

Togarasei, Lovemore, and Ezra Chitando. 2011. "Beyond the Bible: Critical Reflections on the Contributions of Cultural and Postcolonial Studies on Same-Sex Relationships in Africa." *Journal of Gender and Religion in Africa* 17.2: 109–125.

Tolle, E. 2005. *The Power of Now. A Guide to Spiritual Enlightenment*. London: Hodder & Stoughton.

"Transgender Identity: Found in Transition." 2017. *The Economist* (November 18, 2017): 51–53.

Trías Monge, José. 1997. *Puerto Rico: The Trials of the Oldest Colony in the World*. New Haven: Yale University Press.

Trouillot, Michel-Rolph. 1995. *Silencing the Past: Power and the Production of History*. Boston: Beacon Press.

Union for Radical Political Economics. 2009. *Special Issue on the Financialization of Global Capitalism* (December).

United States Conference of Catholic Bishops. "Charter for the Protection of Children and Young People." http://www.usccb.org/issues-and-action/child-and-youth-protection/charter.cfm (accessed January 31, 2017).

van Klinken, Adriaan. 2008. "'The Body of Christ Has AIDS.' A Study on the Notion of the Body of Christ in African Theologies Responding to HIV and AIDS." *Missionalia* 36.2/3: 319–336.

———. 2010. "When the Body of Christ Has AIDS: A Theological Metaphor for Global Solidarity in Light of HIV and AIDS." *International Journal of Public Theology* 4.4: 446–465.

———. 2015. "Queer love in a "Christian nation": Zambian gay men negotiating sexual and religious identities." *Journal of the American Academy of Religion* 83.4: 947–964.

———. 2017. "Western Christianity as Part of Postcolonial World Christianity: The 'Body of Christ with AIDS' as an Interstitial Space." In *Contesting Religious Identities: Transformations, Disseminations and Mediations*, ed. Bob Becking, Anne-Marie Korte, and Lucien van Liere, 39–58. Leiden: Brill.

Van Opstal, Sandra Maria. 2016. *The Next Worship: Glorifying God in a Diverse World*. Westmont: IVP Books, Intervarsity Press.

Vengeyi, Obvious. 2013. *Aluta Continua Biblical Hermeneutics for Liberation: Interpreting Biblical Texts on Slavery for Liberation of Zimbabwean Underclasses*. Bamberg: University of Bamberg Press.

Vincent, John. 2000. *Hope from the City*. Peterborough: Epworth Press.

Wallace, Michele. 1999. *Black Macho and the Myth of the Superwoman*. London: Verso.

Wara Wara. 2016. "Pedagogía Ancestral Amawtica." https://mujermedicina.wordpres s.com/2016/04/18/pedagogia-ancestral-amawtica/ (accessed April 24, 2017).

Warfula, Robert S. 2019. "The Exodus Story as a Foundation of the God of the Father." In *The Postcolonial Commentary and the Old Testament*, ed. Hemchand Gossai, 10–26. London: T & T Clark.

Warikoo, K. 2000. "Tribal Gujjars of Jammu and Kashmir." *Journal of Himalayan Research and Cultural Foundation* 4.1: 3–27.

Weinberg, Albert K. 1935. *Manifest Destiny: A Study of Nationalist Expansionism in American History*. Baltimore: John Hopkins.

Wenham, Gordon J. *Genesis 1–15*. Dallas: Word Books, 1987.

West, Gerald, Charlene Van der Walt, and Kapya John Kaoma. 2016. "When Faith Does Violence: Reimagining Engagement Between Churches and LGBTI Groups on Homophobia in Africa." *HTS Theological Studies* 72.1: 1–8.

Westhelle, Vitor. 2012. *Eschatology and Space: The Lost Dimension in Theology Past and Present*. New York: Palgrave Macmillan.

White, John Bradley. 1978. *A Study of the Language of Love in the Song of Songs and Ancient Egyptian Poetry*. SBL Diss 38. Missoula, Mont: Scholars Press.

Whiteman, Darrell. N.d. "Contextualization: The Theory, the Gap, the Challenge." spu.edu/temp/denuol/context.htm.

Wilfred, Felix. 2008. *Margins: Site of Asian Theology*. Delhi: ISPCK.

Wilmore, Gayraud S., and James H. Cone, eds. 1979. *Black Theology A Documentary History, 1966–1979*. Maryknoll, NY: Orbis.

Wimbush, Vincent L., ed. 2000. *African Americans and the Bible: Sacred Texts and Social Textures*. New York: Continuum.

Woolf, Virginia. 1986. *Three Guineas*. London: The Hogarth Press.

Wu, Tim. 2011. *The Master Switch: The Rise and Fall of Information Empires*. New York: Vintage.

Zakovitch, Yair. 1985. "Assimilation in Biblical Narratives." In *Empirical Models for Biblical Criticism*, ed. Jeffrey H. Tigay, 175–196. Philadelphia: University of Philadelphia.

Zaragocin, Sofía. 2017. "Feminismo Decolonial y Buen Vivir." In *Feminismo y Buen Vivir. Utopias Decoloniales*, ed. Soledad Varea and Sofía Zaragocin, 17–25. Cuenca: Pydlos Ediciones.

Žižek, Slavoj. 2016. *Refugees, Terror, and other Troubles with the Neighbors*. Brooklyn, NY: Melville House.

Index

About the Contributors

Stephen Burns is Professor of Liturgical and Practical Theology at Pilgrim Theological School, University of Divinity, Melbourne. He is a presbyter of the Church of England and has taught in the UK, United States, and Australia. His publications include *Postcolonial Practice of Ministry* (coeditor with Kwok Pui-lan, 2016), *Public Theology and the Challenge of Feminism* (coeditor with Anita Monro, 2014), *Christian Worship: Postcolonial Perspectives* (coauthor with Michael N. Jagessar, 2011), and *Liturgy with a Difference* (coeditor with Bryan Cones, 2018). He is currently writing *Riting the Body* with Nicola Slee.

Cláudio Carvalhaes is Associate Professor of Worship at Union Theological Seminary in New York City. He authored *Sacraments and Globalization: Redrawing the Borders of Eucharistic Hospitality* (2013), *What's Worship Got to Do with It? Interpreting Life Liturgically* (2017), and is the editor of *Liturgy in Postcolonial Perspectives—Only One Is Holy* (2015).

Wanda Deifelt is Professor of Religion at Luther College in Decorah, IA (since 2004). Before that, she worked at Escola Superior de Teologia, in São Leopoldo, Brazil (the largest Lutheran Seminary in Latin America), where she also served as vice president of the seminary and provost of the Graduate Program in Theology. She is an ordained pastor of the Evangelical Lutheran Church in Brazil and has served as theological advisor for the Lutheran World Federation, the board of the Ecumenical Institute of the World Council of the Churches, the Latin American Council of Churches, and the board of the Ecumenical Institute in Strasbourg, France.

Masiiwa Ragies Gunda is an Old Testament and Biblical Hebrew scholar. Gunda has research interests on the intersection of biblical *mishpat* and justice in the contemporary world, with a special focus on the lives of sexual minorities. Gunda has published widely on these areas. He is the author of *The Bible and Homosexuality in Zimbabwe* (2010) and *On the Public Role of the Bible in Zimbabwe* (2015).

Karl Hand is a pastor, working at Crave Metropolitan Community Church in Sydney. He was raised in the Pentecostal tradition, and has engaged deeply with communities informed by Evangelical and Liberation Theology. His area of scholarly interest is in the tradition of Jesus's teaching, especially as preserved in the Gospel of Luke, and was a contributor to *Postcolonial Voices from Downunder: Indigenous matters, Confronting readings* (2017).

Jione Havea is a native Methodist pastor from Tonga who is research fellow with Trinity Theological College (Aotearoa, New Zealand) and the Public and Contextual Theology research center (Charles Sturt University, Australia). Jione has taught at institutions in Tonga, USA, Australia, and Aotearoa New Zealand; recently authored *Jonah: An Earth Bible Commentary* (2019) and edited *Sea of Readings: The Bible and the South Pacific* (2018), *Religion and Power* (2018), and *Scripture and Resistance* (2019).

Dwight N. Hopkins is the author of *Being Human: Race, Culture, and Religion* (2005), *Black Theology: Essays On Gender Perspectives* (2017), and *Black Theology: Essays On Global Perspectives* (2017), among many others. An ordained Baptist, he is Professor of Theology at the University of Chicago.

Adriaan van Klinken is Associate Professor of Religion and African Studies at the University of Leeds, United Kingdom. His work focuses on Christianity, gender, and sexuality in contemporary Africa, employing anthropological, theological, feminist, postcolonial, and queer perspectives. In addition to a range of articles, he is the author of *Transforming Masculinities in African Christianity: Gender Controversies in Times of AIDS* (2013) and coeditor with Ezra Chitando of *Public Religion and the Politics of Homosexuality in Africa* (2016).

Brian F. Kolia is a lecturer in Old Testament Studies at Malua Theological College in Samoa, and an ordained minister of the Congregational Christian Church Samoa. He is currently on study leave undertaking doctoral studies at the University of Divinity (Melbourne, Australia). He is an Australian-born Samoan whose roots go back to the villages of Sili Savaii and Satapuala, and he was a contributor to *Sea of Readings: The Bible and the South Pacific* (2018).

Monica J. Melanchthon is a church worker (ordained by the Andhra Evangelical Lutheran Church, India) and theological educator. She currently teaches Hebrew Bible/Old Testament at the Pilgrim Theological College, University of Divinity (Melbourne, Australia) and has published in various academic books focusing on interpretations of Old Testament texts from the Indian context and the perspectives of the marginalized. Her current projects include a feminist commentary on 1 Kings for the Wisdom Commentary Series (Liturgical Press) and an Earth Bible Commentary on Joshua 1–11 (Bloomsbury).

Sarojini Nadar holds the Desmond Tutu Research Chair in Theology and Social Transformation at the University of the Western Cape. The chair focuses on developing advanced research in the area of religion and social transformation. She was a cofounder of the Gender and Religion program at the University of KwaZulu-Natal, which she headed up from 2008 until 2016. Her numerous publications span diverse fields of research in the area of gender and religion, including gender-based violence, HIV, masculinity studies, and most recently gender in higher education.

Nienke Pruiksma studied theology in The Netherlands and South Africa. She works as a theologian and intercultural educator for COMIN, a mission council working for and with indigenous peoples in various regions of Brazil. Her task is to work with nonindigenous groups in churches, schools, universities, and civil society on the issues of multiculturality and interculturality. Her main interests lie in the intersections of theology, culture, and power, especially the dynamics between hegemonic and non-hegemonic thinking and the lived realities and agency of non-majority groups.

Sarasvathie Reddy is a Senior Lecturer in the Higher Education Training Development Unit at the University of KwaZulu-Natal. She spent the first decade of her academic life at the Nelson R Mandela School of Medicine as the Head of the Skills Laboratory where she was involved in teaching the clinical aspects of the medical curriculum. Her research interests in higher education include a focus on gender and diversity, curriculum studies, doctoral education, and academic development. She is also involved in two international research projects with a focus on gender, religion, and health as well as sexual diversity in higher education curricula.

Luis N. Rivera-Pagán is the Henry Winters Luce Professor of Ecumenics and Mission Emeritus at Princeton Theological Seminary. He is the author of several books, including *A Violent Evangelism: The Political and Religious Conquest of the Americas* (1992), *La evangelización de los pueblos* *americanos: algunas reflexiones históricas* (1997), *Diálogos y polifonías: perspectivas y reseñas* (1999), *Essays from the Diaspora* (2002), *Teología y cultura en América Latina* (2009), *Ensayos teológicos desde el Caribe* (2013), *Peregrinajes teológicos y literarios* (2013), and *Essays from the Margins* (2014).

Jenny Te Paa Daniel is Co-Director of New Zealand-based Ohaki Consultancy specializing in Higher Education and in Public Theology. She was the first lay indigenous woman to hold the principalship of an Anglican seminary—Te Rau Kahikatea, St. Johns College in Auckland, Aotearoa, New Zealand. She is globally recognized for her outstanding commitment to peace and justice activism and to mentoring younger women into higher education and into leadership. Her numerous publications include *Anglican Woman on Church and Mission* (coeditor with Judith Berling and Kwok Pui-lan, 2012).

Printed in Great Britain
by Amazon

64990179R00147